# Welcome to Lust Angeles

> . . . the difference between Los Angeles and yogurt is that
> yogurt has an active, living culture.
> — *Unknown*

**W**elcome to the city, the City of Angels, Hollyweird, the Big Orange, the Naked City. Welcome to *Lust Angeles.* Take a journey into the sexual underside of Los Angeles. Find out where the action is. Find out where the women (or men) are. Find out where the fun is.

Los Angeles has a long, seamy, steamy past. From its days as a frontier town to the beginnings of Hollywood, the heyday of movie stars and their vices, through the sixties when everyone came to California for the sun and fun and the open lifestyles, to the present. OK, I admit that the present isn't as wild as the sixties and seventies were.

Times have changed and Los Angeles has changed with them. Orgies in every house and rampant recreational drug use are probably relics of the past. However, the city is still boiling with passion and lust and there are myriad pleasures out there for you to enjoy (there are still some orgies and drugs around). The purpose of this book is to guide you safely and sanely to those pleasures.

Los Angeles became the city that we know today mostly because of Hollywood. What we see spread out before our eyes when we stand on one of the mountain ranges that crisscross the city would surely be a different sight if Hollywood had been placed somewhere else. A small group of Jewish tradesmen who saw fortune in the nickelodeon made their way west because of low-priced land and great weather. Thus, Hollywood was born! We still have the great weather (if you can see it through the smog!), but low-priced land has gone the way of silent films.

As Hollywood grew, so did Los Angeles. And grew and grew and grew and grew until the valleys were paved, the hillsides terraced, the beaches fenced and the orange groves plowed under. And along with the migration of people came their vices. Prostitutes, massage parlors, strip shows, drug dealers, gambling establishments – Los Angeles would have it all!

During the Roaring Twenties, Hollywood was the place to become a star. Many wanna-bes flocked here in search of fame and fortune. Most didn't find fame and fortune; some of those who failed drifted into more decadent pursuits. Even during the depression years, the influx of newcomers continued. The war years and postwar years brought even greater crowds and greater prosperity.

Even with the demise of the big studios and the advent of television, Hollywood and LA thrived. The Beach Boys, California Dreamin', Charles Manson, hippies, surfer chicks, valley girls, sex, drugs and rock & roll – LA became a magnet for the wild, the weird, the wacky, the wasted. Los Angeles was a universal symbol for weirdness. Yes, the counterculture came and went, but the City of Angels remains.

And here we are . . . having lived through the sexual revolution, a time when erotic movies, sexually oriented businesses, alternate lifestyles and freedom of expression exploded on the scene. Now it's a different era . . . one generation has had its fun and another is dealing with the consequences of all those good times. But . . . even though decadence is not the exciting concept it once was, and even though the term "safe sex" no longer means avoiding pregnancy, there are still ways to have adult fun. There are ways to satisfy your lust. There are still ways to be lustful and lusty and lusting.

So, all you Lust Angelenos . . . welcome to —

## *Lust Angeles!!*

# Lecher McRich's
# *Lust Angeles*

by
**F.M. Philips**
(author of *Sin Diego*)
edited by
**Roger Warren**
(author of *Red Lights of Baja*)
illustrated by
**D.R. Tupper**
(creator of *Lecher McRich*)
introduction by
**Norma Jean Almodovar**

**Warren Communications**
Post Office Box 620219 ◆ San Diego, CA 92160
warren@cyberheads.com

ISBN: 0-945949-06-5

**DEDICATION**
*To those who strive for personal freedom*
"A crime without victims is no crime"




FIRST EDITION
FIRST PRINTING


For additional copies of this book, see
order blank in the back of this book or write to:

# Warren Communications
Post Office Box 620219 ♦ San Diego, CA 92160
Email: warren@cyberheads.com

> . . . I can remember when the air was clean
> and sex was dirty.
> — *George Burns*

# Disclaimer

Don't you hate disclaimers? Just someone trying to absolve themselves of any responsibility. Yep, that's what this is. We take no responsibility. There, we said it! Some would say that we're irresponsible . . . but that's a different issue altogether. Though we have tried and suffered and struggled and endured and exhausted ourselves in an attempt to furnish you with all you need to know about lust and fun and sin in the City of Angels, we know we have fallen short. No book could possibly tell you everything or list each and every wild, kinky, erotic, lascivious, lewd, crude, rude or nude thing in a city so vast and expansive. But, we tried! We tried and we tried and we tried!

We also do not take any responsibility for the actions of any of the establishments or individuals listed here. We don't endorse or guarantee any products or services. We do not promote any illegal activities even though we don't agree with all the laws and regulations that exist in our society. We also cannot guarantee that all of these places will still be in business when you get your sweaty palms on this book. We make a valiant effort to keep this book as current as humanly possible . . . but we know some information will be obsolete by the time you shell out some of your hard-earned cash to buy this great piece of literature.

But we know you will enjoy this book and we hope it brings you many hours of fun and pleasure. If you think that some of those hours of fun and pleasure would be great stories, our crack research staff would love to hear them. Send us all your dirty stories, all your nasty, naughty nuggets of sin and sex . . . or any items we may have overlooked in this book so we can include them in the next edition of this book.

# TABLE OF CONTENTS

Welcome to Lust Angeles................................. ii
Introduction by Norma Jean Almodovar . . . .. xiv

CHAPTER ONE
Naughty In The Nineties ............................... 1
Safe Sex and Risks.................................... 2
About Condoms .......................................... 5
Get Tested!!!............................................... 6
More Facts About AIDS ............................. 7
Ignorance Is Not Bliss ............................... 9

CHAPTER TWO
Sexual Supermarkets ....................................11
Los Angeles Area..................................... 12
San Fernando Valley .............................. 15
Orange County........................................ 16
Other Areas............................................. 18
Love Happens at the Strangest Places .................. 21
The Overly Enthusiastic Salesman ....................... 21

CHAPTER THREE
Tits & Ass .....................................................23
Los Angeles County.................................. 24
San Fernando Valley .............................. 30
Orange County........................................ 32
Inland Empire, Desert Cities & Others .................. 35
Modeling Studios ................................... 38
For The Ladies ...................................... 39

CHAPTER FOUR
Mail Order Videos ............................................41
Mail Order Companies.............................. 42
It Could Have Been You............................ 57

CHAPTER FIVE
Phone Sex.....................................................59
Let's Talk Money .................................... 60
Types of Phone Sex ............................... 60

It Could Happen to You ........................................ 63
Phone Lines ........................................................ 63

**CHAPTER SIX**
**Computer and Cybersex Sex...........................67**
More Boards To Check Out ................................... 72
Other Computer Stuff ........................................... 75
**The Internet .............................................76**
A Little History Lesson ......................................... 76
World Wide Web ................................................... 77
CyberCensors........................................................ 78
Surf'n Sights........................................................ 79
Usenets................................................................ 80
Shopping On the Net............................................. 80
Getting On ........................................................... 80

**CHAPTER SEVEN**
**Sex Workers .............................................83**
Selling Sex Around The Globe .............................. 84
Mexico ................................................................. 84
Europe................................................................. 85
Safety and Disease................................................ 86
Crime and the Law ............................................... 87
Where the Girls Are.............................................. 89
**Escorts ...................................................92**
How To Act........................................................... 93
Escorts, Dancers, Models, Masseuses & More ....... 93
How Much Moolah?............................................... 94
It Could Be You .................................................... 95
Police Stories....................................................... 95
Bring On The Girls ............................................... 97
Desert Area ........................................................ 104
Two Girls in San Diego ....................................... 105

**CHAPTER EIGHT**
**Massage Parlors .....................................107**
Los Angeles Area ................................................ 109
San Fernando Valley ........................................... 113
Inland Empire..................................................... 113
Ventura County................................................... 114
Orange County.................................................... 115

**CHAPTER NINE**
**B & D Clubs............................................117**
Other B & D Businesses...................................... 122

## CHAPTER TEN

**Swinging** ...................................................**125**
   Swinging, Swingers and Sex .............................. 127
   Swing Clubs.......................................................... 127
   Swingers' Dances ................................................ 131
   Swingers' Publications........................................... 132
   It Could Happen To You ...................................... 132
   Publications .......................................................... 133
   More Swinging Stuff.............................................. 137

## CHAPTER ELEVEN

**Personal Ads** .............................................**141**
   Type of Personal Ad.............................................. 142
   What To Say In Your Ad ....................................... 143
   Stories from Telephoneland ................................. 144
   A Bedtime Story ................................................... 144
   The Phone Lines.................................................... 145
   Profile Systems...................................................... 145
   For Swingers Only................................................. 149
   Gay, Lesbian or Bi................................................. 150

## CHAPTER TWELVE

**The Gay/Bi Life** .........................................**153**
   Bars & Clubs ....................................................... 153
   West Hollywood & Hollywood............................... 154
   Other Los Angeles City Bars ................................ 156
   San Fernando Valley ........................................... 157
   Long Beach Area .................................................. 158
   Other Greater Los Angeles Area Bars................... 159
   Inland Empire....................................................... 160
   North Counties...................................................... 161
   Orange County (central) ....................................... 161
   Laguna Beach ...................................................... 162
   Palm Springs Area................................................ 163
   Book & Video Stores............................................. 163
   Adult Stores ......................................................... 163
   Baths .................................................................... 167
   Phone Lines and Personals................................... 168
   Gay Tourism ........................................................ 171
   Publications .......................................................... 172
   Community Support............................................... 175
   Gay Computer BBS's............................................. 176
   Other Resources................................................... 177
   Gay Desert Resorts............................................... 178
   Gay Mail Order Videos.......................................... 179

Gender Bender Goodies ........................................ 182
Gay/Lesbian/Bi/Gender Bender Social Clubs ..... 183

**CHAPTER FOURTEEN**
**Nightlife ................................................................185**
Remember!!! ........................................................ 186
Bars and Clubs ................................................... 187
Los Angeles Area ................................................ 187
Orange County ..................................................... 195
Meeting In The Meat Market .............................. 196
More Nightlife ...................................................... 197

**CHAPTER FIFTEEN**
Nude Beaches & Resorts ..................................... 199
Etiquette and the Problem of Gawkers ................ 202
Nude Beaches ...................................................... 203
San Bernardino County ....................................... 204
Santa Barbara County ......................................... 204
San Diego County ................................................ 205
Nude Resorts & Hotels ........................................ 206
Other Nude Stuff ................................................. 210
Guides To Nude Recreation ................................. 213

**CHAPTER SIXTEEN**
**Gambling ...............................................................215**
Card Rooms ......................................................... 217
Indian Reservations ............................................. 220
Reservations Casinos in San Diego County ......... 222
Race Tracks ......................................................... 223
The Lottery ........................................................... 223
Your Odds of Winning ......................................... 224
Got a Gambling Problem? .................................... 224

**CHAPTER SEVENTEEN**
**Drugs ....................................................................227**
Aphrodisiacs, Recreational & Smart Drugs ......... 227
Herbs ................................................................... 228
Aphrodisiacs ....................................................... 232
Try This Cure For Impotence .............................. 234
Recreational Drugs .............................................. 234
Marijuana ............................................................ 235
Hemp Products .................................................... 236
The Effects ........................................................... 236
Smoke if You Got 'em .......................................... 237
My Opinion ........................................................... 237

Get High on Life ................................................ 238
Drunk (or Stoned) Driving .................................. 239
If You Have a Problem ........................................ 241
Secular Saviors .................................................. 242
Cops and the Law and You .................................. 242
Smart and Life Extension Drugs.......................... 245
Get Smart and Live Longer .................................. 248
Stay Smart!!! ...................................................... 249

**CHAPTER EIGHTEEN**
  **Oddities & Ends ...........................................251**
Carnal Clothing.................................................. 251
Erotic Events ..................................................... 255
Jaded Jewelry .................................................... 258
Tantalizing Toys ................................................. 259
Let's Hear It for the Lawyers ............................... 261
Raunchy Radio.................................................... 262
Private Mail Boxes............................................... 262
Carnal Cakes ..................................................... 263
Maids in the Buff ............................................... 263
Pubic Hair Salon ................................................ 264
Penis Power!! ..................................................... 264
And for those Vast Vaginas .................................. 267
Tantalizing Tours ............................................... 267
Photography....................................................... 268
Girls Who Sell Their Nasty Photos ....................... 270
Phantasy Photographic Models............................. 273
Photographers..................................................... 274
Stimulating Stationery ........................................ 275
Provocative Piercing ........................................... 275
You Be the Director ............................................ 275
Amazing Audio.................................................... 276
Torrid Tattoos .................................................... 277
Bawdy Books ..................................................... 279
Other Oddities ................................................... 281
Motel Meetings.................................................... 281
Sensuous Spa Sessions....................................... 281
Getting It Up on High ......................................... 282
Get Paid to Get Off............................................. 282
Awesome Advertising........................................... 283
Eternal Beauty.................................................... 283
Slide into Bed..................................................... 283
Strange Gifts for Strange People .......................... 284

Let Them Do It ................................................... 204
Feel the Spirit ................................................... 285

**CHAPTER NINETEEN**
  **Censorship**...............................................**287**
  Remember the First Amendment? ...................... 288
  What Harm Pornography?................................... 289
  What Harm Censorship? .................................... 290
  Freedom Isn't Free ........................................... 291
  Other Groups.................................................... 294
  Religion & Censorship....................................... 295
  Freedom to . . . ................................................. 296
  Freethought Books and Publications .................. 297
  Local Freethought Organizations....................... 298
  National Groups................................................ 299

**CHAPTER TWENTY**
  **Sexual Celebrities** ....................................**301**
  Heidi Fleiss ...................................................... 301
  Bill Margold ..................................................... 303
  Norma Jean Almodovar..................................... 304
  Mistress Jayne Alexander.................................. 306
  Robert L. McGinley, Ph.D. ................................ 306
  Jim South ......................................................... 308
  Candye Kane..................................................... 309
  **Adult actresses** .........................................**311**
  Danyel Cheeks .................................................. 311
  Alicia Rio......................................................... 313
  Steve Houston................................................... 314
  Taylor Wane ..................................................... 315
  Brooke Waters................................................... 316
  Traci Lords........................................................ 317
  Kylie Ireland..................................................... 319
  Mistress Brandy................................................ 320

**CHAPTER TWENTY-ONE**
  **The Rear End** .............................................**323**

**APPENDIX A**
  **The Author** ................................................**325**

**APPENDIX B**
  **Lecher McRich's Library** ...........................**327**

**INDEX** ..............................................................**i**

# *INTRODUCTION*

## Words of wisdom from Norma Jean Almodovar . . .

> . . . I'm never vulgar. I kid sex . . . I take it out in the open and laugh at it.
> — *May West*

**A**h, censorship! That age-old tradition of one group of people – usually the government, and/or religious groups – trying to silence the words, thoughts or other non-violent, non-fraudulent, consenting adult, none-of-anyone-else's-business, behavior of another group of people. From the beginning of time, it has been the obsession of some to impose their beliefs on others through coercive tactics.

Whether the group who wished to censor others claimed to have the blessing of a higher authority, or merely claimed to know what was in everyone's best interests, or wished to censor their critics, the lure of the power of censorship is inevitably too strong to ignore.

That's why the framers of the Constitution wanted to limit the power of the government and forbid it from using the weight of the law to impose censorship on the governed.

The insight into human nature of our founding fathers was positively uncanny. They seemed to know there would come a day when lawyers who became legislators would be so plentiful that it would be an easy thing to get laws passed inhibiting the speech of one or more unpopular groups of under-lobbied citizens. Toward that end, the very first amend- ment addressed the rights of a free people to free speech.

"Congress shall make no law respecting an establishment of religion, or prohibiting the free exercise thereof; or abridging the freedom of speech, or of the press . . . " Had they foreseen the many attempts by the very government entrusted to uphold that right to override the Constitution, perhaps they would have felt the need to add, "no ifs, ands or buts!"

Alas, they did not, so over the years, one group or another has attempted, and sometimes successfully, to pass laws that prevent other groups or individuals from freely expressing their ideas. One of the most blatant, flagrant and egregious violations of the rights to free speech has been in the area of sexuality. Often disguised as attempts to regulate morality "for our own good – and the sake of the children!", those who would banish the sexually liberated and their "offensive" ideas, words, pictures, etc. are really abridging the First Amendment.

That damn amendment stands in the way of our govern- ment's ability to gain complete control over us. If only it could be chipped away, a little abridgment here and there, soon there would be nothing left to protect us from whatever group – left or right – that controls our government. All critics of govern- ment policy could be silenced – without the constant invocation of that pesky Constitutional protection!

Thus far, in the brief history of our country, for every group of people who wished to censor, there has been an opposing individual or group willing to stand up and fight against. Some of those who dare to fight are crushed along the way – losing their freedom, their livelihood and their material possessions. Along with them has been destroyed a little more of our freedom. Others have fought valiantly and won – against all odds – and we are all the better for their efforts.

If you want to do something really seditious go out right now and exercise your right to free speech – hire a hooker, view an adult movie, read a pornographic magazine, smoke a joint! And if you enjoy any of these things and hurt no one doing them, then – damn it – get out there and fight for your right to do so! If you are not willing to fight for your rights, who can you expect to do it for you?

\* \* \* \* \* \* \* \* \* \*

*Norma Jean Almodovar is the author of* "From Cop To Call Girl" *and a dedicated worker in the fight for personal freedom. Read her story in the* "Sexual Celebrities" *section of this book.*

© 1995 DR TUPPER

©1993 Jack Messick Photography

# CHAPTER ONE

# Naughty In The Nineties

> . . . don't forget to wear your rubbers.
> — *traditional motherly saying*

**F**or all of you who remember the sixties, seventies and early eighties, it is a whole new world out there. Remember those wild orgies, those good drugs, the string of one-night stands . . . ah yes, it makes me nostalgic for the old days! First it was herpes, and now we have AIDS!! Penicillin doesn't cure those two insidious diseases. And until the scientific and medical community finds a cure or vaccine for herpes, and especially AIDS, we will have to be extremely careful when being naughty . . . and nasty in the nineties.

Though AIDS first gained headlines as an epidemic in the gay community and has spread like wildfire among IV drug users, it should be a concern to the heterosexual community as well. It should be the concern of every sexually active person on the planet . . . and everyone who has a friend or relative who is sexually active.

You have heard of safe sex? Or more appropriately, safer sex? Yes, there are ways to play more safely in the nineties. And to do so, you must know the facts of AIDS, the modes of transmission and the ways to lower your odds of acquiring AIDS.

AIDS is a disease transmitted by intimate sexual contact, the sharing of dirty needles, blood transfusions, and a few other more obscure means, such as a health worker jabbing himself with a needle containing AIDS-tainted blood. There is absolutely no evidence that hugging, kissing, touching, or normal daily contact spreads the disease.

Early in the AIDS epidemic it seemed that only gay men were at risk; in fact, AIDS was first called GRIDS (Gay Related Immune Deficiency Syndrome). But, over time, cases began appearing in the heterosexual community . . . and the general public began to panic. Though AIDS cases still appear to be predominantly, but by no means exclusively, affecting gay men and IV drug users, AIDS is an issue for all sexual beings.

Whatever your sexual preference, gender, class or race, you cannot entirely avoid the risk of contracting AIDS unless you abstain. You can lower that risk. On the following pages we attempt to offer some guidelines to "safer sex." We certainly do not claim to be medical authorities so we strongly suggest that you find out more about AIDS on your own. There are several good books at your local bookstore or library or you can call one of several AIDS organizations in the Los Angeles area.

AIDS is still a mystery; we still do not know all the modes of transmission, we cannot predict its course of action once in the human body, and we still do not have a cure or vaccine for it. So, knowledge is power and the more knowledge you have, the more power you have to control your own destiny.

The following are our classifications of sex in the nineties:

# Very Safe

**. . . ..(anything is better than nothing)**

- Hugging

- Dry social kissing

- Mutual masturbation

- Body massage

- Touching, caressing, feeling, body-to-body rubbing

- Fantasy (wishing you were at a disco, dressed in a leisure suit and sex was in the air)

- Use of sex toys if they are not shared

- Light S & M activities (no bleeding or penetration)

- Voyeurism (watching everyone else having fun!)

# Low Risk

**. . . . . . (there's still hope in the nineties)**

- French (wet) kissing with no sores in the mouth

- Oral-genital contact with no sores in the mouth

- Water sports with urine (no contact with sores)

# Some Risk

**. . . . . . (if you're going to play
. . . play as safely as possible)**

- Anal or vaginal intercourse with a condom

- Oral sex to completion

# More Risky

**. . . . . (for those of you who complain
about condoms!!)**

- Vaginal intercourse without a condom

- Oral sex when there are open sores in the mouth

# Very Risky

**. . . . . (or, another game of Russian Roulette)**

- Anal intercourse without a condom

- Oral-anal contact

- Water sports, if urine comes into contact with sores

- Sharing of sex toys

- Sharing IV drug needles

Remember, we are not experts in AIDS research or prevention, but offer these guidelines as a motivation to obtain more information about your own particular sex practices.

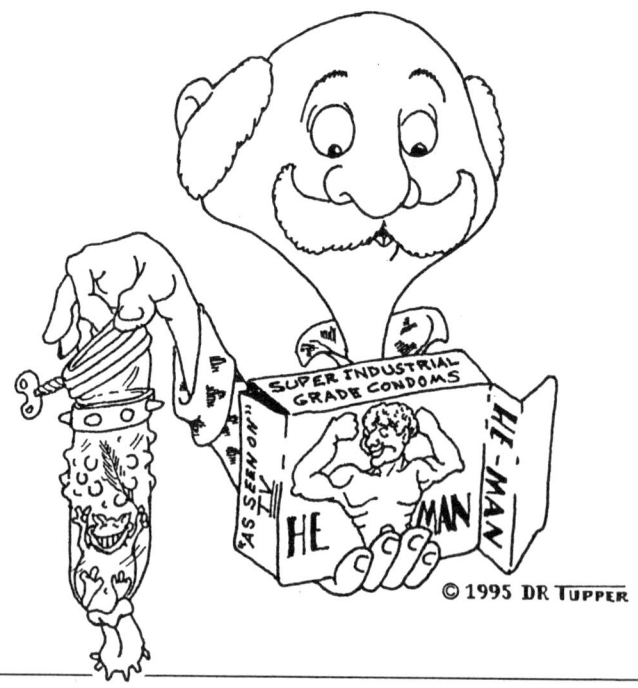

© 1995 DR TUPPER

# What Are The Chances . . . ?

Scientists at the Centers For Disease Control and Prevention have estimated the chances that HIV will be transmitted by vaginal, oral or anal sex. They estimate that a man who is infected with HIV has a 1 in 500 chance of transmitting the disease to a woman in a single act of unprotected vaginal intercourse.

The odds are even less that a woman will transmit it to a man in one solitary act of intercourse. Anal intercourse increase the chances significantly, but the exact risk is uncertain. The odds of transmitting HIV while using a condom correctly drops almost to zero. These odds increase tremendously with frequent unprotected sex.

Scientists do know that AIDS is much more difficult to transmit than other diseases, including other sexually transmitted diseases. That does not mean that restraint, safer sex and protection should be ignored.

# About Condoms

- Condoms are not 100% safe and effective

- Use only latex condoms

- Use a spermicide in addition to a condom

- Use condoms pre-lubricated with nonoxynol-9

- Use a water-soluble lubricant such as KY Jelly

- Do not . . . EVER . . . NEVER . . . use oil based lubricants such as petroleum jelly, body lotions or oils

- Use a new condom every time you have sex

- Learn how to use a condom . . . condom effectiveness is very high if utilized properly

- Hold the tip of the condom to squeeze out air while unrolling it

- After the act is complete, hold the base of the condom while pulling out

- Do not use old condoms that have been in your wallet since the Nixon administration. Condoms are cheap . . . get new ones!!!!!

For more information on condom effectiveness, write to:

### The Mariposa Foundation

*3123 Schweitzer Drive, Topanga, CA 90290*

They do research of human sexuality and the prevention of sexually transmitted diseases and would certainly appreciate a tax-deductible donation to help continue their work.

# Get Tested!!!

Know your HIV status. And know if you have any other sexually transmitted diseases (STD). Other STDs such as syphilis, gonorrhea, and chlamydia are curable, but they can cause severe complications if left untreated. And untreated STDs may be a contributing factor in the contraction and development of AIDS. Call the *Los Angeles AIDS Hotline* at: (213) 876-2437.

# The Old Fashioned Condom

If you think putting on a condom nowadays is a bitch, you should have been around in the Middle Ages. They used various kinds of animal or fish guts or skin. One method occasionally used was to place a piece of animal or fish tissue over the head of the penis and under the foreskin. They would then take some gut or twine and tie the foreskin tightly over the head of the penis. Ouch!!

Early condoms (or sheaths) in the mid-1500s were a standard eight inches long (some men were very optimistic), and were tied at the base with a pink ribbon (to make the penis? . . . or the condom?? more appealing to the female???)

And for you history butts, it is theorized that the word condom comes from the Earl of Condom, who was personal physician to King Charles II of England who ruled in the mid-1600s. Condom (or Earl as he prefered to be called) created a stretched sheath of sheep intestine to help protect his wild, uninhibited king from syphilis. The first "rubber" was introduced in the 1870s and the first latex rubber came out in the 1930s. And, the rest, as they say, is history!

# Choose Sex . . .    Choose Life!!

To be sexual or not to be sexual . . . that is the question. It isn't as easy being naughty in the nineties as it was in the seventies, but before you strap on that old chastity belt or retire to a monastery in the mountains, take a look at your options. What can you do to continue being sexually active and stay alive?

Learn all you can about sexual diseases and their means of transmission. Always . . . **always** keep the concept of "safer sex" in mind, use condoms, don't allow alcohol or drugs to destroy your judgment, use good old common sense . . . and go out and have some fun.

Abstinence and monogamy in a long-term relationship between two HIV-negative partners are the only ways to be absolutely, positively certain of avoiding STDs, but you can minimize your risk tremendously! Choose life . . . and sex!

# More Facts About AIDS

- We live in a world inhabited by infectious organisms. We are protected from these nasty organisms by our immune systems. AIDS kills by destroying our immune system.

- AIDS does not discriminate. There may be some statistical preferences, but it can strike anyone . . . rich, poor, gay, straight, white, black, male, female. Although certain people are at higher risk due to lifestyle choices and demographics, we all need to be concerned.

Photo by F.M. Philips

- Though AIDS does not discriminate and despite dire warnings to the contrary, HIV infection remains highly concentrated among IV drug users and their sexual partners, and gay men.

- A parasite; it cannot reproduce on its own, it needs human cells to survive, it is fragile and extremely minuscule with an amazing survival instinct.

- You don't get AIDS from sharing a glass of water, sharing towels, from mosquitoes, from toilet seats, by kissing, through socializing, from a swimming pool or by shaking hands.

- AIDS is still spreading, especially in the Third World . . . Brazil, India, Thailand appear on the verge of a crisis.

- The more you know, the easier it is to make intelligent decisions. Listen, learn and live!

- Get used to it . . . AIDS is here and there is no cure yet. Be careful and cautious.

# Donations Needed . . .

One group which will put your money to good use in the fight against AIDS is:

## AmFAR

*5900 Wilshire Blvd., Los Angeles, CA 90036*
*(213) 857-5900 or (800) 38-AmFAR*

# For More Information . . .

For more information on AIDS and AIDS prevention call:

### The National AIDS Hotline

*(800) 342-AIDS*
*(800) 344-7432 (Spanish)*
*(800) 243-7889 (TTY) (deaf access)*

# Ignorance Is Not Bliss

As individuals and as a society, we should not ignore AIDS. Whether you know someone with HIV or not, whether you are in a high-risk group or not, whether you are sexually promiscuous or monogamous or celibate, AIDS is a relevant health care issue. Somehow, someway, someday the AIDS crisis will affect your life. It is important to you as a member of a free society to know all the facts. Learn and live. Ignorance is not bliss!!

© 1995 DR TUPPER

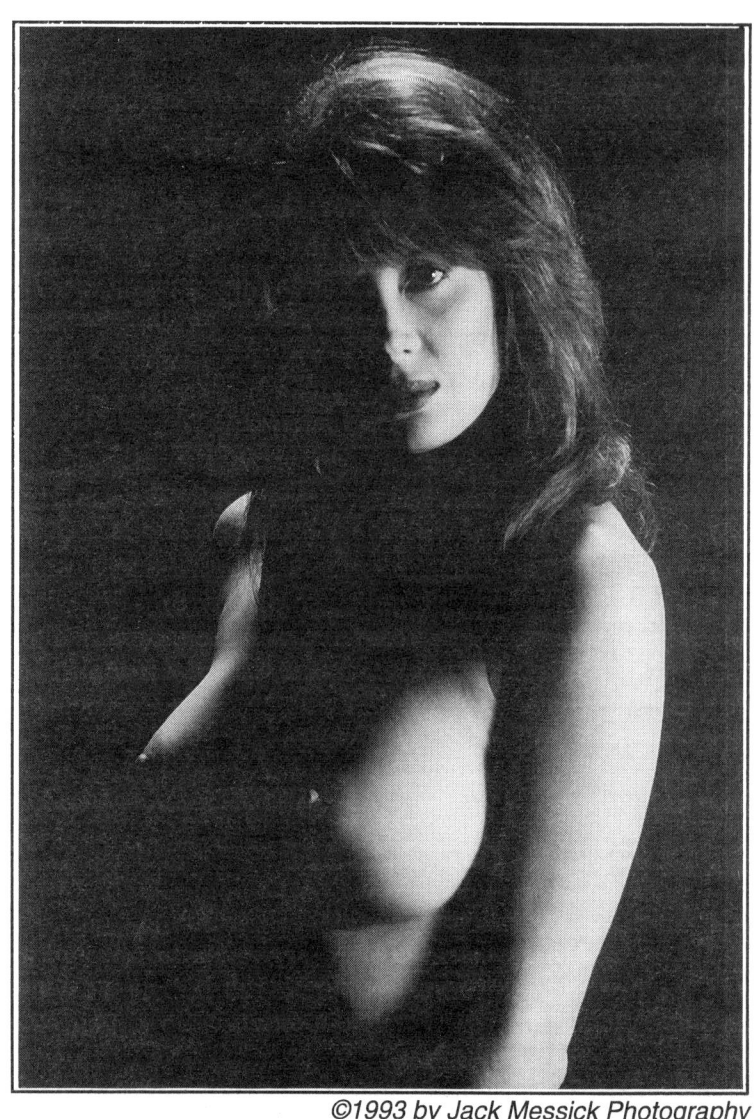

©1993 by Jack Messick Photography

# CHAPTER TWO

# Sexual Supermarkets

. . . .too much of a good thing can be wonderful
— *Mae West*

There are X-rated bookstores all over the Los Angeles city and metropolitan areas. Most of them are fairly similar; some are cleaner and better stocked than others, but they basically have the same merchandise. Some are milder, and cater more to couples while others are the typical porn palace catering to horny single guys. You can find glossy magazines covering every subject including oral, threesomes, bisexuals, anal, orgies, interracial, transvestites, bondage, she-males, gay and more. Everything!!

Movies of all types are found in these stores; both professional and amateur. Sex toys (marital aids for those of you with a ring on your finger) of all shapes, sizes, colors and speeds can be purchased. Swingers' newspapers and magazines, dirty dime-store novels, X-rated novelties, gifts and much more can be found in most of the following stores. Also, many of these book stores have video arcades: peep show booths where you can watch sex flicks until your money and energy run out. If you are interested in watching sex on tape, reading about it, staring at (and drooling over) pictures of it, or enhancing it with toys, this is the chapter for you. Read on!

# Los Angeles Area

Following in no particular order, are the sexual supermarkets in the greater L.A. area:

## The Pleasure Chest

*7733 Santa Monica Blvd.*
*(213) 650-1022*

Enter this store and you enter a wonderful world of erotica. They cater to all your needs: lingerie, oils, lotions, toys, gifts, cards, leather, videos and much more. Clean and well-stocked.

## Le Sex Shoppe

- *6315 1/2 Hollywood Blvd. — (213) 464-9435*
- *45 E. Colorado Blvd., Pasadena — (818) 683-9468*
- *10618 Whittier Blvd., Whittier — (310) 699-9458*
- *6816 Eastern Ave., Bell Gardens — (213) 560-9473*
- *3147 San Fernando Rd., Los Angeles — (213) 258-2867*

These are all well-stocked sexual and sensual supermarkets with all the usual (and some unusual) paraphernalia: books, glossy magazines, swingers' papers, toys, gifts, and videos for sale or rent. They have a great selection of everything at great prices.

## International Love Boutique

*7046 Hollywood Blvd.*
*(213) 466-7046*

A well-stocked erotica store; lingerie, leather, toys, cards, games, condoms and more.

## The Cave

*6315 Hollywood Blvd.*

There are books, toys, novelties, magazines, and if that isn't enough to "wet" and satisfy your appetite, there's a live nude show in back. The nude show will cost you $7 to enter.

## C West Books

*5601 Century Blvd. — (310) 641-9784*

Located near the airport, it's just the place to pick up some interesting reading for that long flight. It's 50 cents to enter and it's your typical adult book store.

## Casanova's Adult World

*7766 Santa Monica Blvd., Hollywood*
*(213) 848-9244*

They carry a large selection of magazines, videos, marital aids and more. They also have poppers, if you're into enhancing your sex life through chemicals. Open 10 to 2 am.

## Hollywood Video

*1651 N. Cahuenga Blvd. — (213) 461-9691*

All the usual stuff: novelties, magazines, videos and more. They also have a 30-channel video arcade. Open 24 hours.

## Stan's

*1117 Western Ave., Hollywood*
*(213) 467-1640*

Part of a five-store chain that has hundreds of videos for sale or rent. They also have a 25-cent video arcade.

© 1995 DR TUPPER

## Odyssey Video

- *11910 Wilshire Blvd., West L.A. — (310) 477-2524*
- *4240 Lincoln Blvd., Marina Del Rey — (310) 823-1100*

They have a vast selection and assortment of videos for rent or sale at prices starting as low as $5.99. Lots of hot stuff!

## Adult Books

*2286 Firestone Blvd., South Gate — (213) 581-6043*

Recently opened place with novelties, magazines, gifts, lingerie and a multi-channel video arcade.

## Drake's

- *7566 Melrose Ave. — (213) 651-5600*
- *8932 Santa Monica Blvd. — (310) 289-8932*

These two erotica stores have all the essentials. Clean and friendly places with condoms, lubes, lotions, vibrators and more.

## Andy's Adult World

*4624 Whittier Blvd., East Los Angeles*
*(213) 269-4123*

Wide selection of paraphernalia and goodies, and a 63-channel video arcade.

## Circus of Books

- *8230 Santa Monica Blvd., West Hollywood*
  *(213) 656-6533*
- *4001 Sunset Blvd., Silverlake — (213) 666-1304*

Adult erotica store with a huge selection of fun and sensual goodies.

## Main Theater

*438 Main Street — (213) 236-0652*

A relic from the past . . . a porno movie house that shows three movies per day and runs them continuously . . . 24 hours. $5 to get in. Located downtown . . . so be careful!

### Crenshaw Adult Books
*15232 Crenshaw Blvd., Gardena*
*(213) 327-5186*

### Atlantic World
*5525 Atlantic Ave., Long Beach*

### Pacific World
*1529 W. Pacific Coast Hwy., Long Beach*
*(310) 431-9312*

### TC World
*6037-39 Atlantic Ave., Long Beach*
*(310) 423-9991*

### Joe's Adult Books
*4535 W. Century Blvd., Inglewood*
*(213) 419-9064*

More goodies for your pleasure.

### Adult Book Store
*440 S. Main — (213) 614-0844*

# San Fernando Valley

### Le Sex Shoppe

© 1995 DR TUPPER

* *21625 Sherman Way, Canoga Park — (818) 992-9801*
* *4877 Lankershim Blvd., N. Hollywood — (818) 760-9529*
* *4539 Van Nuys Blvd., Sherman Oaks — (818) 501-9609*
* *12323 Ventura Blvd., Studio City — (818) 760-9352*

A large chain of stores where you can purchase most anything erotic: magazines, papers, videos, toys, gifts and more. They have a giant video selection, 25-cent video arcades, on-site private viewing rooms and much more.

### Northridge Video
*17646 Lassen St., Northridge — (818) 772-0939*

This place has adult and family videos. They have all major titles and low sale prices.

## Odyssey Video

*4810 Vineland Ave., N. Hollywood*
*(818) 769-2001*

They have thousands of videos for sale or rent. Sale prices begin as low as $5.99.

## Diamond Adult World

*6406 Van Nuys Blvd., Van Nuys*
*(818) 997-3665*

Adult store with all the usual goodies, mags and toys. Also has a 100-channel video arcade for your viewing pleasure.

## Twisted Video

*10530 Burbank Blvd., N. Hollywood*
*(818) 508-0559*

Loads of videos with a tremendous selection of gay videos.

## Valley Bookstore

*6749 Lankershim Blvd., N. Hollywood*
*(818) 765-9170*

All the usual stuff.

## Jason's II

*6408 Tujunga ,North Hollywood*
*(818) 506-6840*

## Sherman Boostore

*11841 Sherman Way, North Hollywood*
*(818) 765-1217*

# Orange County

## The Book Store

*8502 Garden Grove Blvd., Garden Grove*
*(714) 537-2723*

Has all the usual items for you horny Republican bastards out there!

## Midnight Rental & Preview Center

*8743 Garden Grove Blvd., Garden Grove*
*(714) 534-9922*

This is the place to preview all those hot new flicks . . . and then rent them for the night. Well-stocked with all the new releases.

## Midnight Adult Book & Video

* *8745 Garden Grove Blvd., Garden Grove*
  *(714) 534-9823*

* *12686 Garden Grove Blvd., Garden Grove*
  *( 714) 638-8595*

Well-stocked places with magazines, periodicals, swingers' papers, toys, gifts and novelties. Lots of videos for sale or rent. You can also watch movies in their video arcade. Part of a large chain with several stores in the San Diego area.

## The Party House

*8751 Garden Grove Blvd.,*
*Garden Grove*
*(714) 534-9996*

This is part of the Midnight chain . . . and it has all the usual goodies and some unusual ones, too!!

## Academy Video

*18122 Brookhurst, Fountain Valley*
*(714) 964-1691*

They have a large selection of videos; some priced as low as $7 for sale.

## Condom Revolution

*1799 Newport Blvd., Suite A102,*
*Costa Mesa*
*(714) 646-1967*

An erotic giftshop with toys, games, cards, novelties, oils and lingerie and more.

© 1995 DR TUPPER

# Other Areas

## Le Sex Shoppe

- *3945 Market St., Riverside — (909) 788-5194*
- *14589 Valley Blvd., Fontana — (909) 350-4717*
- *2320 Vineyard Way, Oxnard — (805) 981-4611*

Part of the large chain of stores serving all of the Los Angeles area. Well-stocked with all your favorite playthings.

## Sunshine Gifts

*38519 Sierra Hwy., Palmdale — (805) 265-0652*

Part of the Midnight chain, this has all the fun and erotic things you desire. Videos, gifts, toys, magazines and more.

## Video Fantasies

*5327 Mission Blvd., Rubidoux — (909) 782-8056*

Also part of the Midnight chain, this has all the usual great things you expect from Midnight.

## Stan's

- *19266 Walnut Ave., Rowland Heights — (818) 854-3575*
- *7505 Foothill Blvd., Tujunga — (818) 352-8735*
- *4651 Holt, Suite J, Montclair — (909) 625-4277*
- *530 S. Citrus, Azusa — (818) 966-1900*

All stores have a super selection of videos for sale or rent. Also have video arcades playing your favorite X-rated movies.

## Mustang Adult Books & Video

*961 N. Central, Upland — (909) 981-0227*

This place stocks it all: books, magazines, videos, bondage equipment, lingerie, condoms, toys and more. Great prices on fun and fantasy items.

## Toy Box

*1999 Arrow Rtout, Upland — (909) 982-9407*

More stuff for your lpleasure.

## Unmentionables

*1200 S. Diamond Bar Blvd., Diamond Bar*
*(909) 861-2000*

Erotic store with a variety of goodies: toys, gifts, lingerie and more.

## Fantasy 66

*835 E. Foothill Blvd., Rialto*
*(909) 820-9386*

You can find all the usual mags, rags, flicks, tricks and toys here. Videos for sale or rent.

## Baseline Books

*25557 E. Baseline St., San Bernardino*
*(909) 889-3284*

They advertise as the "cleanest" dirty book store in town. I'm not certain if that is true, but I attest to the fact that it is very neat and clean. They have videos for sale or rent and all the other usual playthings.

## Mount Vernon News

*328 Mt. Vernon, San Bernardino*
*(909) 888-4210*

Along with regular magazines, comics and paperbacks, they have a complete selection of adult and swingers' publications.

## Liberty Books

*15106 Valley Blvd., Fontana*
*(909) 357-3421*

They advertise that they are the store that has everything in fine adult entertainment . . . and that about says it all. Videos, leather, lingerie, magazines, newspapers, novelties, games, a 99-channel video arcade and more.

Le Sex Shoppe                          *Photo by F.M. Philips*

## Spice For Life

*1391 Arrow Hwy., San Dimas*
*(818) 963-6924 or (909) 592-0569*

An upscale lingerie boutique with tons of goodies for sale.
They will also plan and arrange local romantic escapes from
limos to hot tubs to dinners to flowers.

## V & B Adult Book Store

*15651 Valley Blvd., City of Industry — (818) 968-4475*

They have all the usual goodies . . . with lots of low-priced
videos and computer CDs for sale. Novelties, gifts, magazines,
a video arcade and more.

## Three Star Adult News

*359 E. Main St., Ventura — (805) 653-9068*

Adult magazines and books for your reading pleasure.

## A.A. Video & Novelty

*42257 6th Street Warehouse #301, Lancaster, CA 93534*
*(800) 624-2444 or (805) 949-9583*

A warehouse full of videos and adult toys and novelties. Sells
wholesale and retail only . . . no mail order.

# Love Happens at the Strangest Places . . .

Here's a story about something that happened to me several years back. I was in a local X-rated book store browsing through the cards and gifts when I caught the eye of a pretty girl who was browsing through the magazines. We kept giving each other the eye until I finally worked up the courage to say "hi." We laughed at the magazines and she acted like a kid in a candy store.

After a short time, she asked me about the video arcade. She had never been in one and she wondered what all those guys did in there. I laughed and told her that I "think they, ah, pleasure themselves." "Oh, you mean they jerk off in there." She laughed and then asked if I wanted to go in a booth with her. Now there was an offer I couldn't resist!! So, I did.

We flipped through the channels for a few minutes before she decided she wanted to go. I thought she would run away before I asked for her phone number . . . but she asked for mine as we walked to our cars. We had a great date that night and a hot and heavy relationship for several months before she moved away. You just never know when and where you'll meet that someone special!!

# The Overly Enthusiastic Salesman

My girlfriend and I were in a store looking for a "present" for her. The salesman seemed overly pleased to show her the vibrators. He followed us around the store pointing out the best models. He talked about various speeds and sizes and colors and materials. My girlfriend turned several shades of crimson, but the salesman's enthusiasm paid off . . . she left the store with a beautiful magenta-colored variable-speed vibrator. He enthusiastically asked if he could show her how to use it . . . but she told him she was already an expert!!

©1993 Jack Messick Photography

# CHAPTER THREE

# Tits & Ass

> . . . I'm not against naked girls
> – not as often as I'd like to be.
> — *Benny Hill*

**I**f you like seeing naked, half-naked or scantily-clad women shake their stuff, this is the chapter for you. Los Angeles has topless, go-go dancers and all-nude clubs. At the topless and go-go clubs you can order your favorite cocktail, but at the all-nude clubs you'll have to satisfy your thirst with juices or sodas. If the girls take it all off, no alcohol is served. That's the law.

Whether you drink or not, you must always remember to behave yourself in the clubs. If the sight of a bare breast gets your hormones raging so much that you can't control yourself, perhaps you better not go. If you can't stop yourself from playing grab-ass with the girls, forget it; stay home. Most of these places have bouncers the size of large buildings, and they will not hesitate to throw you out by the seat of your pants if you don't mind your manners.

I know a friend of a friend who reached out and touched one of the girls at a table dance . . . one of the hulking bouncers reached out and touched him . . . touched him all the way to the parking lot where he was told to keep his ass off the premises!

And don't forget to tip the girls generously. Even though it may not look like work, the dancers work their butts off. And tips are usually the only income they receive. So, give them tip for tit, so to speak.

The following is a list of some of the clubs in the greater Los Angeles area. Check them out and have a good time.

# Los Angeles County

## (excluding the San Fernando Valley)

All you city dwellers, get out of the tiring heat of the city and into the stimulating heat of the strip clubs!!

## Alladin

*5214 Sunset Blvd., Hollywood*
*(213) 660-1410*

Nothing special here to get your testosterone overly excited. It's $4 to get in and the drinks are expensive. Some girls are quite attractive and sexy . . . some aren't that great.

## Angels Nite Club

*2310 W. Pacific Coast Hwy., Long Beach*
*(310) 435-7320*

Your typical topless club. A lively place, but I thought it was more fun when they had sexy go-go dancers. The table dances are now "no touch." There are pool tables for when you get tired of the action. Open from 2 pm to 2 am.

## Bailey's Twenty-Twenty Gentlemen's Club

*2020 Avenue of the Stars, Century City*
*(213) 933-2020*

A topless club that serves lunch, dinner and a late night menu. Upscale club with some great looking dancers; about 25 working per shift. Open 11:30 am - 2 am (Monday - Friday), 6 pm - 2 am (Saturday and Sunday).

## Barbary Coast

*14320 S. Western Ave., Gardena — (310) 532-3406*

Topless dancers shake their stuff in a friendly, casual atmosphere. About $5 to get in. Table dances are $5.

## Bare Elegance

*4824 Imperial Hwy., Hawthorne (near the airport)*
*(310) 649-1100*

There's total nudity here. Yea! No alcohol served. Booo! There are some sizzling girls working here. $10 gets you in the door. It's all neon and modern decor where you get to drink cokes and juices and watch some very hot bodies strut their stuff. Table dances are $20 and some of the table dances are very hot . . . up close and personal.

Three of my favorites dancers are Mia: a very pretty blonde with an excellent body; Ashley: a decent looker who dances up a storm; and Obsession (I bet that's not her real name!), who is a dark exotic beauty with an extraordinary body. They serve food, and proper attire is required.

## The Body Shop

*8250 W. Sunset Blvd. — (213) 656-1401*

A famous burlesque house where the girls dance for you totally nude. There is an $8 cover charge. It's an average place where you can see it all. It's open until 2am.

## The Cave Theater

*6315 Hollywood Blvd.*
*(213) 465-0473 or (213) 465-3208*

Live nude show that will cost you $7 to get in. They have seven shows daily. There is also an adjacent adult book store for your shopping convenience.

## Cheetah's

*4600 Hollywood Blvd. — (213) 660-6733*

Topless dancers, full bar, pool tables and no cover . . . what more could you ask for.

The Tropicana in Hollywood                    *Photo by F.M. Philips*

## Century Theater 7 Lounge

*5601 W. Century Blvd.*
*(213) 641-6833*

Naked girls! Naked girls! Naked girls!! 3 to 10 big ones to enter. Open 11 am - 2 am. Located near the airport. Table dances cost $12 and they can be very revealing! Amanda is my favorite here; she's a very pretty brunette with a great body, and her table dance is very revealing and stimulating!!

## Crazy Girls

*1433 N. LaBrea Ave., Hollywood*
*(213) 969-0055*

It's only $3 to get in, but drinks are around $5. Some very pretty girls here, but I found the girls to be rather aloof and unfriendly (though I would still let one of them take me home if they begged and pleaded!). Table dances cost $25. Private and secluded booths are available for your viewing pleasure, but that doesn't mean you can touch. One girl to look for is Tara, a very pretty brunette with a great body and good dance moves who usually works the day shift. Open noon to 2 am.

## Extasy

*2470 Fletcher Drive*
*(213) 644-1122*

Totally nude dancers. It's $5 to enter. They offer hot private table dances for $20, and also serve food. Catch their Thursday night amateur contest. Open noon to 2 am (Friday and Saturday: Noon to 3 am).

## 1st King

*14401 S. Western Ave., Gardena*
*(310) 532-5801*

This club offers topless dancing and it will cost you about $5 to get in (it varies).

## Fritz That's It

*9747 E. Artesia Blvd., Bellflower*
*(213) 925-2308*

A topless place with lots of dancers working each shift. Has hot table dances, pool tables and some sexy girls. It's $5 to get in at night. A friend of mine used to work here . . . she was a very hot dancer and is a very sexy woman. Unfortunately, she has moved on to a different career!

## Frontview Cabaret

*1612 Pacific Coast Hwy.*
*(310) 539-6122*

Located in the Harbor City area, you get a "front view" and a back view and a side view of lots of bare-breasted girls. Cover from $3 to $5 and table dances $10. Open 11 to 2 am.

## The Holiday

*10915 Norwalk Blvd., Santa Fe Springs*
*(310) 944-6581*

A fun topless place with about 25 dancers working per shift. During football season it's worth it to check out their Monday Night Football promotions.

## Jumbo's Clown Room

*5153 Hollywood Blvd. — (213) 666-1187*

Basic guys watching basic girls strut their basic stuff. A neighborhood type bar; a "Cheers" with go-go dancers. Open 2 pm to 2 am.

## Monte Carlo II

*5222 Sunset Blvd., Hollywood — (213) 664-4702*

It's another basic topless place with a few sexy girls vying for your stares and money. Open 2 pm to 2 am.

## The New Jet Strip

*10624 Hawthorne Blvd. — (310) 671-1100*

A totally nude place that has hot stage, table and couch dances. The cover charge varies from $5 to $10. They seem to have about ten to twenty dancers working each shift. Some of them will fog up your glasses!! Lunch is served from 11 am to 5 pm. There is a big-screen TV for major sporting events. They're open from 11 am to 2 am (11 am - 3 am Fridays and Saturdays, 4 pm - 1 am Sundays). Look for their hot dance contest on Wednesday nights.

## Seventh Veil

*7180 Sunset Blvd., Hollywood — (213) 876-4761*

Another totally nude place. It's $8 to enter during the day and even more at night! The cokes and juices will cost you plenty also. You may see a few knockouts here . . . then again, you may not. On my last visit, I did see a few standouts (pun intended!). There are three stages for your viewing pleasure.

## Sly Fox

*2528 W. Rosecrans, Gardena — 310) 327-2796*

Topless dancers show you their stuff! There are a few hot dancers here. It's inexpensive to get in and they have some hot nude table dances.

# Star Strip

*365 N. La Cienega Blvd. — (213) 652-1741*

Totally nude place that has several small stages and some sexy girls. You may find a porno star strutting her stuff on stage from time to time. Look for specials on certain nights when F.O.X.E. brings some of the top porno stars to strip. Large club with eight stages that opens at 5 pm and closes at 2 am.

## Tiki Theater

*5462 Santa Monica Blvd. — (213) 462-0345*

Twenty-four hours a day of total nudity! They show adult movies all day and night, with live erotic dancing during the intermissions.

## Sunset Strip

*5214 Sunset Blvd. — (213) 660-1410*

A new upscale topless club with some hot dancers. It's $5 to get in. They have pool tables and serve lunch on weekdays.

## Tropicana

*1250 N. Western Ave., Hollywood — (213) 464-1653*

Also known as the "Hollywood Tropicana," it's $10 - $15 to get through the door. There's a multitude of lovely ladies working here. You should see some fantastic foxes baring their souls and breasts.

One of their specialties is nude oil wrestling. You get the opportunity to hose down a girl or to wrestle with one (and don't think they can't pin your wimpy ass to the ground in a New York minute!). Look for midweek passes in free local newspapers.

## Wild Goose

*1160 Aviation Blvd., Inglewood — (310) 643-9769*

It's a topless place with a large stage and some attractive women. They have table dances, food, pool tables, and video games (who's interested in the video games when there are half-naked women all around??). Open 11 am to 2 am. Located near the airport.

# San Fernando Valley

Come on all you voyeuristic valley boys . . . see some hot valley girls in the flesh!!

## Bob's Classy Lady

*14626 Raymer St., Van Nuys*
*(818) 787-2627 (BOBS)*

Has nude stage, table, booth and shower dancing. $5 cover during the day and $10 at night. Has some top adult film stars every week. Also serves food.

## Candy Cat I

*21625 Devonshire St., Chatsworth*
*(818) 341-0134*

A topless place that's free to enter and has some of the hottest girls around. They serve beer, wine, and sodas. They also have pool tables and video games.

# Star Strip

Totally nude place that has several small stages and some sexy girls. You may find a porno star strutting her stuff on stage from time to time. Look for specials on certain nights when *F.O.X.E.* brings some of the top porno stars to strip. Large club with eight stages that opens at 5 pm and closes at 2 am.

**365 N. La Cienega Blvd.** • **(213) 652-1741**

## Candy Cat Too

*6816 Winnetka, Canoga Park*
*(818) 999-3187*

Sister club to Candy Cat I. It's topless with a few nice looking dancers.

## The Classy Lady

*8314 Sepulveda Blvd., Sepulveda*
*(818) 891-9544*

Your basic topless dancing place with your basic topless dancers. It's free to get in. It's $5 for a table dance.

## Fantasy Island

*11434 W. Pico Blvd.*
*(310) 473-5678*

Large place with very sexy go-go dancers and a $5 cover.

## The Gentlemen's Club

*5175 San Fernando Rd.*
*(818) 552-3686*

Upscale totally nude strip club with private shows, table dances and a free lunch buffet. Open noon - 2 am (Noon - 3 am, Friday and Saturday).

## Hollywood-A-Go-Go

*10542 Hollywood Blvd., North Hollywood*
*(818) 763-3090*

The girls don't take it off here . . . they dance around in their bikinis. There are some pretty and sexy girls. They serve beer and wine and there is never a cover charge.

## Odd Ball Cabaret

*8532 Sepulveda Blvd., Van Nuys*
*(818) 893-3392*

Sister club to Bare Elegance and New Jet Strip. There's a $10 cover at night. They have good kitchen service, hot table dances, and a dance contest on Tuesday nights. It's open 11 am to 2 am (4 pm to 1 am on Sunday).

## Playtime

*13324 Sherman Way, Van Nuys*
*(818) 765-0718*

Basic topless dancing place with no cover. Table dances are $5.

## Star Garden

*6630 Lankershim Blvd., N. Hollywood*
*(818) 764-9766*

Your basic topless club with your basic bare-breasted girls. $4 cover charge

## Venus Faire

*6452 Lankershim Blvd., North Hollywood*
*(818) 763-0400*

It's a totally nude twenty-four hour dance peep show. Live nude girls stripping for your peeping pleasure in what's termed "New York style" dancing. Open 24 hours, 7 days a week.

# Orange County

Take a journey behind the "Orange Curtain" and see what's shaking and stripping!

## California Girls

*1109 N. Harbor Blvd., Santa Ana*
*(714) 554-0491*

It's free to enter and you can see go-go dancers shaking and strutting their stuff. Some attractive, some not-so-beautiful. Hit or miss here.

## Humdinger

*12581 Harbor Blvd., Garden Grove*
*(714) 750-2051*

Go-Go dancing from 1 pm - 2 am. $2 cover at night with about 5 to 7 girls working per shift. Has two stages and pool tables.

## Captain Cream's

*23642 Rockfield Blvd., El Toro*
*(714) 951-5052*

It's a large club with some attractive topless dancers. They have a complete lunch menu and also offer happy-hour food. They have televisions, pool tables and videos. There are some outstanding girls at this place; some "11's" on the scale of 1 to 10. There is also plenty of silicone and peroxide walking around. They offer hot cream wrestling (hence the club's name). It's a fun, friendly and stimulating club. Look for Elise, a gorgeous blonde, although she is so gorgeous she may be in the movies or Playboy's centerfold by the time you read this. It's open 11 am to 2 am.

## Che Che Club

*1109 N. Harbor Blvd., Santa Ana*
*(714) 554-0491*

The girls dance in bikinis here. Some sexy girls. Open 11 am - 2 am.

## Funhouse

*11572 Beach Blvd., Stanton*
*(714) 898-9933*

Basic place with basic exotic bikini dancers. The cover charge is $5.

## Harvey's Bar & Grill

*3020 Coronado St., Anaheim*
*(714) 630-0810*

Has great American and Mexican food. Also has exotic dancers who will do table dancing.

## Marbles

*1160 N. Kraemer Blvd., Anaheim*
*(714) 630-0147*

Topless club with full kitchen and many special events.

The Tropical Lei                    *Photo by F.M. Philips*

## Mr. Jay's

*2101 E. Edinger, Santa Ana*
*(714) 667-5000*

It's free to get in and you'll see some good bodies and some so-so bodies strut their stuff topless.

## Paddy Murphy's

*2920 W. Warner Ave., Santa Ana*
*(714) 556-8956*

Your average place with some above-average, average, and below-average girls. Topless and nude dancing for your voyeuristic delights. $3 will get you in before 6 pm and $5 will get you in after 6.

## Sandi's Wounded Knee Cabaret

*815 Brookhurst St. Anaheim*
*(714) 635-8040*

Topless dancers, pool tables, video machines and some fun times. $5 cover at night.

## T J's Theater

*10350 Beach Blvd., Stanton*
*(714) 995-1534*

Nude dancing place with about 15 girls working per shift. It's about $10 to get in and it's open until 2 am. There's one stage in the middle and seats all around the room. Table dances cost $10 and the girls get up close and personal; they touch you and grind against you and get you all worked up!

I found the girls to be quite friendly. My favorite is Angel, a dark-haired beauty with a knockout body and an oh-so-very-hot table dance. Located in a cookie cutter mini-mall; it's pretty hot inside!

# Inland Empire, Desert Cities & Others

It's time for all you desert rats and country club fanatics to get out of the blazing sun and stimulate the senses!

## Eyefull, Inc.

*5282 Mission Blvd., Ontario*
*(714) 591-7005*

They offer both topless and nude dancing. The dancers take it all off on stage. There is couch dancing, table top dancing, oil wrestling, amateur contests, banana eating contests (I'd love to see one of those!!), and featuring some famous dancers from time to time. The cover charge averages $5. You can also get your picture taken with one of the gorgeous dancers. The club is part of the Deja Vu chain. Good place to get an "eyeful"!!

## Fantasy Topless Theatre

*1019 S. LaCadena Dr., Colton*
*(714) 370-1574*

Topless stage and table dancing. About 15 or 20 girls working per shift. Cover is $5 and it's open 11 am - 2 am.

The Pink Lady            *Photo by F.M. Philips*

## The Pink Lady

*67-990 Hwy. 111 (pink building), Cathedral City*
*(619) 328-1434*

Located in the Palm Springs area, this club offers some sexy ladies for your viewing pleasure. It costs $3 to get in and it's open noon to 2 am. It's a very classy club that has go-go dancers (they don't take it off). They offer a happy hour and reasonable drink prices.

## Spearmint Rhino Club

*630 Maulhardt Ave., Oxnard*
*(805) 988-65818*

Nude stage and couch dancing. Open 11 am - 2 am.

## Pope's Back Street

*508 B Industrial Way, Palm Springs*
*(619) 327-1902*

They offer nude dancing which means you'll be drinking expensive sodas and juices all night. They usually have about 10 to 15 dancers working. Open 11 am to 2 am. They also offer food service with good chili and cheeseburgers.

## Spearmint Rhino Club

*573 N. Central Ave., Upland — (909) 946-5378*

Nice bar with some hot dancers and no cover charge.

## Tropical Lei

*2121 W. Foothill Blvd., Upland — (714) 985-1575*

A nude dancing place that offers some sexy dancers on stage. Couch dances are available for $20! Plus $15 to get in on weekends and $8 on weekdays. There are about 10-15 girls working each shift and some of them are very sexy. Hours are 11 am to 2 am (3 pm to 2 am Sundays). Many of my friends rate this place an "A+." A few readers of our Sin Diego book wrote and mentioned this place as their favorite.

## Villa-A-Go-Go

*1420 W. Holt, Ontario — (714) 986-3607*

Typical nude dancing place. It will cost you $5 to get in. Open 11 am to 2 am (1 pm to 2 am Sundays).

© 1995 DR TUPPER

# Modeling Studios

These are not your typical dancing establishments. No, they are more personal and private. You get to watch a girl dance just for you . . . in a private room. It's just you and the sexy dancer. Of course, the modeling studios cost more than the typical strip joints. But, for those of you who like it up close and personal, these may be just the places. What goes on behind the closed doors? . . . you'll have to find out for yourself.

### Flash Modeling Studio

*11321 San Fernando Rd. — (818) 890-6650*

They offer totally nude dance shows in a private room. They will do face dancing (sounds like a good time to me!!), bend-overs, spreads, fantasy and two-girl shows. You can also take photos of the girls (they have cameras available). You have a choice of several sexy models. Niki (if she's still there) is very seeexxxxxxy!! Open noon to 8 pm Monday through Friday (noon-6 pm Saturday).

### Suzette's Studio

*4224 E. Florence Blvd., City of Bell — (213) 560-9007*

This place is open twenty-four hours for your voyeuristic pleasure. They have a good assortment of girls to choose from. Many of them do not speak English very well; so you may have to use body language.

### Paris House

*7527 Santa Monica Blvd., Hollywood*

You can see totally nude girls in private rooms. They will dance and bend and stretch and reach and . . . whatever. There are approximately 30 girls to choose from. Open 7 days a week noon to 10 pm.

### Lingerie & Accessories

*22706 S. Western Ave., Torrance — (310) 212-7280*

Open 11-11, Tuesday through Saturday. Same rates and concept as the other places.

## Lingerie Dreams

*20769 S. Avalon, Carson*
*(800) 616-6335*

If you want to buy some lingerie for your wife or girlfriend, you can see how it looks on some hot models first. They offer private modeling sessions; just you and the girl, modeling her lingerie and taking it off. If you buy some, don't tell your woman where you got it! Hours are 9 am to midnight (10 to midnight on Saturdays and noon to 8 pm on Sundays).

## Lingerie Oasis

*1212 Pacific Coast Highway*

Have sexy girls in private rooms. $40 for 20 minutes. (Wish someone would pay me $120 an hour to prance around in my skivies.)

# For The Ladies

Here are a few clubs that offer hot-bodied erotic dancing men for those lusty ladies out there.

## Bailey's 2020

*2020 Avenue of the Stars, ABC Entertainment Center*
*(213) 933-2020*

They offer you "the centerfold men of Playgirl Magazine." Look for the hot hunks every Thursday, Friday and Saturday night. The night my girlfriend went, I had to wipe the drool off her face when she got home!!

## *Chippendale's*

*(310) 396-4045*

Here's the most famous male dance show in the world. They are a touring show and constantly change locations, so you need to call for more information.

page for Lust Angeles

Danyel Cheeks

©1993 Danyel Cheeks Fan Club

# CHAPTER FOUR

# Mail Order Videos

> . . . the difference between pornography
> and erotica is lighting
> — *Gloria Leonard*

**T**homas Alva Edison developed the first commercially successful motion picture camera in 1889, and by the early 1900's, the pornographic film industry had begun. Many of these early films were made in Buenos Aires and shipped to the rich and horny aristocrats in Europe. French whorehouses showed their customers these early sex films for $20 . . . a great deal of money back then!! When customs officials in Europe cracked down on the importation of these films, innovative entrepreneurs in France and Germany began to make their own films.

Americans didn't really become involved in porn until after World War I. New York City became the center of the industry at that time. In the twenties, thirties, forties and fifties, these "stag" films were often shown at the local Elks Lodge, Rotary Club, Lions Lodge, Kiwanis Club or other fraternal organizations. Even though there were strict laws against showing and viewing sex films, these places were rarely busted . . . usually it was because the local police chief belonged to the organization showing the film!!

In the sixties, arcades showing these sex films began popping up in all the big cities. The films were called "loops" because they ran for ten minutes or so and played over and over again. As laws loosened up and people did too, films moved into X-rated theaters and eventually, with the advance of technology, into our living rooms and bedrooms with the invention and proliferation of VCRs.

Just as the movie industry once moved into Los Angeles and called it home, the porno industry has done the same. In the sixties and early seventies, San Francisco was known as "the porn capital of the world" despite earnest attempts by then-city councilwoman (and now U.S. Senator) Dianne Feinstein to close down the dancing places and arcades. Places like the Mitchell Brothers, O'Farrell Theater and the Condor Club all have their place in San Francisco (and the sex industry's) history. But, as the X-rated industry grew exponentially and more films were needed and made for the VCR market, many film companies and distributors set up shop in "Lust Angeles."

Los Angeles is now the center of X-rated movie production and mail order activity. More movies, professional and amateur, are produced here than anywhere else. There are big companies, small companies, old companies and new companies. Some mail order companies are also production companies while others merely market the flicks. Mail order companies are everywhere and you can obtain the full spectrum of skin flicks from them: mainstream, gay, bisexual, bondage, kink, amateur and any other sexual activity you can think of. Some market and distribute only the films they make, while others market everything they can make money from. Some market to Mr. and Mrs. and Ms Public, while others only distribute to dealers.

# Mail Order Companies

The following is a list of some of the mail order and production companies in the L.A. area. Some are large companies that produce and market major adult releases while others may be just a girl trying to support herself by selling some of her home videos. Most producers offer direct mail order sales to individuals, though a few only offer sales to distributors. Many publish catalogues and brochures;

some will cost you a nominal fee. For more information about a particular company, call the listed phone number or write to the company's address.

When you write, always include a signed statement attesting to your age (you must be over 18 !!). This should save a great deal of time and get those dirty movies in your sweaty palms much sooner. These companies were all in existence at the time of printing, but we cannot guarantee that they will still be around when you read this. Some video companies are fly-by-night operations, while others are extremely steady and reliable. Find out for certain before you order anything or send any money.

I know a girl who used to work for an amateur mail order video distributor. She worked the desk and the phones and sat around all day watching porno videos! I guess you could say she had a "hard" job!

OK all you porn princes (and princesses) and video voyeurs . . . and potential video vixens and amateur studs . . . here's where you can get those hot videos through the mail.

## AFV Releasing

*9619 Canoga Ave., Chatsworth, CA 91311*
*(818) 407-0900*

Markets a full line of professional films under the names *Arrow, Eruption, Flame* and *Down & Dirty.*

## AFVC

*13160 Raymer St., North Hollywood, CA 91605*
*(818) 765-8091*

Puts out a good selection of orgy films: *Amateur Orgies, Black Orgies,* and a good selection of other films.

## Anabolic Productions

*P.O. Box 12456, Marina Del Rey, CA 90292*
*(800) 233-2264*

Produces the *Totally Nasty* home video series, a down and dirty line of amateur porn.

# Ataxi

*3243 Arlington Ave. Suite 375, Riverside, CA 92506*
*(No phone)*

Sells some great amateur and professional films.

# Avica Entertainment

*P.O. Box 545 9018 Balboa Blvd., Northridge, CA 91325*
*(No phone)*

An amateur seller whose Dick & Jane series is very hot hot hot!

# Bon-Vue Enterprises

*901 West Victoria #G, Compton, CA 90220*
*(800) 827-3787*

They put out a great selection of B & D films, some girl-girl wrestling flicks and much more.

# Caballero

*15041 Calvert Street, Suite B, Van Nuys, CA 91411*
*(800) 269-4457*

They produce *Sweet Pink* and *Swedish Erotica* films. Top-notch feature films.

# Catalina Video

*P.O. Box 7016, Los Angeles, CA 91357 (No phone)*

They release girl-girl, bisexual, and a great selection of all male videos.

# Cinderella

*8021 Remmet Ave., Canoga Park, CA 91304*
*(818) 884-6681*

They market Pepper Productions *(Jalapeno Peppers, Yellow Peppers, Cherry Peppers, Black Peppers)*, and much more. You can get the CDI Home Video catalog, which has hundreds of videos for sale.

## Curtis Dupont

*7046 Hollywood Blvd. #203, Los Angeles, CA 90028*
*(213) 462-6745*

Markets female wrestling, boxing and catfighting films. If you like girls fighting each other: scratching, crawling, ripping, pawing – you'll like these.

## D.O.M. Corporation;

*Post Office Box 9786, Marina Del Rey, CA 90295*

Carries most major lines. Reliable company that also offers toys, phone lines and more.

## D.G. Distributors

*1736 Erringer Rd. #104, Simi Valley, CA 93065 (No phone)*

They produce the *Hot Body Video Magazine* (softcore), *Playboy* and *Penthouse* videos, and other non-explicit softcore releases.

© 1995 DR TUPPER

## Evil Angel Video

*14141 Covello St., Unit 8C, Van Nuys, CA 91405*
*(818) 787-1414*

Markets films under the *Evil Angel, Elegant Angel* and *Bruce Seven Productions* labels. A wide range of hot films for your viewing pleasure.

## Excalibur Films

*3621 West Commonwealth, Fullerton, CA 92633*
*(714) 773-5855*

They put out a few films per year. Their catalog is free.

## Eye Shadow

*1626 North Wilcox #348, Hollywood, CA 90028*
*(213) 466-0728*

Markets single girl masturbation and lesbian lingerie fantasy films.

## Factory Home Video

*19521 Business Center Drive, Northridge, CA 91324*
*(818) 701-6555*

Three films say it all: *Seymore Butts' Buttwatch* and *Seymore Butts in Paradise.*

## Fantastic Pictures

*21526 Osborne St., Canoga Park, CA 91304*
*(800) 742-4411*

They have produced the *Harry Horndog, Love Bunnies, Anal Knights,* and *John T. Bone's Starbangers* series. Very successful pro-am producer.

## F.I.N. Entertainment

*520 Washington St., Suite 305, Marina Del Rey, CA 90292*
*(310) 82108476*

Distributes all lines with great quality and services.

# 4 Play Video

*9701 Canoga Ave., Canoga Park, CA 91311*
*(818) 715-0008*

They put out some excellent amateur films. Their lines include *More Dirty Debutantes, Deep Inside Dirty Debutantes* and *Black Debutantes.*

# Glitz Video

*942 Calle Amanecer Suite E, San Clemente, CA 92673*
*(714) 498-1934*

Has produced a variety of series including *Rump Humpers, Our Bang, Glitz Tits, Bodacious Boat Orgies, Risque Business, Prime Time Slime, Video Vamps,* and much more.

# Gloria

*P.O. Box 3837, Fullerton, CA 92631 — (No phone)*

Gloria, a very sexy 5'0" Latina with rather large breasts, and who is a former "Miss Nude America", has many homemade videos for sale. Most of them are good quality gangbang flicks with loads of action. And from what I've seen, she really enjoys the "work" as she truly loves men.

# FJS International

*7605 Santa Monica Blvd., Suite 633,*
*Los Angeles, CA 90046 — (213) 845-5600*

Softcore erotica

# Gourmet Video

*13162 Raymer St., North Hollywood, CA 91605*
*(818) 765-8720*

Releases a wide range of flicks from the *Hispanic Orgies* series to the *Amateur Lesbians* series. Lots of tasty morsels for you video voyeurs.

# Hollywood Video

*9547 Cozycroft Ave., Chatsworth, CA 91311*
*(818) 773-9100*

Makes and distributes a variety of lines. Also sells playing cards.

## J.B. Video

*P.O. Box B-21 7313 Owensmouth, Canoga Park, CA 91303*
*(No phone)*

They specialize in pantyhose worship videos. Haven't seen any of them, so someone will have to write and tell me what they are all about.

## KBBS Video

*P.O. Box 10282, Canoga Park, CA 91309*
*(No phone)*

If you are interested in making some big bucks in the porno industry, get a copy of their video, *How to Make Your Own XXX Video for $$$.*

## Las Vegas Video

*21540 Praire St., Unit D, Chatsworth, CA 91311*
*(818) 346-2587*

Produces professional and pro-am films starring some of the more popular porno stars of the moment.

## Laser Disc Entertainment

*2040 Broadway, Santa Monica, CA 90404*
*(310) 453-5068*

They market laser disc releases of feature films from various manufacturers. They also market CD-ROM adult-oriented software for you horny computer nerds.

## LBO Entertainment

*7959 Deering Ave., Canoga Park, CA 91304*
*(818) 407-3800*

They produce a horde of releases under various titles including *Mr. Peepers Amateur Video*, *Analvision* and *Bun Busters*.

## Leisure Time Entertainment

*7050 Valjean Ave., Van Nuys, CA 91406*
*(818) 781-2345*

They produce *Infinity Video*, *Video Exclusives*, *Leather Lovers*, *European Amateurs*, *Raunch-O-Rama* and much much more.

## Leoram

*P.O. Box 1622, Studio City, CA 91604*
*(818) 898-1591*

If you like your chicks with dicks or your men with tits (depending on how you look at it), you can get some she-male videos from this company, including Kim Christy's *She-Males*.

## *Letro Limited*

*P.O. Box 2966, Mission Viejo, CA 92690 — (no phone)*

Has put out a few amateur releases including the *San Francisco Lesbians* series.

## Moonlight Entertainment

*10000 Canoga Ave. #5, Chatsworth, CA 91311*
*(818) 709-5635*

More porno entertainment with some well-known X-rated stars.

## Odyssey Video Group

*P.O. Box 77597, Los Angeles, CA 90007*
*(800) 369-6214*

They have homemade tapes made in private bedrooms from all around the United States. Some of their video lines include *Bedtime Theater, Amateur Home Video, Triple Play, The People's Choice, Private Video Magazine* (European imports), and much more. Send $3 and they'll send you their catalog.

## Ona Zee Productions

*10234 Jefferson Blvd., Suite 152, Culver City, CA 90230*

Produces fetish, specialties and B & D videos.

## Pacific Media Entertainment

*9135 Alabama Ave. Suite B, Chatsworth, CA 91311*
*(800) 262-7367*

They produce non-explicit videos with such titles as *Bikini Girls, Wet T Shirt,* and *Big Bust Screentest.*

## Pro Video

*14666 Titus St., Suite 4, Panorama City, CA 91402*
*(818) 786-7623*

## Platinum

*4501 Van Nuys Blvd. Suite 215A,*
*Sherman Oaks, CA 91403 — (no phone)*

They sell a complete line of totally lesbian, totally amateur fetish videos.

## Player Home Entertainment

*22647 Ventura Blvd. #131, Woodland Hills, CA 91364*
*(800) 783-7558*

They produce and market a variety of soft core releases which star some mainstream models.

## Quackenbush Video
*16760 Stagg St., Suite 217, Van Nuys, CA 91406*
*(818) 780-1396*

They have hundreds of mail order videos for sale. All types . . . great prices . . . great selection.

## Raincoat Productions
*Exceptions Enterprises, 5632 Van Nuys Blvd., Suite 426, Van Nuys, CA 91401 — (No phone)*

They are the mail order seller for the *Positively Pagans* line, which is produced by *SB Sales*.

## Rosebud Productions
*22425 Ventura Blvd. #110, Woodland Hills, CA 91364*
*(818) 702-8040*

They specialize in anal features (is that what "rosebud" stands for??) including the *Rosebud Girls* line.

## RTP
*520 Washington Blvd., Suite 426,*
*Marina Del Rey, CA 90292 — (310) 391-7982*

They produce many amateur and gangbang films. Their new *House of Sex* line sounds fascinating. The *House of Sex* is a combination disco, swing party and X-rated video production company. A couple of weekend nights a month, the proprietor, Stan Brunt, rents out a place somewhere in Los Angeles and has a dance party. However, this is not your normal dancefest; in the back room there's a swing party/ orgy going on.

Late at night or early in the morning, depending on your perspective, Stan's cameramen start shooting all the wild action. The tapes are compiled and edited and sold to you, the lucky consumer. I'm not sure how you get invited to the parties, but you can write for more information. I've heard that anyone is allowed in on the fun if they have proper IDs and a proof of HIV-negative status.

If any of you readers get in on the fun, let us know about it. At the time of printing, there was a hot line for more information on the *House of Sex* parties: (310) 391-7982.

## Sandy's

*P.O. Box 3892, Thousand Oaks, CA 91359*
*(No phone)*

She has a few amateur videos for sale. Her sample photos cost $5.00.

## S.B. Sales

*942 Calle Amanecer, Suite E-1, San Clemente, CA 92673*
*(714) 498-1940*

They produce a variety of films including the good bisexual series, *Bi Bi Love*.

## Shadow Lane

*P.O. Box 1910, Studio City, CA 91614-0910*
*(818) 985-9151*

If you like watching female butts getting spanked, paddled, stroked and strapped, then you should try this place.

## Sinclair Blue Productions

*2763 Avenue L, Suite 258, Lancaster, CA 93536*
*(805) 940-9411*

They do fetish videos. So, if you enjoy latex, rubber, B & D, or women fighting like cats in heat, check out the films from this company.

## Sorel Productions

*2005 Palo Verde Ave., #214, Long Beach, CA 90815*
*(No phone)*

Films from *Mistress Leah LeFleur*. I haven't seen any of her films; let me know how hot they are. (If I watched all these videos, I wouldn't have time [or energy] to write this book!!)

## Star

*P.O. Box 6993, Burbank, CA 91510*
*(No phone)*

A company that sells various videos and other sexually oriented paraphernalia. Their catalog costs $2.

## Topper Video

*4501 Van Nuys Blvd., Suite 121A,*
*Sherman Oaks, CA 91403*
*(818) 503-9598*

They have a great selection of videos for sale of women with rather large breasts. Also, you can call their "Bust Line" at (900) 745-0710 or (800) 395-JUGS. It's $2.50-$3.99 per minute and you get to talk with one of their big-breasted women.

## Totally Tasteless Video

*3034 Glendale Blvd., Los Angeles, CA 90039*
*(213) 668-2281*

The name say it all!! Totally tasteless and exciting!!

## Twist Productions

*520 Washington Blvd., #445, Marina Del Rey, CA 90292*
*(no phone)*

They have B & D films for sale.

## VCA Pictures

*9650 DeSoto Ave., Chatsworth , CA 91311*
*(818) 718-0404*

Produces many major releases with some of the biggest current stars.

## Victoria's Videos

*P.O. Box 1664 Brea, CA 92622*

Victoria is a very sexy girl who loves gangbangs. And she has a few videos for sale to prove it. They are good quality, hot action films.

## Video Vortex

*5699 Kanan Road, #320, Agoura, CA 91301-3358*
*(818) 889-7277*

These films, with Nancy Novak, are of female domination and wrestling. If that's your scene, check them out.

## Visual Direct

*8821 Shirley Ave., Northridge, CA 91328*
*(818) 885-7771*

Two of their top lines are *Uncle Roy's Amateur Home Videos* and *Hollywood Exposed.* They recently put out a big-budget transsexual film with Sharon Mitchell entitled *Be Careful What You Wish For.*

## Vivid Video

*15127 Califa St., Van Nuys, CA 91411*
*(818) 908-0481*

A company with big productions and big stars and big sales and big everthing!! They also have a line of boy-boy videos.

## Western Visuals

*15745 Stagg St., Van Nuys, CA 91406*
*(818) 621-1190*

Some of their lines are *Pink & Plentiful, Blacks & Blondes,* and *Dirty Movies.* One of their recent releases is *So I Married A Lesbian* (I like that title!).

## Wicked Pictures

*9025 Eton Ave., Suite C, Canoga Park, CA 91304*
*(818) 349-3593*

More movies from wicked minds for us wicked folks with our wicked fantasies who enjoy these wicked scenes.

## X-citement Video

*7118 DeCelis Place, Van Nuys, CA 91406*
*(818) 909-9200*

More movies from excited minds for us excited folks with our exciting fantasies who enjoy these exciting scenes.

## Zane Entertainment

*21526 Osborne St. Canoga Park, CA 91304*
*(800) 742-4411*

Some of their lines are *America's Raunchiest Home Videos* (some of these are among my favorite amateur videos), *American Connection Video Magazine, Anal Gangbangs* and *Oral Gangbangs.*

## Versatile Productions

*Post Office Box 10511, Tustin, CA 92681*
*(714) 538-6498*

Mistress Antoinette (a very imposing mistress indeed!) markets her fetish videos for you fetish fans.

# For More Information . . .

You can find advertisements for mail order distributors and sellers in most men's magazines. You can usually write to the companies for a catalog. Some of them charge for their catalog, so you may have to send along some cash just to see what they are selling. They also keep you up to date on all the new releases. The following are a few periodicals that keep you informed about the adult film industry.

## *Adult Video News (AVN)*

*8599 Venice Blvd., Suite J, Los Angeles, CA 90034*
*(310) 842-7450*

A monthly magazine that keeps you informed about all the latest releases, stars and news in the adult video industry. If you enjoy adult videos, this is the publication for you.

## *Video Xcitement*

P.O. Box 187, Fraser, MI 48026 — (no phone)

This is a monthly newspaper found at adult bookstores that will keep you informed of all happenings in the amateur adult video world; from big distributors to the girl just having a little sexual fun and making some cash at the same time. If you are an amateur video fanatic and want subscription information, send a note to the above address.

### *Adam Film World Guide*

Knight Publishing Corp., 8060 Melrose Ave., Los Angeles, CA 90046-7082 — (no phone)

A monthly magazine that extensively covers the world of erotic films. Lots of hot photos, too!

### *Adam Presents Amateur Porn*

*Same address as above*

A periodical that covers the wonderful world of amateur porn. More hot action photos here, too!

### *The Directory of Adult Films*

*Same address as above*

This is an annual directory of all the best new and old adult films, descriptions and ratings of the films, plus biographies of all the major adult video stars. Order it from Adam or find it in your local bookstore.

# It Could Have Been You (Or Me) . . .

I have a friend who was a little hard up for cash so he thought . . . hmmm . . . why not film a few X-rated home videos and attempt to sell them? So, being the swinger that he is, he got his wife and a few friends together to have some fun and film a few videos. And what do you know . . . they had some fun, shot a few hot videos and made a little bit of cash. Enough that they took a trip to Australia and Southeast Asia for two months. And they had enough left over when they returned to take all their "actors and actresses" out for dinner at a fancy, over-priced restaurant in Beverly Hills!

Now it's back to overdrawn bank accounts and overdue bills, and his wife wants to get pregnant instead of making sex videos . . . so he'll have to think of something else. But, it was oh so much fun while it lasted. The amateur porn market is open to anyone with a video camera, a reasonably steady hand and a few willing participants. If your films are hot, full of action and reasonably well shot, there are many companies willing to buy your work. Just think, you might not become the next great Francis Ford Coppola, but you could become the next great horny *Buttman!*

I'm talkin' to ya!"                                    *Photo by Jack Messick*

# CHAPTER FIVE

# Phone Sex

> . . . if a man talks dirty to a woman, it's sexual
> harassment. If a woman talks dirty
> to a man, it's $3 a minute.
> — *Anonymous*

It's the safest sex. It's a connection without contact. Aural sex (not oral sex!) has been with us for awhile, but it exploded on the commercial sex scene in the late 1980's and early 1990's due to the public's increasing recognition and fear of HIV infection, the easing of regulations for advertising and perhaps, to an increasing sense of detachment in society. In the 1920's ear sex was labeled by the psychiatric community as coprolalia, a sexual deviance: the love of obscenities and filth.

Modern technology has made phone sex, recorded phone fantasies, phone personals, party lines, phone orgies, and other types of phone play easily available, but it took the horrifying specter of AIDS to create an insatiable demand for sex over the telephone wires.

There are hundreds, if not thousands, of phone sex lines to choose from. Some have been in business for awhile, others have just begun operations, while still others will be out of business by the time you read their ads and dial the phone.

# Let's Talk Money

These calls cost money. Sometimes big money. If you're a big talker . . . or a big listener, be prepared to lighten your wallet. If you take more than a few minutes to get off over the phone, it will cost you plenty! I have seen phone sex lines costing anywhere from 49 cents a minute up to $5 per minute. Sometimes, companies charge a flat fee such as "$30 for 15 minutes." Watch out for hidden costs such as toll charges or rates that are quoted in half-minute amounts. For example, many companies will state their rates as "only 99 cents" and then in small print it says "per half-minute". This call will actually cost you nearly $2 per minute.

Just keep in mind that these type of calls are expensive. Five . . . ten . . . fifteen . . . twenty minutes, it goes by very, very fast! The girls will usually attempt to keep you on the phone for as long as possible; they'll talk about the weather, their school, your job, whatever . . . anything to keep you anticipating some sexy talk while running up a big tab!

# Types of Phone Sex

There are a few different options when considering phone sex. You can choose between party lines, recorded fantasies, one-on-one live, and phone personals. Phone personals is not really phone sex, but more of a way to meet people and is discussed in a separate chapter.

A party line is where you are connected to an open forum of people. Several callers may be on the same line and you can talk with them all. It's kind of the orgy of phone lines. Sometimes two, sometimes six, sometimes more are on simultaneously. These party lines are utilized for both meeting people and talking dirty and are generally the cheapest. The best time to call these lines is late at night when everyone is drunk, lonely or exceptionally horny after a night out at the clubs.

A recorded fantasy line is where you get to listen to some taped message from a sexy voice telling you how hot and wet she is and how big and virile you are. If you enjoy over-exaggerated sexy voices and telephone actresses faking moans and groans, this may be for you. Remember . . . It's not live . . . it's Memorex!

A live one-on-one line is just that: you talk privately with a girl (or guy). Try to get her talking dirty as quickly as possible . . . remember, the meter is running! All the girls you speak with will have big boobs, flat stomachs, gorgeous long hair, tantalizing asses . . . yeah right! But we can all fantasize, can't we?

These one-on-one lines are the most expensive. Many of them have 900 numbers where you pay by the minute. For some of them, you must obtain a special access number which allows you to use all their services. Many of them can charge your credit card; others use a prepayment method and a direct call-back system where they call you back at a designated time. There are a variety of lines and options out there for you to choose from. Give one of them a call and enter the world of "aural sex."

© 1995 DR TUPPER

# It Could Happen to You . . .

I have a friend who used the phone lines on a regular basis. He was very busy trying to make himself a millionaire and didn't have much time for dating and meeting women, so he got off over the phone. Sometimes he talked to a girl one-on-one for hot, sexy talk, other times he tried the party lines where he talked to other regular people looking for fun. One late night, talking on a party line, he "met" this attractive-sounding girl. They were the only two on the line and talked about all the usual stuff. After some small talk, he asked her to call him at home, and when she did it turned into a hot talk session.

They made a date for the next night, but she canceled on him; she admitted that she only talked so nasty because she was drunk and feeling good, and after sobering up she was afraid he was a dangerous pervert or something. But they spoke on the phone a few more times and she eventually acquiesced to a date. And that date led to a whirlwind romance which led to a happy wedding. Now they are married and talking dirty to other people on their computers (more on that in another chapter).

# The Phone Lines

### Mistress Jayne Alexander
### & The Velvet Voices

*P.O. Box 24020, Los Angeles, CA 90024*
*(213) 479-4210*

A phone service that specializes in phone domination. You can speak live with Mistress Jayne or one of her beautiful associates. They do it all: slave training, feminization, bondage, body worship, S & M, and other role playing. Mistress Jayne is a nationally known mistress whose columns appear in many magazines, and whose beautiful physique has graced the pages of several publications, including *Playboy*, *Penthouse* and an international bikini calendar. This is a first class operation all the way.

## Michelle's Forbidden Pleasures

*2 FPD & Associates, P.O. Box 7516,*
*Van Nuys CA 91409-7516*
*(818) 413-9191 or (818) 776-3434 or (818) 893-006*

They offer live, private calls. It's $35 for 15 minutes and $55 for 30 minutes. They specialize in hot domination and fetish calls.

## Mistress Jacqueline

*7095 Hollywood Blvd. #350, Hollywood, CA 90028*
*(900) 844-5552*

She offers S & M, B & D, TV, TS, spanking, slave training and more. Write for her free brochure.

## J.H. Phonics – Bedtime Stories

*(900) 288-2710*

Listen to "bedtime stories" told by major porno stars such as Ginger Lynn, Jamie Summers, Tori Welles, Christy Canyon and many others. It's $2 per minute and you can listen 24 hours a day.

## Frenchie's Fantasy Tales

*(818) 986-3308*

They caters to fetishes and those into dominance, cross-dressing, bondage and more. Many different billing options are available.

## Chateau Phone Fantasies

*(800) 291-2255 or (900) 745-1213*

Operated by *The Chateau,* a premier fetish establishment. They offer a variety of phone fantasies. Prices range from $1.99 to $3.99 per minute.

## The French Connection

*(714) 828-7470*

They offer live one-on-one phone fun and they also do domination. Use your Visa or Master Charge and chat away to your . . . er, heart's content!

## Talk Dirty To Me
*(714) 563-0008*

The name says it all! $12.50 will get some fun. Use your Visa and Master Charge.

## Bev Carlson
*P.O. Box 57, Fullerton, CA 92632*

She offers personalized phone sex. I talked with her just once . . . and it was well worth it! A great voice that just says "SEX"!! Write for information.

## Laura Lynn
*4141 Ball Rd., Cypress, CA 90630*
*(714) 648-2127 or (714) 220-0640*

Prepaid calls are $15 for 10 minutes with a $20 minimum. She offers discounts for frequent callers.

## Tina
*Post Office Box 48408, Los Angeles, CA 90048*
*(800) 777-8462 (TINA)*

A phone service that has a few different lines depending on your tastes. You pay by credit card and the cost is around $3 per minute. Write for information on all their services.

## Communaphone
*P.O. Box 4185, Malibu, CA 90265*

A phone sex card that sells for $10. It allows you to utilize low-cost phone sex lines (around 60 cents per minute). With the card you get 800 phone line access. You can either write to the company or look for it in your local adult book store.

## Eroticard DataDriven Inc.
*23626 Messina Laguna Hills, CA 92653*

A phone sex card that comes in $10, $20, and $50 denominations. This is a prepaid debit card that offers the caller a number for taped erotic messages and other phone services. As the card is used and the minutes go by, the telephone system debits your account until your card is all used up!

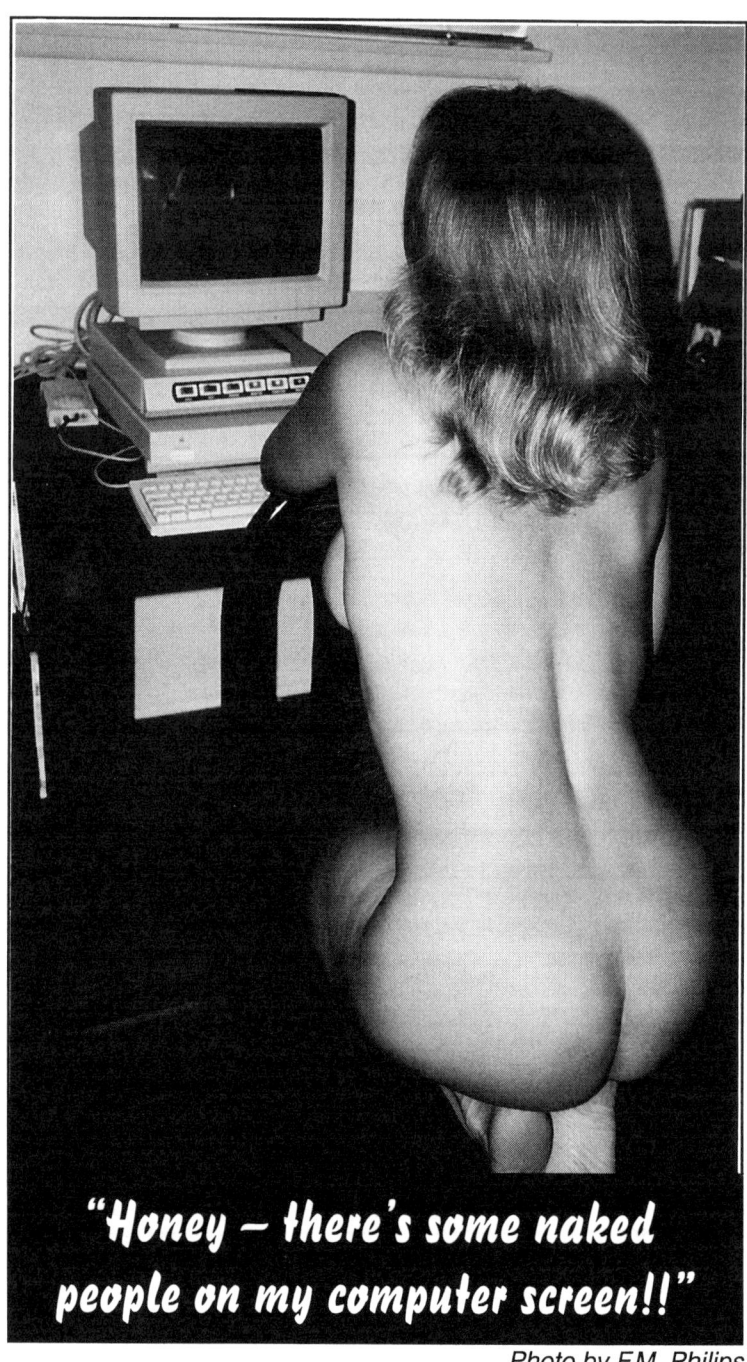

"Honey — there's some naked people on my computer screen!!"

Photo by F.M. Philips

# CHAPTER SIX

# Computer Sex

> . . . to error is human, but to really fuck up
> you need a computer.
> — *unknown*

**D**o you think those early computer geeks ever imagined the kind of fun people are now having on their computers? Did Mister Nerdly with the giant coke bottle glasses and the pocket pencil holder even have a clue what mature adults would be doing with a modem in the 1990s? Back when computers comprised entire rooms, I doubt anyone envisioned the day when every John and Jane Doe would have a computer in their house . . . or in their lap . . . or in their hand. And I surely doubt that anyone, even in their wildest fantasies, could imagine the kind of nasty "talk" that would one day go on from modem to modem to modem.

Well, that day is here. Welcome to the computer age . . . welcome to computer sex. You can "listen" to other people "chat" on your computer monitor through the magic of modern technology. All you need is a computer, a modem, a phone line and an imagination. If you have all the required "hardware," all you need do is get on-line with one of the thousands of computer bulletin boards (called BBSs in computerspeak) out there in cyberspace.

# Cybersex

Some of these BBSs are national, such as *America On Line*, *Prodigy* and *CompuServe*, while others are local. The national ones provide you with information on business, politics, news events and personal finance as well as a place to chat with people from all over the country. The local ones offer you everything ranging from church news to hot sex talk, and everything G-rated to X-rated and all ratings in between. Obviously, the BBSs we are concerned with here are the ones of a more adult nature.

These adult boards usually have open chat forums, information on a variety of events, access to a cornucopia of data files and GIFs. GIFs are computer pictures that you can download from the BBS and often are of a very adult nature. Just because these BBSs are for adults only, it doesn't mean you have to "talk" nasty and it certainly doesn't mean that it is an instant orgy. Calm down guys, just because you get on-line, it doesn't mean you are going to get off!! Most of the talk is strictly G-rated. But you'll never know what goes on at computer keyboards all over America unless you get on-line and do a little exploring. That's the only way to find out all the pleasures a local BBS has to offer.

One of my friends is a computer BBS junkie. He's had hundreds of dates, been to a few wild parties and has met one of the ex-loves of his life through the computer. His current girlfriend won't let him near the computer – she knows what goes on!!

# More Information About Computer Sex . . .

If you are a novice to computers, bulletin boards and hot chat, it may all seem a bit confusing to you. The best way to learn about this fascinating world of erotica is to call one of these boards and just do some exploring. If you want more information, there is an excellent book on the market. Look in your local bookstore for:

## *Erotic Connections: Love and Lust on the Information Highway*

*by Billy Wildhack* (a pseudonym, I presume!).

It's filled with all the information you need to know about signing on and getting off!

What are you waiting for??!! You may meet your future bride on a BBS. You may meet your next lover on a BBS. You may finally meet that dominating mistress you've been dying to submit to on a BBS. So . . . turn on your computer, dial up one of the following numbers and enter the world of computer sex!

## Video Vortex BBS

*(310) 395-3808 or (310) 471-6408*

They have hot chat, on-line games, many adult and kinky GIFs, and you can chat on-line with Mistress Nancy.

## Pathway BBS

*(714) 236-4247*

Owned by *Pathway Communications* which publishes several swingers' and fetish periodicals, this BBS has 16 lines, GIF, adult and public domain files, public and private chat and more. The rates range from $9.95 per month to $189 per year. They also have a northern California line at (408) 956-5600. You can meet many local swingers on this board. I know a guy who met a swinging couple here a few months back and has had several sexy encounters with them since then. He sure is glad I told him about this BBS.

## Odyssey

*(818) 358-6968*

This is one of the largest and most active BBS's around. Lots of wild chat here. They also have parties from time to time where you can meet that nasty talker face to face!! Lots of files, GIFs and more.

## Chateau Computer BBS

*(818) 503-8819*

Owned by *The Chateau,* one of L.A.'s best dungeons, there are many people on here who are involved in the B & D lifestyle. It's a fun BBS.

## Legend Graphics On-Line

*(909) 689-9229*

They offer the user all types of pictures and many hot, hot, hot adult images for downloading. Also have games and other services. Many, many GIF and story subjects to choose from including group sex, lesbians, toys, B&D and more.

## KBBS

*(818) 994-0442, (310) 558-0145, (714) 441-1839*

A big, busy BBS with lines from the 818, 310, 714, 213, and 805 area codes. Live chat, internet games, files, and more. Lots of fun-loving adults here.

## The Hedonism BBS

*(310) 631-7697*

Mainly a fetish and bondage board. Women get free access. Has chat, stories and files.

## The Castle

*(213) 953-0040 or (818) 785-6920*

Another busy board with lines from the 213, 310, 714, and 818 area codes. Has hot public and private chat, public messages, private mail, games and more. Over 40 lines to connect with.

## The Westside

*(213) 933-4050*

A colossal BBS with much adult activity. Many couples have met through this board. I have a friend who uses this board all the time. He hasn't met the love of his life yet, but he has met a few "lusts for the moment." Softcore and hardcore GIFs, games, files and more. Many open channels with their own themes are set up for chat.

## The Colossal Collection BBS

*(310) 421-5591*

A BBS that caters to all lifestyles. Has chat, files, messages, GIFs, shareware and much more.

## Eden BBS

*(714) 548-1900, (714) 530-6335, (310) 421-2420*

Has games, chat, files, messages and more. I have a friend who met his fiance on this line . . . and she is a knockout. You can chat nasty in *The Garden,* talk about women's issues in Eve's Room or get all tied up in chat in Caligula's Dungeon.

## Bits and Bytes

*(909) 356-4636*

Hot chat for the Inland Empire. It's a general interest board with many adult files and people looking for hot chat.

## GIFshoppe

*(818) 989-0975*

You can download hot sexy pics from here. Also have games, files and more.

## Modem Boy

*(310) 417-5157*

Chat and much more catering to the gay lifestyle.

## OWE BBS

*(818) 969-7955*

Catering to the gay, lesbian and bi crowd.

## Cybersex

*(818) 447-9268, (818) 447-9850*

You can view sexy photos on-line or you can download them.

## Unzip It

*(900) 844-2200*

You can download hot, sexy GIFs from this line. The cost is 69 cents per minute . . . so watch out, those charges can add up quickly.

### L.A. Connex BBS

*(805) 273-9456 or (805) 266-0171*

Serving the alternative lifestyle community with chat, E-mail, adult reviews, lists, events and more.

### Scanin: Southern California Area Nudist Information Network

*(619) 581-9262*

A computer BBS for those interested in the nude lifestyle.

# More Boards To Check Out . . .

### Annex
*(818) 786-5600*

### Expressions West BBS
*(818) 368-0027*

### Valley West
*(818) 888-8419*

### The All Nighter BBS
*(310) 421-5591*

### Image Core
*(818) 752-1380*

### Prime Time
*(818) 982-7271*

### Baudtown
*(818) 893-0340*

### The Downtown BBS
*(213) 484-0260*

### Funtime BBS
*(310) 793-8701*

### Homegrown BBS
*(213) 664-1706*

### California Girls
*(909) 682-1055*

### Head's Up Adult BBS
*(909) 681-3721*

### Night Vision
*(909) 369-6556*

### Sleepless Knights
*(714) 523-8838*

### Suburbs BBS
*(714) 871-9000*

### The Night
*(714) 495-3784*

### Art Gallery – South BBS
*(310) 791-7278*

### After Hours
*(310) 842-7995, (213) 269-2393, (818) 997-1863*

### Compu - Net
*(310) 822-0038*

## 69 Fantasy Line

*(310) 986-9705*

## Interstate 1

*(310) 989-2360*

## Hotel California

*(310) 407-1300*

## Midnight BBS

*(213) 936-5706*

## Interludes

*(714) 828-7093*

## The Chateau

*(714) 455-2790*

## Fantasia BBS

*(714) 579-7022*

## Eat My Shorts BBS

*(714) 827-7776*

## Tom Cat Pictures

*(805) 482-8030*

## The Late Show

*(805) 832-6173*

## Adult Services BBS

*(213) 627-8230*

## Vivid Interactive

*(818) 909-9424*

© 1995 DR TUPPER

# Other Computer Stuff . . .

## Virtual Connection

*(800) 465-6423*

You can watch girls strip on your computer . . . not digital images but real girls!! For $29.95 you download their software, then hook up over the phone lines. The calls are $3.98 per minute with the first five minutes free. Open from 2 pm to midnight and credit cards accepted. Look them up on the Internet at: http://www.cts.com/~talon

## Compu T's

*662 W. Huntington Dr. #655, Monrovia, CA 91016*

They sell XXX custom computer discs with sexy adult GIFs. 3½ and 5¼ formats. IBM or Mac. Write for info.

## XIS

*Box 19292, Los Angeles, CA 90019*

They sell adult amateur images software for PC and Mac. They have bi, gay and straight. Write for more information.

## A6 CD ROM

*(714) 773-5412*

They offer a variety of adult CD ROM images.

## Pixis Interactive

*P.O. Box 3684, Tustin, CA 92681*
*(800) 697-4947or (714)669-1818*

More adult CD-ROM images for your horny computer.

## REG Publishing

*P.O. Box 5138, Chatsworth, CA 91313*
*(818) 993-5629*

More CD-ROM stuff to get your sweaty palms on!

## LACE

*(818) 709-4275*

An adult on-line magazine where you can download sexy images. The board features original adult images from Richard Stevens, a well known professional photographer. Most of the GIFs here are R-rated instead of X-rated.

# The InterNet

Well, now that you have been roller skating on the BBS's, maybe you think it is time to get up to speed on the InterNet itself. If a local BBS is a telephone switchboard in a small village and if large commercial BBS's like *America OnLine, CompuServe*, etc., are like a small city with many operators (sysops), the "Net" is like the entire communications system in the whole world.

However, unlike AT&T, the Net is not well organized yet. You have to "surf" your way around to find interesting things. It can be a great place to chat with people with similar viewpoints. And, it can get pretty damn hot on the 'Net!!

Unlike the smaller BBS's, the Net has no censorship (yet). You can find everything from child pornography and instructions on making your own bombs to fundamentalist prayer groups and everything in between. Have you posted a personal ad on a BBS? Well, there are many personals on the Net. One has over 14,000 personal ads that you can scan for gender, sexual preference, race, preferred sexual actions, age, locations, etc.

## A Little History Lesson

The InterNet; everyone has heard of it, but almost no one understands it. Because my understanding of the InterNet is about equal to my understanding of quantum physics, don't look to me for an explanation of it.

The InterNet was started as a research project by the Defense Department in 1969 to be utilized as a military communications tool to help move data during nuclear attacks. The InterNet linked various computers together so that the bombing of one site wouldn't disable our mighty military machine.

Since this new technology was military in origin, it received one of the million acronyms that the military loves; the acronym for early InterNet was TCP/IP. The next group to discover the usefulness of the InterNet was the academic and research communities. They loved it because it facilitated free exchange of ideas and information.

Next, bulletin boards, both local and national burst on the scene, copying the openness of the InterNet. In 1981 there were about 200 host computers linked to the InterNet. But, technological advances brought the cost of connecting to the InterNet down and contributed greatly to a dizzying spurt of growth in the late 1980's and early 1990's. By 1994, the estimate was over 3 million host computers and rising!

On the InterNet, you can send electronic E-mail all across the globe, you can access data bases at research facilities, universities and other major information points from your home and you can chat with people in remote corners of the world. Yes, the world is shrinking and true globalism is here!

# World Wide Web

The newest thing to hit the InterNet is the *World Wide Web*. It is supposed to make things easier to find on the InterNet. It is about as helpful as a compass when you are lost in the wilderness. The compass can tell you what direction you are headed, but it won't point you to the nearest paved road, motel or ice-cold beer. Of course, anywhere you have a free exchange of ideas and information, you will also have the words and pictures of sex!!

Sex on the InterNet and the WWW is quite prevalent but can be rather difficult to find. You may be able to just stumble on some hot conversation or accidentally find a room where people are trying to meet others for wild fun.

On the other hand, if you are attempting to look for a particular address or a specific type of activity, you may have a tough time navigating the 'Net. InterNet addresses are lengthy; miss one character and you're going to be at the wrong place, probably talking about the current state of contemporary literature with some eggheads instead of talking about wild foursomes with swinging couples. For those of you who have trouble dialing the correct phone number, the InterNet may be a study in frustrating futility for you.

# CyberCensors

As one would expect, where there is sex, there is censorship. One case that is very damaging to the pursuit of freedom is the case of Robert and Carleen Thomas of Milpitas, California. They ran an adults-only bulletin board and were busted when a U.S. postal inspector in Tennessee obtained sexually graphic images from their board. The couple was tried and CON-VICTED in a Memphis courtroom of 11 obscenity counts.

Because the case can be tried anywhere the information can be received and not where it is transmitted from, the most conservative community in the country will be the one setting the standards for everyone. Although this was not the InterNet, it has serious implications for InterNet users. This is a dangerous precedent and one that can lead to a severe restriction of our freedom.

But . . . can the thought police actually censor those on the InterNet. Because it is such a loose network of host computers and users, it would be quite difficult to police. However, national on-line services such as America OnLine, in a worst-case scenario, would have to adhere to stringent anti-pornography laws and this could virtually eliminate that fun nasty chat on line!!

But, be forewarned!!! There is a bill making its way through the various government channels. It is the Communications Decency Act of 1995. It has already passed the Senate Commerce Committee and would make it a crime to transmit obscene or harassing text or images through any electronic media. It is an all-encompassing bill and covers the InterNet, and all national and local on-line services.

This would put an impossible burden on all universities, bulletin boards and on-line services: they would have to read all E-mail and check for pornography and other illegal information lest they be liable for criminal and civil damages. The sponsors of the bill say that the principal goal of the bill is to protect children, and while that may be a truly worthwhile motivation, the answer isn't censorship and the destruction of our First Amendment right. Aaaahhhhhhhhh... another infantile and inane example of politicians interfering with our freedom!

# Surf'n Sights

If you want some hot action on the InterNet, the following are a few addresses of newsgroups, discussion areas and world wide web sites that are rated X! Be aware that these areas on the 'Net come and go faster than you can type the word "sex." Some of these sexually oriented InterNet addresses may have already vanished into eternal cyberspace before you can check them out.

- **http://www.best.com/~craig/netsex.htm#IRC** The location of the *Complete InterNet Sex Resource Guide.* You get it all here.

- **http://www.gus.com/PlayCouples** This is the home page of the Lifestyles organization, promotors of the *Lifestyles Convention* and *Lifestyles Tours.*

- **http://www.paranoia.com/~gyrotech/tits.html** Tits of the week!!

- **http://www.paranoia.com/faq/prostitution/** Info on prostitution around the U.S.

- **http://www.paranoia.com/faq/Los Angeles.txt** Info on fun in L.A.

- **http://www.web-link.com/sda-list.htm** Info on the adult scene in San Diego.

- **http://www.psych.nwu.edu/biancaTroll/vibrations/index.html** For those of you into auto-erotic fun.

- **http://olt.et.tudelft.nl/fun/pictures/porno.html** You can download some nasty pics from here.

- **http://www.cts.com/~talon** This is the home page of *Virtual Connection* where you can watch live girls strip.

- **http://www.cmpharm.ucsf.edu/~troyer/safesex.html** If you decide to have sex in "real time" stop here for instructions first.

# Usenets

Usenets are somewhat like BBS's in that you can read and post messages for others to read. Some of the postings on USENET are photos and graphics. You wouldn't know it by looking at them on-line (they look like a collection of garbage characters). So how do you get these this ASCII soup to look like pictures? Well, you first have to use a program called "uudecode" (a common shareware program you can easily obtain from a variety of sources, including the Internet).

Many graphic files contain two parts. Download and save each part as a separate file on your hard disk (for example, "file1.uue" and "file2.uue." Each file needs to have a ".uue" extension ). You enter the command "uudecode file1.uue" and the program does the rest, including moving on to "file2.uue," decoding it also and combining both files to form a workable graphics file -which you then call up with an appropriate file viewer.

- **alt.sex.breast** Usenet forum devoted to breasts

- **alt.sex.movies** Forum on X-rated films.

- **alt.sex.pictures** This is the place to download mega-bytes of pics.

- **alt.sex.spanking** For those of you who have been naughty! Think they will ever have virtual spanking?

- **alt.amazon-women.admirers** For those of you who like your women strong. Let's hope they don't cut off their right breast like the first ones did.

- **alt.personals.bondage** For those of you fit to be tied!

- **alt.sex.enemas** You figure it out!

# Lecher McRich's Mansion

*http://www.electriciti.com/~warren/index.htm*

Just enter the Library and follow the instructions to order books or to hyperlinck to other sites. tTo cruise the personals, enter the Master Bedroom. We don't know what we are going to put in the Dungeon yet.

**HELP WANTED!!** If you want to be involved in the maintenance of the mansion, drop us an E-mail message. We can use all the help we can get, and we might even be able to pay you something.

Feel free to drop us a line with comments and suggestions. But please! We don't have time to read about all your sexual exploits. Our email addresses is:

*warren@cyberheads.com* or *SinDiego@aol.com*

# Lastly . . .

If you get on-line with one of these boards, don't think everyone is on just in pursuit of carnal pleasures. There are a variety of reasons to be on-line: friendship, companionship, relationships, to pass the lonely hours, to get information, and to get laid! Have a good time on-line and you never know what you may find.

I have a friend who was on-line for a few years on many different boards. He was always looking to score. Sometimes he did, but most times he didn't. He was always complaining about the "flakes" on-line. He finally met someone who would "chat" with him but refused to meet him. After about six months of "chatting," she finally agreed to meet. And it was nearly love at first sight.

In those six months of "chatting," he got to know her as a person, instead of just worrying about the score. And now he is very happily married in an open relationship to a beautiful woman and they have one beautiful daughter (they didn't get their daughter on-line).

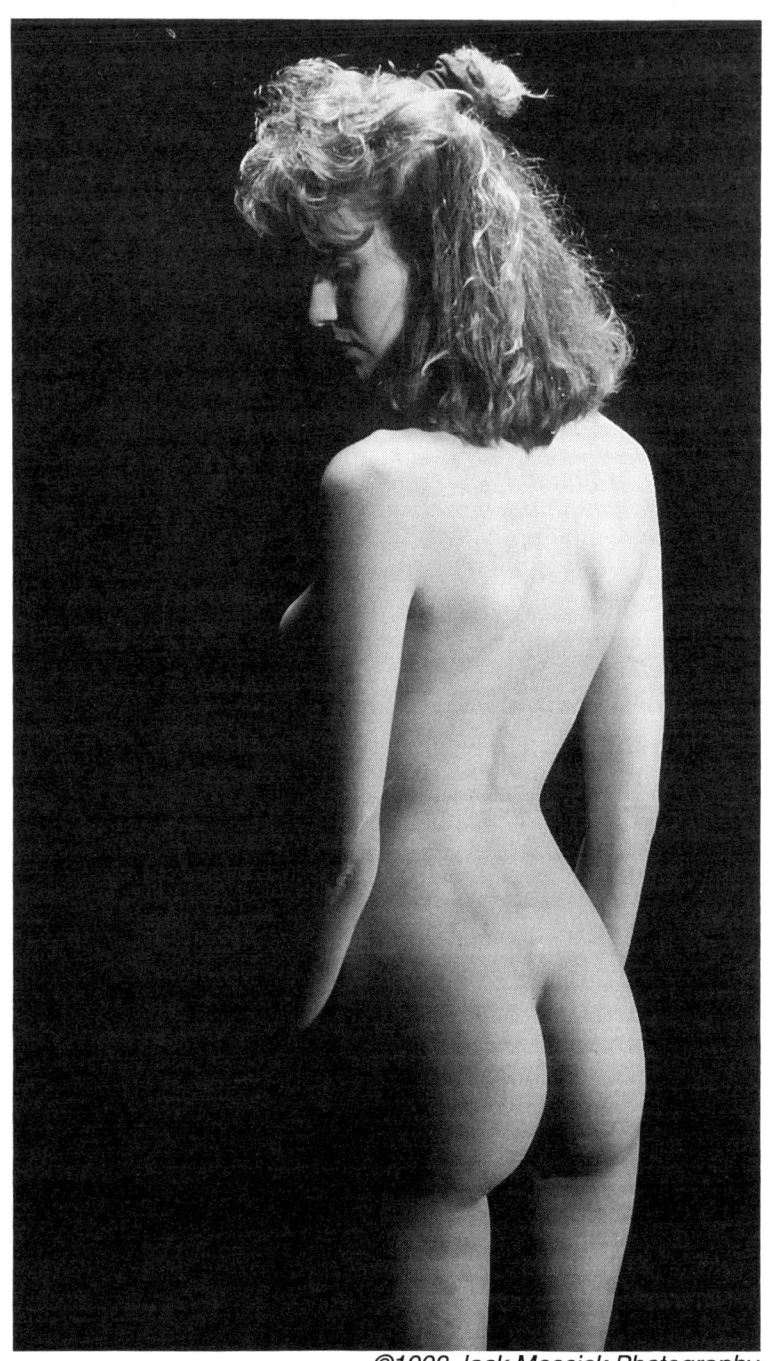

©1993 Jack Messick Photography

# CHAPTER SEVEN

# Sex Workers

> . . . prostitutes believe in marriage. It provides
> them with most of their trade.
> — *"Suzie," as quoted in "33Knave magazine"*

**S**treetwalkers are the prostitutes who receive the most attention from the media and it is easy to understand why that is. *Hookers are the most visible. They are out there . . . walking the streets. They are out there in their short skirts, their spandex, their high heels, their black leather, their fishnet stockings. They are out there trying to lure customers off the street, out of their cars; with subtle eye contact, with a wave of their hand or with a not-so-subtle, "wanna party?"

Call girls, masseuses and erotic dancers are tucked away, unseen by the general public, in their cozy apartments, while streetwalkers pound the pavement in search of customers.

Streetwalkers are a legitimate concern of hard-working business owners. Unless you own a condom store, what business owner would want a parade of streetwalkers in front of his or her store every night or day? High-heeled

---

\* Some historians think that the name "hooker" came from the Civil War general, Fighting Joe Hooker. The General was known for his proclivity of visiting "ladies of the night." At first they were called "Hooker's Girls," and then shortened to just "hookers." What a way to be immortalized!

---

hookers are an eyesore for business owners, scaring away potential customers and increasing crime. That is why, in some countries, the red-light district is a distinct and separate area from other business areas; designated, tolerated and regulated.

However, there are other not so legitimate concerns over streetwalkers. Right-wingers, religious zealots and moral do-gooders are always sticking their noses in your business and attempting to take all your fun away from you. They don't like street girls just because they are selling SEX! And sex is a dirty little word to them. If anyone, anywhere, at any time is having sex outside the institution of marriage, they feel an urge to stop the action. Sex is sin . . . and we all know that sin is very bad for you.

# Selling Sex Around The Globe

In certain parts of the world (and in certain parts of the United States) prostitution is legal . . . and this being legal helps keep girls off the street and away from other businesses. Legalization is not without its flaws, but it seems to me to be a much better alternative than what we have now.

## Mexico

Take a trip south of the border someday and see how prostitution is handled. It is quasi-legal; not exactly legal, but it is accepted, tolerated and policed to a certain extent by the authorities. A girl who wants to make a living selling (or renting) her body can register with the local authorities and obtain a health certificate. She then must be checked once a month for disease. Some people will tell you that the problems of disease are non-existent due to this regular check-up. Don't believe it. Even though girls can register and get checked, many do not do so; they operate outside the law the same as girls do north of the border.

Also in Mexico, much of the prostitution takes place in a specific area called "zonas de tolerencia" (or zones of tolerance). Most cities or towns of any size have a zone of tolerance. The town that most Southern Californians are familiar with, Tijuana, is somewhat different from other cities and towns away from the border. In Tijuana, prostitution is found in several areas; this is due to the fact that it is and always has been a major tourist town and "sin city" for gringos (especially the military). In Tijuana, it has been estimated that for every registered prostitute there are two who operate without registration and health checks.

Though Mexico tolerates prostitution to a degree and has its "zonas de tolerencia," it attempts to keep things quiet. You certainly will not see any Mexican tourist brochures advertising the availability of prostitutes and easy sex for sale. But, once you are in a city or town you can usually find out the location of the girls and the Zona Tolerencia by asking the taxi drivers. They generally know where all the action is!! They will be glad to show a tourist (especially a gringo tourist) where he can spend his money!!

If you would like information on sex across the border, send for *Red Lights of Baja*, by Roger Warren. It is an informative guide to Tijuana, Mexicali, Rosarito, Ensenada and other Baja cities' sex industries. There is an order form in the back of this book or our can order it from our InterNet home page (see Computer Sex).

# Europe

You can go to Amsterdam in the Netherlands and see the "evil" effects that legalized prostitution has on the city and its people. Amsterdam is one of the most beautiful and one of the safest cities in the world. The people are friendly, intelligent and hard-working. Even though a virtual cornucopia of sex and sin are there for the taking, the people have not been consumed with decadence.

The red-light district encompasses a small area in the city center and it is here that all the prostitutes, sex shops, live sex shows and strip clubs operate. The prostitutes sit in storefront windows and wait for customers to make their choices. The area is a bit seedier than the rest of Amsterdam and you will undoubtedly see a few social pariahs, misfits and outcasts, but it is quite safe and not a den of horrific crime as some Americans would imagine.

Since prostitution is regulated by the government, the girls are checked for disease and have protection against pimps and abuse. Of course nothing is ideal. There are problems with runaways, girls sold into prostitution slavery and drugs. But the problems are minimal when compared with the prostitution and sex industry here in the United States.

Another city, Hamburg, Germany, has a designated red-light district, which is located along the Reeperbahn. It is a wild and uninhibited area. Again, most of the sex industry is confined within these designated boundaries. If you want to get a prostitute or see a live sex show, you go there. And you can do it and see it all here. However, if you don't desire to be involved with the sex industry, you stay away from the area. Problems do exist but it seems to be a much better alternative than what we are doing here in America. If we have to error, let's err on the side of freedom.

# Safety

Well, so much for the world tour and back to American reality. Safety should always be a major consideration when dealing with streetwalkers. There are myriad problems associated with street prostitutes.

## Disease

Gone are the good old days when a shot of penicillin would rid your body of any sexually transmitted diseases and you could be out and carousing in no time. Yes, those old standbys, syphilis and gonorrhea are still with us and are still a major health concern. But now we must also concern ourselves with AIDS and herpes: both incurable, one deadly, one a pain in the crotch (literally and figuratively!). Don't ever forget to take your rubbers when cruising the streets for girls (or when cruising for girls anywhere!!). And certainly don't forget to use them . . . they can save your life! Read more about what you can do to protect yourself against disease and safer sex in the chapter "Naughty in The Nineties".

# Crime

Always be aware of your surroundings . . . crime exists! Unfortunately, most of the areas where streetwalkers ply their trade are high-crime areas. Also, be warned that street girls do rip off their customers at times; they may lift your wallet or their pimps may be lurking in the shadows waiting to pounce on you, knock you out and steal your valuables. Always know your surroundings, keep your eyes open and if for any reason you don't feel one-hundred percent safe and secure . . . get out of there. You can always find another girl down the road or try again another night.

# Drugs

Many of the street girls in the United States are heavy drug users. Many of them are strung-out junkies just trying to make enough money to pay for their next fix. And heavy drug use and addiction lead to crimes of desperation and deadly diseases ( i.e. AIDS!!!). As you don't need a resume to work the streets, the business attracts all types.

# The Law

The cops are watching you. Be aware that there are cops posing as prostitutes, and they will be glad to bust you on a soliciting charge. Picture this: you pull up to a sexy, mini-skirted girl standing on the street, she flashes you a smile and some leg and asks if you "wanna party". You ask her the price and she tells you "fifty bucks". You agree to the amount and follow her around the corner, admiring the rounded curves of her buttocks underneath her tight black skirt. She puts out her hand and you give her the wad of bills. The next

*Jack Messick Photography*

thing you know she is flashing you something else – a shiny badge while she whips out some handcuffs and motions for her partners to come out of the shadows. You have been arrested!! You may be booked, fingerprinted, jailed, fined, and have the family car impounded. Try explaining that one to the wife and kids. Yes, that could be your nightmare. Caveat emptor . . . buyer beware!

Even though this book is about sex and fun, we do not recommend picking up girls off the street. As we have explained above, it is a dangerous adventure. But if you do go cruising for streetwalkers, remember to keep your eyes open, watch out for cops, watch out for strangers lurking in the shadows, don't carry more money than you think you'll need, don't wear expensive jewelry and always carry and use your rubbers. Always!! If we haven't turned you off by now, you must be a masochist.

Remember, prostitution is illegal in the State of California. We do not endorse any illegal activity. Let's push to make prostitution legal . . . and then we can endorse it and make it safer and keep it off the streets and out of the neighbor-hoods!

# Where the Girls Are

We know that anyone with the smarts to read this book will not be so dumb as to take a chance of picking up a hooker from the streets. But just for informational purposes, the following is a partial listing of locations where you are more than likely to find some prostitution activity. Maybe you just want to cruise the street to see who is working. It's OK to look, just don't touch!!

Keep in mind that the vice cops make periodic sweeps of certain areas and clean out those locations for a time. Usually the girls just move down the street a few blocks. Locations usually float to some extent; bear this in mind when searching areas for a sexy, mini-skirted girl. Even if the cops have cleaned out an area . . . the girls usually move back in eventually.

Prices for various activities vary slightly from place to place, night to night and girl to girl. It seems that the going rate for oral sex at this time is approximately $20. Sexual intercourse can be had for around $40 to $50 – a lot less than a call girl, but then you get what you pay for (sometimes).

Don't forget . . . the men and women in blue are out there, driving around, keeping the streets safe for democracy, and waiting to arrest an unsuspecting horny soul like you. Remember, whether we like the laws or not, the cops are just doing their jobs and enforcing the rules and regulations of our society. Don't hassle them!

# Areas

- **Sepulveda Blvd.** Between Roscoe Blvd & Devonshire in North Van Nuys. They move around a bit, but they are there somewhere. Sometimes the girls can be found below Roscoe as far south as Burbank.

- **Echo Park.** Near the Stadium and near the Glendale Expressway. The streets change depending on where the cops are. Be careful here. The cops have been known to confiscate your car. That would be a tough one to explain to your wife!!

- **Hollywood Blvd.** You can walk among the stars on Hollywood Blvd . . . .and you can also find a play-for-pay girl if you want. The girls move around frequently as the cops like to keep them away from the tourists. They can be found on side streets just off the boulevard; last time I was there I saw some on Cahuenga. You may also find them in the area near the 101 freeway. You may spot them both in daylight and under the cover of darkness. You will also find a great deal of gender-bender activity here. So, if you're looking for a girl, make sure she really is one!

- **Sunset Blvd.** Girls located on a two-mile stretch between LaBrea and Western. There have been recent crackdowns here . . . so the streetwalkers may have moved on.

- **Lankershim Blvd**. North Hollywood, between Vanowen and Burbank.

- **Vineland.** No. Hollywood between Victory and Burbank.

- **Cahuenga Blvd.** North Hollywood south of Victory.

- **Glen Oaks Blvd**. San Fernando around Hubbard Street.

- **Hubbard Street.** San Fernando on both sides of the intersection with Glen Oaks Blvd.

- **Glen Oaks Blvd**. In Pacoima.

- **Van Nuys Blvd.** Pacoima west of Glen Oaks Blvd.

- **Beverly Blvd.** Hollywood from Western west to Fairfax. This area sees a great deal of transsexual and transvestite activity. Check their body parts before you pay (unless that is what you want)!!

- **Whittier Blvd.** Between Findlay and Garfield.

- **Pasadena** At the east end of Colorado Blvd. The cops frequent this area . . . watch out!

- **El Monte** On Garvey Avenue.

# In Conclusion

Remember, the areas where streetwalkers ply their trade are neighborhoods where people work, live and bring up families. That is another reason we discourage the use of streetwalkers. Call an escort instead. Let the streets be free and clear of lewd activity. Do what you want behind closed doors, but remember to respect the rights of your neighbors.

# Escorts

> . . . my method is basically the same as Masters and
> Johnson, only they charge thousands of dollars
> and it's called therapy. I charge fifty dollars
> and it's called prostitution.
> — *Xaviera Hollander*

> . . . last time I tried to make love to my wife nothing was
> happening, so I said to her, what's the matter,
> you can't think of anybody either?
> — *Rodney Dangerfield*

## The World's Oldest Profession

**O**K guys and girls, it's time to put away those magazines, turn off the porno tapes on the VCR, and deflate those blow-up dolls . . . you need a real live girl. And that's what this chapter is all about.

Here you will find a listing of escort services and individual girls who will do lingerie or nude modeling, dance for you or give you a rubdown. And they may do more. Of course, you do know that prostitution is illegal in Los Angeles as well as most parts of the United States, and even though you may want something more than just a model or a dancer or a masseuse, you may not get it. The girls do not want to get busted for prostitution and they are very careful about what they do. In fact, some girls don't ever do anything more than what they advertise. It all depends: on the girl's mood, on her feelings about you, on the tip, and on the current state of siege by the vice cops.

# How To Act

Don't act like a cop!! How do cops act, you ask?? Generally, vice cops are rather pushy and aggressive. They have spent some time and energy setting up a bust and they want it to work. He attempts to badger the poor working girl into giving him something more than a private strip show so he can pull out his shiny badge, shove it in her face and say "smile, you're on vice cop camera".

Of course, not every vice cop acts like a pushy New Yorker in a traffic jam, but that is the general feeling among the working girls. If you are too aggressive, the girl may believe you're the heat and refuse to do any more than that allowed by law. Give the girls a little time to get used to you; don't try to push things. Keep it cool, treat the girls with respect and let things take their course.

# Escorts, Dancers, Models, Masseuses & More

What's the difference between escorts, dancers, models and masseuses, you ask?? Does it really matter, I respond . . . they are all fun, fun, fun and more fun!

It would be safe to say that escorts are girls who work for escort services. These are businesses that generally consist of a small office, a telephone line (or a few telephone lines), a receptionist, possibly some drivers, and several girls. You call and speak with a receptionist who will discuss the type of girl you desire and the appropriate fee, and will then send a girl out to your place. The service gets a part of the fee, usually splitting it with the girl.

These services are generally more expensive than independent girls because of the fee splitting. Some girls feel safer working for a service as they expect the receptionist to screen out all the wackos, the psychos, and the truly deranged.

It would also be safe to say that escorts are girls whom you hire to go out on a date, to a social function or serve as some sort of companion for the evening. And it would be safe to say that dancers and models also work for escort services. The dancers and models usually describe their service as lingerie modeling or nude entertainment.

Whatever, it basically amounts to the same thing . . . a girl comes over to your place, puts on some sexy lingerie, dances a little, takes off that sexy lingerie, and may or may not get more intimate. You see, these terms – "escort," "model", "dancer" – are just advertising words, not absolute job descriptions.

Of course, it would certainly be safe to say that masseuses give massages. Sometimes they are sensual, non-sexual massages. Sometimes they are full-body massages during which you get all your tensions released (yes . . . even that tension!!). Sometimes, the massages lead to more intimate play. It just depends.

Now that you know something about escorts, models, dancers and masseuses, we can move ahead.

# How Much Moolah??

Are you ready for my answer? It all depends. That's my answer! Great help, huh? The going rate for escort services is $150-$250. You can get two girls for $200-$300. And some places offer three-girl specials for about $250-$400. And don't forget to include the tip when figuring out how much damage this is going to do to your wallet.

Some services include the tip in the basic rate, but buyer beware, if you want additional services, a tip may be required. From my experience, tips run about $100 (that's why I stay with my girlfriend, she only requires a $50 tip!!!).

Individual girls or services with only a few girls are usually less expensive, but not always. They generally charge $100-$200 and the tip is included, but not always. Some girls expect you to reach into that wallet and pull out even more greenbacks. You just have to play it by ear . . . but don't say I didn't warn you. I'll be glad when they legalize it so the prices will drop with all the competition.

# It Could Be You

I have a friend who works on a part-time basis for a local escort service. She's a real looker: 5'11" with an athletic body, long blonde hair and gorgeous long legs. She makes enough cash to pay the rent, pay for college, and put some away for a rainy day. She's very personable, a great conversationalist and truly loves her work. She met a traveling businessman one night at his hotel. He took a real liking to her (she never told me exactly what she did to make him fall for her). He offered her a free ticket to fly to New York to visit him. What's a girl to do . . . she accepted.

They must have had a great weekend because for the next year, he invited her with him on all his business trips. And his trips took him to London, Paris, Geneva, Rome and a few other tempting locales. Eventually, the romance and lust withered away and she is back to the escort service, college and her Westside apartment. But, she has some wonderful photos and great memories. So girls, the escort service isn't all hard work and sleazy customers!!

I have another friend who used to patronize escort services on a regular basis. I swear he would spend more on escorts in a week than I made in a month (he's a busy lawyer so I suppose he can afford it). And guess how he met his wife. You guessed it . . . on an escort call. She was a struggling college student with a perfect 36-24-36 body. They hit it off immediately and the next thing you know, they were walking down the aisle and living happily ever after. And along with that great body, she has a tolerant personality. She still lets him see an escort from time to time. Jeez – some people have all the luck!

# Police Stories

In one southwestern city, police placed a classified ad in a local paper looking for men to work as paid escorts. When the men responded, they were arrested for violating the prostitution laws.

In another city, police paid private citizens to pick up prostitutes, have sex with them, and then drive them to the police for immediate arrest.

In other cities, police have wired hotel rooms to catch call girls in the act. Do you think they are watching tourists and other hotel guest just for fun??

# Bring On The Girls . . .

The following is a partial list. (not in any order of preference) of some of the escort services and independent girls offering nude entertainment, lingerie modeling, massage and more in the greater Los Angeles area. I personally did not try all these services and girls – I'd be exhausted!! Keep in mind that these services open and close faster than a vice cop can whip out his badge.

When you call some of these phone numbers you may be greeted with that familiar "the number you have reached has been disconnected and is no longer in service." You can locate other services and individual girls in the Yellow Pages under "Escorts" or "Massage," or in local papers such as *L.A. Weekly*, *L.A. Reader* or some of the swingers' papers such as *Swing*, *The L.A. X Press*, *Hollywood Playmates*, or *New Reality*.

I have listed the escort agencies and a few of the individual girls. There are hundreds of individual escorts, dancers, models and masseuses in the LA area; you can locate them in the previously mentioned papers and publications. Remember: have a good time, don't be aggressive, treat the girls with respect, and everyone will have a great time!

## *Teasers*
*(800) 300-8327*

They have over 50 girls to choose from. It will cost you $200 for an hour for one girl and $350 for two girls. They also do bachelor parties and stripping telegrams. They can fax or mail you their brochure. I've seen their portfolio and they do have some very gorgeous girls.

## *Class Act Dancers*

*(213) 663-7399*

A girl for one hour will cost you $150, two girls will cost you $250. Recently I had one of their girls come to my house. She was a real dark-haired beauty. She danced in some lingerie, stripped it off and danced nude, and then got real intimate with herself (if you know what I mean!!). She was either an Oscar-winning caliber actress or she had a great time with herself. Of course, I had a great time with myself, too! I was so turned on I forgot to ask if she did anything more! This service also does bachelor parties and will fax pictures of their girls. They have an office in Silver Lake where you can view their portfolio (open 10 am to 7 pm). There are approximately 35 girls to choose from.

## Night Rhythm

*(818) 895-0458 or (310) 514-4341*

They have female and male dancers. It's $160 for an hour of fun. For bachelor parties, it's $140 for one girl and $210 for two girls. Last time I called, they needed two days advance notice to book a girl. Whatever happened to spontaneity???

## Your Search Has Ended

*(310) 288-4143*

Cute name, top-notch service. They offer escorts from the exotic to the erotic (at least, that's what they tell you). They "on parle francaise, si parla italiano, falsa se Portuguese" (they speak French, Italian and Portuguese!!!) Give them a call and find out if they speak your language.

## Nikki's Bare Assets

*(818) 768-8849*

They have many gorgeous girls to choose from. It's expensive to get an hour with one of these girls: $225. Bachelor party dancers cost $160 for an hour or $260 for two gorgeous girls. They're open twenty-four hours and they only take your hard-earned cash; no plastic!!

# Ten Plus Entertainment

*(800) 410-7587*

They offer bachelor party entertainment, private shows, fantasy shows for singles and couples. They offer a color portfolio to choose your girl from. It's $190 for the hour.

# Hot Bodies

*(213) 463-0306 or (818) 761-8816*

Making an appointment with a girl from this place will run you about $200-$300; you discuss the price with the girl after she calls you back. Incalls may be arranged depending on the girl's situation. They will gladly take your plastic (and your cash, too!!)

# Tawny's Twilight Liaisons

*(818) 766-7993*

It's $185 an hour for private dances. And if you're planning a bachelor party, it's $155 an hour for one girl, $240 for two girls, and if you can handle it, $340 an hour for three girls. They take your credit cards and they have a portfolio for you to see.

# California Girls

*(310) 305-8885*

The prices here vary; I have received several different answers. They have a good assortment of models/dancers.

# Madison's Avenue

*(714) 831-WHIP*

A fantasy outcall service specializing in dominance and submission. They travel south of Newport Beach to San Clemente. A high-class service. Starts at $200 to $300.

# Midnight Modeling

*(714) 438-1744*

An outcall service in the Orange County area. It's $150 for the hour and they have plenty of girls to choose from.

## $99 Outcall

*(818) 955-5350*

You can guess the price, but what about the tip?

## The Fun Company

*(818) 779-1052*

It's an expensive hour at $225. Bachelor parties are $175 for one girl and $275 for two girls.

## Carol

*(310) 288-1798*

An individual girl who lives in the Beverly Hills area. She's pretty, has a great body and is very friendly.

## Large & Lovely

*(310) 285-9334*

If you're into round and Rubenesque women, this is the phone number you'll need to remember.

## A Mystic Arousal Entertainment

*(800) 837-9338*

## Talk of the Town

*(310) 858-1009 or*
*(818) 761-8816*

## Hy-O-Silver

*(818) 988-7710*

## Covergirls

*(310) 930-6024*

## Sweet Dreams

*(818) 757-0856*

## Heavenly Bodies

*(805) 540-1479*

## Table Dance Delivery

*(310) 823-5522*

## Victoria

*(818) 893-1294*

A very pretty girl in her mid-twenties who has videos for sale. You get to preview the videos with her and possibly play. She sells 10 videos for $175. Her husband is also available to join you. She is very nice and sexy and wants only very nice and easy-going people.

## Sara

*(310) 366-8662*

A mature and experienced woman who gives a great massage. She is very voluptuous and tall.

## *Malibu*

*P.O. Box 862 Hollywood, CA 90078*
*(213) 874-7788*

A girl with some hot feminine muscle. She was an American Gladiators TV contestant. She offers private, fun wrestling and posing sessions. She's a busty bodybuilder.

## Angie

*(213) 436-0188*

This girl is the one for you Greek freaks. She claims to love Greek and I don't doubt her. She's very sexy and 38D-26-38. It will cost you around $200-$250.

## Gina

*(310) 281-7778*

A very, very sexy girl in her twenties. She's pretty, petite and in great shape. She charges around $200 for an hour or so, and believe me, it's well worth it. She operates out of an apartment in Beverly Hills and she will knock you out with her extraordinary looks.

## The Honey Bunnies

*(818) 842-2284*

Two girls, Honey and Bunny (names changed to protect the sexy!), who do incall massages. One blonde, one redhead; both extremely sexy and deliciously voluptuous. . . have fun!

## Chaynelle

*(213) 663-2203*

You get a great incall massage from this perfectly proportioned young blonde. She charges $120 topless and $160 nude. If the receptionist on this line attempts to get you a different girl, wait until you can get Chaynelle . . . she's worth it! She is located in the Silver Lake area.

## Laurie Lewis

*(213) 241-6003*

A porno star who gives you her all for $300. She works on an outcall basis only.

## Kissin' Sisters

*(213) 896-1496*

Two girls, Rose and Christie, who claim to be sisters. It's a fun session if you have the $500 required. Located in the mid-Wilshire area..

## Jennifer West

*(818) 782-1624*

An adult film star who does outcalls on the west side of town only. She's 36C-25-34 with long blonde hair. She charges $250 cash for the hour.

## Mistress Roxanne

*(714) 891-6458*

An attractive, "in-shape" mistress who is into wrestling, spanking, B&D and other fetishes.

## Absolutely The Best

*(714) 434-0933*

This is a platonic companionship service. They have men and women who only go to public places. They do not present themselves as an escort or dating service. If this is what you're looking for . . . check them out.

## The XXX Connection

*(818) 883-7931*

This escort service features the hottest adult stars. Prices start at $300 and go way up for the bigger stars.

## Streakers on the Run

*(818) 342-4475*

Don't know how the girls here are but they have a cute name.

# Desert Area

For those of you who live out in the Palm Springs and Coachella Valley area or those of you who enjoy visiting the area, here is a list of some of the services and girls waiting to heat up those already hot desert nights.

## Sensations

*(619) 342-8269*

Outcall service with a few girls. Full body massage costs $120. Sometimes they are all out of girls for the night, so you may want to plan ahead.

## Heather & Jane

*(619) 779-4767*

They offer full body massage. Call for their current rates.

## Dolly

*(619) 770-0624*

Her advertisement states that she will give you the "best massage you've ever had." After all the massages I have had doing the strenuous research for this book, I cannot dispute her claim. It's $80 for 45 minutes and $100 for the hour. She does incall only and is located in the Desert Hot Springs area.

## Mon Cherie Lingerie Strippers

*67575 E. Palm Canyon Dr., Cathedral City*
*(619) 328-2826*

This is a lingerie shop and an outcall service. The lingerie shop only sells lingerie (no dancers there!!). The outcall service charges $200 for an hour or $150 for half an hour. You can also buy lingerie from the strippers (that's one way to get it off their bodies!!!)

## A-1 Teasers

*(800) 300-8327*

They have male and female strippers. They have a wide assortment of girls to choose from and they will fax photos to you if you like. A stripper will cost you $200 for an hour of fun.

## Erotica
*(619) 864-9896*

They do private parties, bachelor and bachelorette parties and stripping telegrams. They offer some hot two-girl shows for your viewing pleasure. They have many male and female dancers to choose from. Call for their current rates.

# And Two Girls in San Diego

For a much more extended list, grab a copy (after paying for it) of *Sin Diego* (see back of this book).

## Brittany
(619) 645-1204

Centerfold curves, sophistication and sensuality in La Jolla.

## Sexxy Sadie
*(619) 685-0804*

A fit, classy and sophisticated blonde.

© 1995 DR TUPPER

"Now it's my turn to get a rub down!"

©1993 Jack Messick Photography

# CHAPTER EIGHT

# Massage Parlors

. . . License my roving hands, and let them go.
Before, behind, between, above, below.
— *John Donne*

The mere mention of a massage parlor sends me off to a fantasy land where petite, dark-haired geisha girls run their tiny hands across my shoulders, walk gently on my back, and tend to my every wish. I lie back, naked as the day I was born, and enjoy all the sensual pleasure my personal geisha girl can offer.

OK, I know, it's a fantasy. But one can dream, can't he?? Where's the fun in life without a few fantasies??

Actually, the massage parlors around town are mostly "Oriental"; staffed by Korean, Vietnamese or other Southeast Asian girls who do run their tiny hands all over your body (I haven't had any walk on my back yet). Whether they cater to your every wish . . . you'll have to find out for yourself. A few of the places listed are not "Oriental"; they are staffed by blondes, brunettes, redheads or whatever. Their prices are usually higher than the Oriental places, somewhere around $100-$200.

Even if we were in the business of rating places, it would be difficult to rate these establishments as they seem to change from day to day. I may report to you that a certain place has the best-looking girls and by the time you read this the place down the road may have the prettiest and finest.

One day a particular place may offer the friendliest and best service, but the next day you may get choice service at another place.

I find most of these places to be similar; prices are the same, services offered are very uniform and the buildings and decor are basically identical (except for the non-Oriental places). You'll have to try them all out and see for yourself. By the time you read this, some of the massage parlors may be out of business and new ones opened up to take their places. Call before you go.

What do you get at these places, you ask?? Good question; unfortunately I don't have a good answer for you. Basically my response is . . . it depends! It depends on the place, the girl, the girl's mood at the time, the recent police activity, your attitude, your wallet, and a whole host of other factors. You do get a massage; sometimes a pleasant and sensual fingertip massage, sometimes a mildly invigorating rubdown. And you may get more. Sometimes you get a "full-body" massage included in the price, sometimes you don't. Sometimes you have a great time – sometimes you feel like you've been ripped off.

The basic massage rate at most of these establishments is $40 for a half-hour and $60 for an hour. Sometimes you get a "full-body" massage if you tip the girl (usually $20 - $40), sometimes your money won't buy you anything. And sometimes you may even get more than a "full-body" massage if the money and the mood are right. Again it depends!

The poor hard-working masseuse has to be ever vigilant in her vice watch as the men in blue are out there ever ready to pounce if she steps over the legal line. Every customer is a potential ticket to the slammer or bureaucratic hell. And you may catch her at the wrong time or remind her of a vice cop who once busted her . . . it depends!

The girls who work at these places run the gamut of beauty. Some are very attractive, some are average and some are well below the median for beauty. But, you can keep your eyes closed as she gently stinulates your flesh with her soft touch. Lie back and enjoy, you never know, fantasies sometimes can come true.

Speaking of fantasies coming true, I have a friend who used to visit the massage parlors on a regular basis because Oriental girls were his turn-on. He got one of the best massages of his life, made a date with the girl, they fell in love and eventually got married. That's what I call a fantasy coming true! Now, he gets his massage for free and he always knows he will getting more than just a massage!

Now that you know absolutely nothing about what to expect when you go to a massage parlor . . . here's the list of places around town. Enjoy!!

# Los Angeles Area

## Century Acupressure

*4252 W. Century Blvd., Inglewood*
*(310) 412-5050*

I had one great massage here from a very attractive girl. She was friendly, with beautiful long dark hair and hands of silk. I've been back a few times, but I haven't found her again. It's open 9 am to 10 pm, 7 days a week.

## Fuji Oriental Spa & Massage

*1439 Lincoln Blvd., Santa Monica*
*(310) 394-0733*

Last time I visited this place I saw a few young, attractive girls. The massage was good, too!

## Ginza Spa

*733 N. LaBrea #204, Hollywood — (213) 932-9580*

Haven't seen too many attractive girls here, but I have had a few skillful massages (and a few poor excuses for one). The mama-san tries to keep watch over the girls. Turnover is fast here as I see different girls every time I go.

## Hollywood Massage

*5909 Hollywood Blvd., Hollywood*
*(213) 465-2833*

Not an "Oriental" place. But it is a massage parlor with many girls to choose from. It's open 7 days a week from 11 am to midnight. They have a relaxing sauna and exciting two-girl specials. You probably will only get a massage here.

## Leo's

*N. Hillhurst & Los Feliz, Hollywood*
*(213) 664-3029*

It is a strange experience going to Leo's. It is a women's hair salon where you can get a massage from one of the young Asian girls in the back room. It's a strange feeling waiting for your massage sitting with a few older Asian women waiting for their hair appointments. I've enjoyed some excellent deep tissue massage here and more.

## Oriental Massage

*621 Broadway, Santa Monica*
*(310) 394-9060*

Open 7 days a week, 9:30 am to 10:30pm. The last time I visited, I received a great massage from a young and extremely beautiful girl. She barely spoke English and had such a strong accent that I never understood her name. Oh well, I'll have to force myself to go back and find out.

## Shiatsu Japan

*2922 Pico Blvd., Santa Monica*
*(310) 450-5237*

They have several girls to choose from, with a few very young attractive ones. Open 7 days a week from 9 am to 10:30pm.

## Shiatsu Spa Center

*14129 S. Van Ness Ave., Gardena*
*(310) 329-7529*

Nice friendly place. You can get a sauna and a massage here. Open 10 to 10 Monday through Saturday.

## Sun Oriental Acupressure

*654 E. Manchester Blvd., Inglewood*
*(310) 671-7913*

Hit or miss here. Sometimes the girls are young and attractive, sometimes they're not. Sometimes you need your Oriental-to-English translator.

## Shiatsu Massage & Acupressure

*12118 1/2 W.Washington Blvd., Culver City*
*(310) 390-4831*

I recommend this place as they offer good service and a few Asian girls in their twenties.

## Tokyo Acupressure

*1019 W. Manchester Blvd., Inglewood*
*(310) 348-9008*

Hit or miss here – sometimes you'll be pleasantly surprised, sometimes you won't! Depends on the mood, time of day and alignment of moon and stars, I suppose.

## Tokyo Massage

*817 Pico Blvd., Santa Monica*
*(310) 450-6559*

The last time I visited, the girls were young and pretty. Open 7 days a week from 9 am to 10:30 pm.

## VIP Massage

*20346 Hawthorne #99, Torrance*
*(310) 214-9294*

They offer Japanese massage, jacuzzi, dry sauna and steam sauna. Open 9 am to 10 pm.

## Little Hong Kong Acupressure

*11607 Washington Blvd., Culver City*
*(310) 390-1609*

They have Hispanic and Oriental girls.

## Japanese Bath Massage

*2823 Pico Blvd., Santa Monica*
*(310) 453-9908*

## Mimiko's

*2629 Santa Monica Blvd., Santa Monica*
*(310) 828-5088*

© 1995 DR TUPPER

# Green Garden

748 E. Washington St.reet
Venice
(310) 823-9531

# Fuji Shiatsu
# & Massage

8434 E. Telegraph Rd.,
Downey
(310) 927-9147

# Ginja Oriental
# Massage

2512 Wilshire Blvd., Santa
Monica
(310) 828-9017

# Oriental Massage
# & Acupressure

12719 Washington Place,
Los Angeles
(310) 390-3858

# Oriental Acupressure

421 E. Hillcrest, Inglewood
(310) 677-9239

# Oriental Massage

3311 Pico Blvd., Santa
Monica
(310) 829-4241

# Oriental
# Shiatsu Massage

1913 Santa Monica Blvd.,
Santa Monica
(310) 453-6310

# Oriental
# Spa Massage

7625 S. Eastern Ave., Bell
Gardens
(310) 927-9158

# Sanwa Health Spa

120 S. Los Angeles Street
(213) 687-4597

# Shiatsu Massage

523 W. Manchester,
Inglewood
(310) 672-5141

# Sue Acupressure

261 S. LaBrea Ave. #102,
Inglewood
(310) 672-0630

# Sun Oriental Massage

1439 Lincoln Blvd., Santa
Monica
(310) 587-1121

1111 Pacific Coast Hwy.
#7, Harbor City
(310) 325-6552

# Tawa's
# Shiatsu Massage

362 East First Street
(213) 680-9141

# Townhouse Massage

1447 Sixth Street, Santa
Monica
(310) 394-2999

# San Fernando Valley

## Oriental Acupressure

*10700 Burbank Blvd. #4, North Hollywood*
*(818) 980-4249*

Typical Oriental place. Last time I was here I received a massage from a girl who wasn't attractive and who only knew about five words of English ("you like me massage there?"), but she smiled constantly and gave a great massage.

## Flamingo Massage & Sauna

*13522 Ventura Blvd., Sherman Oaks*
*(818) 990-1020*

# Inland Empire

## Shiatsu Massage

*13031 Central Ave., Chino*
*(909) 590-7444*

## Sun Acupressure

*142 A Turnbull Rd.,*
*City Of Industry*
*(818) 968-0043*

Recommended for its fun and friendly girls.

## Oriental Shiatsu Clinic

*1133 E. Sixth St., Corona*
*(909) 735-6233*

## Japanese Massage

*1200 Arizona, Redlands*
*(909) 798-5643*

© 1995 DR TUPPER

# Ventura County

## Golden Touch

2600 Vineyard Ave.,
Oxnard
(805) 981-9554

There were a few nice-looking and friendly masseuses the only time I visited this place.

## Jade Massage

2720 S. Ventura Rd.,
Oxnard
(805) 486-5997

I had an excellent massage from an older Oriental woman here. It's open 10 am to 11 pm.

## Japanese Shiatsu Massage

205 North "A" Street,
Oxnard
(805) 483-6676

## Oriental Spa Massage

3606 S. Saviers Rd.,
Oxnard
(805) 486-8533

## Sun Massage

1251 Saviers Rd., Oxnard
(805) 486-4456

## Tokyo Spa

1732 Saviers Rd., Oxnard
(805) 487-8434

## Health Center Oriental Massage

125 St. Mary's Dr., Oxnard
(805) 487-9954

A decent place with one or two attractive girls

## New Seoul

1237 N. Ventura Rd.,
Oxnard
(805) 983-2707

Good place with some young, attractive and fun loving girls.

## Nichole's Therapy Massage

660 N. Ventura Rd., Oxnard
(805) 983-2707

Good place with some young, attractive and fun girls.

## Oriental Acupressure Massage

4235 Saviers Rd., Oxnard
(805) 487-7899

## Myako Massage

156 E. Pleasant Valley Rd.,
Oxnard
(805) 488-3559

A good place with some fun and friendly girls. I's a run-down building – but don't judge a book by its cover!

### Oriental Acupressure

885 E. Main St., Ventura
(805) 653-9979

### Oriental Massage

1653 E. Main St., Ventura
(805) 648-6453

### Oriental Massage

1763 E. Thompson St.,
Ventura (805) 653-6633

### Okinawa Massage

1763 E. Thompson St.,
Ventura
(805) 653-6633

# Orange County

© 1995 DR TUPPER

### Narita Spa

4222 Campus Dr., Newport
Beach (714) 756-1953

### Japan Shiatsu

436 32nd St., Newport
Beach (714) 675-6718

### Nagoya Acupressure

4063 Birch Street, Newport
Beach (714) 852-8456

### Hana Acupressure

767 W. 19th St., Suite 109,
Costa Mesa
(714) 645-6442

### New Fuji Spa

4251 Martingale Way #G,
Newport Beach
(714) 553-0231

### Jh Acupressure

5242 Katella Ave., #106,
Los Alamitos
(310) 598-2222

### Century Acupressure

2576 Newport Blvd., #C,
Costa Mesa
(714) 722-8640

### Oriental Garden Spa

17061 Newland, Huntington
Beach (714) 848-6446

If you're interested, you can
get a massage from a male,
too but you will need an appointment. This way, you
and your wife can both get
one if you get tired of giving
each other massages.

*I like it
hard
and
Rough!!*

Danyel Cheeks

# CHAPTER NINE

# B & D Clubs

> . . . you gotta be cruel to be kind.
> — *Nick Lowe*

**O**h . . . spank me, whip me, beat me . . . oh yes, mistress, I'll do anything you say." For those of you who understand that there is most definitely a fine line between pleasure and pain, this chapter is for you.

Los Angeles, and its environs, is world-famous for the proliferation of Bondage & Domination parlors, dungeons and the multitude of mistresses. Most of these places are not brothels; many of them do not offer sex in the usual sense of that word. These places are on the fringes of the law and they certainly want to remain open; they tend to follow the rule . . . NO SEX. Don't expect that when you go to one, you will get a little B & D and then have sex. Expect B & D or whatever fetish you are into and that's all. If anything else occurs, consider it a bonus.

Some of the fetishes you will usually be able to indulge in at a B & D establishment include female over male dominance (the most popular indulgence), male over female dominance with trained submissives, cross-dressing, spanking, whipping, latex, leather, infantilism, foot fetishism, and more. Just pick out your favorite fetish and go explore your fantasy.

The following is a partial list of B & D clubs and mistresses operating in the greater Los Angeles area. So . . . get off your butts, you worms, you scum of the Earth, you worthless pieces of dirt, go and submit to your deepest, darkest fantasies!!

## Lady Laura's Dominion

*(310) 559-7111 or (310) 204-6777*

This is one of the most popular and well-known B & D establishments in the country. They have approximately twenty women working here: dominants, submissives, switchhitters, whatever. This place has four fully equipped dungeons. They do it all: spanking, whipping, paddling, cross-dressing, bondage, latex and much more. The cost is $80 for the half hour and $140 for an hour.

The ladies are fun and friendly (or mean and nasty, if you like), and they seem to enjoy their work. If you are a dominant, two of the best submissives here are Xavia (a blonde with a great body) and Zeena (a dark-haired exotic beauty). They are open 7 days a week, 11 am to 11pm Monday through Saturday and 2 pm to 7 pm on Sundays.

## The Chateau

*7310 N. Atoll Street, North Hollywood*
*(800) 696-4414 or (818) 503-3034*

Their rates are $70 for thirty minutes, $90 for forty-five minutes, and $110 for an hour. They have approximately five to seven girls working per shift. They are open noon to 2 am and they do most every fetish. One of the best switchhitters here (she'll dominate you or let you dominate her) is Regina, a dark-haired, busty and muscular Mexican girl. Two of the best submissives are Nina and Asia, both extremely sensuous and pretty Oriental women.

## Diva's Dungeon

*(310) 398-8811*

They offer it all: B & D, S & M, role playing, cross-dressing, and many other fetishes. The sessions begin at $100. There are mistresses, slave girls or masters available. Also, they allow voyeurs to watch certain "live sessions". They offer a special 4 hours of play for only $100. Call for details. Phone sessions are also available for $2.66 per minute; you can charge it to your credit card or prepay.

## The Web

*(310) 287-2128*

A very upscale club that charges $200 for a session, which usually lasts from 1 hour to 1 1/2 hours. They don't watch the clock or rush you out if you are having a good time. They follow the "no sex" rules, but they show you a very good time.

They are located in Culver City and are open 10am to 10pm (10am to midnight on weekends). To make an appointment you will need to call at least an hour in advance as their girls are on call, not sitting around waiting for customers to drop in.

## Mistress Storm

*904-3499*

A sexy dominant awaits your call.

## Mistress Elvira

*(213) 851-0947*

She is one mean and nasty lady and enjoys heavy bondage and whipping; if you're only into light B & D, don't call her. She's located in Hollywood and charges $120.

## Mistress Paloma

*(818) 348-7228*

She operates in the Woodland Hills area and her rates vary depending on how heavy or light you like your dominance; from $75 on up. She has a nice apartment and a reasonably well-equipped dungeon.

## Mistress Bijon

*(714) 491-0761*

A slightly older Mexican lady who works in Orange County. She charges around $135 per session.

I Like to Play Horsie!                    *Mistress Jayne Alexander*

## Mistress Dee

*(310) 821-5633*

She is a mature and experienced dominatrix who works out of the Marina Del Rey area. She is very good at most aspects of dominance including spanking, cross-dressing and Greek. She charges $60 for a half-hour and $120 for an hour. She works Monday through Saturday, 1 pm to 8 pm.

## Gentle Enemas

*(213) 739-1749*

You can guess what they do here. If this is your thing . . . give them a ring. It's a couple of cute, young girls who have set up a hospital in their apartment.

## Mistress Shannon

*(310) 559-7111*

A very sexy light-skinned black dominatrix who works out of Lady Laura's Dominion. She is into all fantasies and fetishes and enjoys the scene.

## Mistress Vanessa

*(818) 891-4082*

A very sexy mistress who lives in the San Fernando Valley. She orders you to buy five X-rated videos for $150 and you will get a free B & D training session. Or you can buy two videos for $75 and get a half-hour training sesion. Or, if you've been a very naughty boy, you can purchase ten videos for $325 and get four hours of sensual dominance. Her husband is also available as her servant or as an additional dominant. She is worth a visit.

## Mistress Elizabeth

*(213) 257-2938*

She's a very sexy mistress who does most anything that turns you on. B & D, S & M, foot fetish, infantilism, cross-dressing; you got a fetish and she'll do it.

## Angella

*(310) 576-3972*

If you like to wrestle with a sexy woman, here's the phone number for you. Don't think it will be easy as she is strong and very competitive. It's her way of making you submit . . . and you will submit.

## Mistress Aries

*(818) 985-6969*

A very busty girl with bright red hair who will fulfill your B & D fantasies for $100 per hour. She works out of her Toluca Lake apartment.

# Other B & D Businesses

## Threshold

*2554 Lincoln Blvd. #1004 Marina Del Rey, CA 90291*
*(hotline #) (213) 845-0889*

Threshold is a non-profit educational and support association for adults interested in the safe, consensual exchange of power between partners into S & M, B & D, D & S, and foot fetishes. It is one of the largest S & M educational and support groups in the U.S., open to all interested people over 21.

It is not a swingers club, an orgy house, or a dating service. It sponsors several activities including demonstrations, workshops and social events. You must attend an orientation before becoming a member. Yearly dues are $40.

## Mistress Jayne Alexander& The Velvet Voices

*(310) 479-4210*

This is a phone sex service, one that specializes in phone dominance. If you are into submitting over the telephone, this is the ultimate experience for you. You get to speak live with Mistress Jayne or one of her gorgeous mistresses. They specialize in slave training, feminization, cross-dressing, bondage, body worship, S & M, role playing and more.

Mistress Jayne is a nationally known mistress whose beautiful face and body have appeared in numerous magazines and publications, including *Penthouse* and *Playboy*. Give them a call, this is a first class-operation.

## Majick & Fetish Shop
*3934 W. Sunset Blvd., Silverlake — (213) 660-1575*

They have fetish equipment and other goodies like candles and incense. Also have "spanking socials" on ocassion. Call for more details.

## *Whips & Chains*
*(213) 878-0300*

A new publication specifically catering to the needs of B & D aficionados. Call them for information or pick one up at your local bookstore.

## *Fantasy Fashion Digest*
*Post Office Box 950, Palom Springs, CA 92263*

A magazine that keeps you informed on all the fetish fashions and happenings.

© 1995 DR TUPPER

©1993 Jack Messick Photography

# CHAPTER TEN

# Swinging

> . . . when two people make love, there at least four people
> present - the two who are actually there
> and the two they are thinking about.
> — *Sigmund Freud*

**S**winging: swapping partners, wife swapping, open relationships, orgies, threesomes, exhibitionists, voyeurs,
swing parties. Whatever you call it, it all adds up to wild,
uninhibited sex play. Swinging certainly isn't for everyone;
it requires an open mind, a rein on your jealousies and
insecurities, and a passion for wild fun. If that describes you
. . . read on!!!

The swinging life dramatically gained popularity in the
sixties. The age of flower power, psychedelic posters and
music, hippies, social upheaval, and drugs also created a
subculture devoted to the pursuit of pleasure regardless of
marital status. Underground newspapers ran ads from couples looking for other couples, couples looking for women,
single men looking for fun couples, bisexuals looking for
other switchhitters, and many other combinations. The L.A.
Free Press was one of the underground papers which com-
bined the serious and the fun: pushed for social changes and
featured ads from wild and sexy swingers. Party houses,
commonly referred to as swing houses, began popping up
all over. And California was one of the hedonistic pleasure
centers of the globe!

Swinging matured through the seventies. While many singles were dancing to disco beats and screwing their brains out in one-night stands, couples were discovering the joys of swinging. Some jumped into the lifestyle with both feet while others just dabbled in it occasionally. The early eighties saw a continuation of the lifestyle, but all that changed for a time in the mid and late eighties. The reality of the AIDS epidemic hit home.

Once people became aware that AIDS wasn't a "gay disease," swingers slowed down their wild times. Swing parties all over the country closed down and many people dropped out of the lifestyle altogether. However, swinging did not become a relic of our wild past. No, it still exists and is enjoying somewhat of a rebirth. Of course, people are thinking twice (or more) before jumping into bed with someone else, but it's still going on.

Others are into voyeurism and exhibitionism. If you visit a swing house, you'll see much less group sex than during the sixties, seventies and early eighties. And, the most prominent aroma in the rooms of swing houses is not the sweet smell of sex . . . no, it's the slightly acrid scent of latex. Rubbers, rubbers everywhere. And if you are going to swing, use your rubbers!

# Swingers

People who are involved in the swinging lifestyle come in every shape, size, color, class and personality. The woman next door, the lawyer down the street, the foxy girl you see at the gym, the man and woman who walk their dog by your house every evening . . . it could be anyone. Couples dominate the swinging scene and single women are treated like precious treasures.

Single women are always in demand . . . and single men are always in abundance. It's one of the realities of swinging. Look in any of the swing publications; there is a preponderance of single men and everyone is looking for single ladies, especially bi-ladies. If you are a bisexual female, you can have it all!

There are swingers and swing parties all over the country. Even in such bible-belt states as Georgia, Alabama and Tennessee you will find swingers, swing parties and swingers' periodicals.

There are swingers in other countries as well. When I was in France I picked up a few swingers' magazines and read through the advertisements. Basically they are the same as here except for one difference: all the measurements were given in centimeters, not inches. It sure sounds great when that most precious part of your anatomy measures over a whopping "20"!!

## Swinging, Swingers and Sex

Swinging is about freedom of choice, expression of one's sexuality and the exploration of fantasy. It is about friendship as well as sex. It is about doing one's own thing. About being free. And we should all be concerned with our freedom; our freedom to be swingers, our freedom to express our sexuality, our freedom to explore our sexuality. Swinging can be a lifestyle, an occasional diversion or merely a fantasy. Swinging, swingers and sex are a part of freedom's landscape, and we must be ever vigilant in preserving that landscape, whether we are swingers or not.

# Swing Clubs

Now you need to know where to find other swingers. Swing clubs would be a good place to start. Swing clubs are houses which host parties, usually on weekends, that cater to swingers. There are places to socialize and have sex. You will usually find a jacuzzi, a few bedrooms, a social room and a small spread of food. Most clubs are for couples only, but some clubs allow single men. All clubs allow single women (aren't you ladies lucky!!!).

When you go to a swing club, it is no guarantee that you will have sex. Some people go only to watch, others go just for the fantasy of being watched, while others go to meet new sex partners. If someone says "no", it means **"NO"**! Also, no

Adult Actress Kylie Ireland

illegal drugs are allowed . . . please do not even think of bringing them to a party. You usually must bring your own alcohol if you want to drink.

There is generally a fee to enter, anywhere from $25 to $50. If you go to have a good time, without any expectations, you will usually have a good time. Don't be rude, crude or lewd (unless asked to be), and everyone will have a good time.

Following is a list of the swing clubs in the greater Los Angeles area. Have fun!!

## Club Worldwide

*P.O. Box 5366, Buena Park, CA 90622-5366*
*(714) 821-6117 or (213) 608-0722*
*or for the dances call (714) 821-9953*

This club is run by the people who bring you the *Lifestyles Convention* every year. This is a membership organization which hosts excellent parties with fun people. They also sponsor Friday night socials which are couples dances where you can meet other open-minded couples for conversation and dancing.

There are Friday socials on the first and third Friday of each month. The first Friday social is in Fullerton and the Third Friday social is in Long Beach. You can enjoy the dinner and the dance for $60 or the dance only for $35. Make a reservation by the preceding Monday and you'll get $5 off the price. Call and ask for their membership information and newsletter.

## Freedom Acres

*P.O. Box 6024, San Bernardino, CA 92412*
*(909) 887-8757 or (909) 887-6898*

A large club that has been in existence for quite some time. I have been to a few good parties there and a few slow ones . . . but it's usually a fun time. You must become a member to go to a party. Cost for the membership is $15 for the year, and the cost of each party is $35. The year runs from August through July and everyone must renew in August.

## Gemini Club

*P.O. Box 105, Claremont, CA 91711*
*(909) 622-8544*

They have parties for couples and singles at a house in Pomona every Friday and Saturday. You must purchase a membership before you attend a party. The cost for membership is $80 for single males and $40 for couples. Each party you attend costs $60 if you're an unattached male and $25 if you're a couple. They have an indoor jacuzzi, pool table, social area, video area, private rooms and a group room.

## Orgy Club

*Pager # (805) 274-3574 (beep your number and code 111)*

Located in the Palmdale area, they have parties for females and couples only. Haven't been to any of their parties so I don't know what they're like. Let us know what you think of it if you go.

## Panther Palace

*(714) 631-5485*

A private house party run by Wild Bill and Dottie, who have parties on the first and last Saturday of each month. It's for couples only and is located in Costa Mesa. They have one of the largest hot tubs you'll ever see!!

## Swingers Anonymous

*P.O. Box 4005, W. Covina, CA 91791 — (818) 918-4957*

They hold parties for couples and singles in a newly remodeled house. It's $80 for single guys and $25 for couples.

## The PC Group

*211 S. State College Blvd., #5095, Anaheim, CA 92806*
*(714) 533-5933*

Membership contact group for couples.

## D.J.'s

*P.O. Box 854, West Covina, CA 91793 — (818) 918-6233*

A recent addition to the swing party scene. There is a $40 membership fee (complimentary party included) and parties cost $30. They have a jacuzzi, pool table, group and private rooms.

## The Sybrians

*Post Office Box 2525, Seal Beach, CA 90740*
*(714) 964-7775*

Couples only membership club.

# Swingers' Dances

## Southland Social Club

*Post Office Box 459, San Dimas, CA 91773*
*(909) 593-6110*

Hosts social events in the L.A. area.

## The Love Network

*Post Office Box 16272,*
*Encino, CA 91416*

Resource group for singles and couples exploring alternative livestyles.

## Friday Night Socials

*P.O. Box 7128, Buena Park, CA 90622*
*(714) 821-9953*

These are dances sponsored by The Lifestyles Organization that are held on the first and third Friday of every month. The 1st Friday social is held at a hotel in Fullerton and the 3rd Friday social is held at a hotel in Long Beach. The cost is $35 for the dance and $60 for the dinner and dance. There is a $5 discount if you pay a week in advance. These are fun, no-pressure dances . . . that are just dances and places to meet people in the swinging lifestyle. You can also get a discounted room if you want to spend the night at the hotel.

### After Midnight Parties

*4354 Laurel Canyon, Blvd., Suite 198,*
*Studio City, CA 91604 — (310) 281-8293*

These are very exciting dances for couples held at a hotel in the Los Angeles area on a monthly basis. The cost is $30 per couple and reservations are not required. These are fun, sensual parties with attractive alternate lifestyle couples. Call for more information and details on becoming members.

### Dream Makers

*(714) 632-6969*

Adult social dances in the Orange County area. Dances are $40 each.

# Swingers' Publications

There are many swing publications serving the greater LA area. You will find them in your local X-rated bookstore. They contain personal advertisements from swinging couples, single men and single women, commercial ads from "working girls", ads from escort services, transsexuals, bookstores and more. Some of them have more personal ads than others and some cater to a specific crowd or fetish.

## It Could Happen To You . . .

I have a friend who has been answering swing advertisements for years. As a single guy he usually scored a big fat zero. So many letters written to ads, so few responses. But, all that effort has paid off twice.

Once, he answered an ad from a couple who was looking for a few guys for a "gang bang for wife." It turned out to be a fantasy of the woman's and her first time. Well, my friend was one of the three guys they responded to. On a Friday night the three guys and the couple met at a local hotel and rented a room. My friend says the girl was about 30 years old, about 5'5" with long blonde hair and an athletic body. And she had great tits!! (His description).

Everyone was a little shy at first, but after a few drinks the girl did a slow striptease for the guys and everything just followed from there. I guess she took on all four guys (her husband joined in) and was left wanting even more!! A few months later, she invited my friend over for a threesome and he had another great night!

A few months after the threesome he answered another ad in a swing paper. This one was from a single girl (there aren't very many of them!!) and surprise, surprise, surprise, she responded to him. She was looking for a partner who would be interested in introducing her to the swinging lifestyle. And guess what??? They are now living together and happily swinging ever after!!

Yes, it could happen to you! But only if you pick up one of these periodicals and start sending out some responses.

Following is a list and brief description of some of the swingers' publications you will find in the area. Read up and I hope you find what you're looking for.

# The Publications

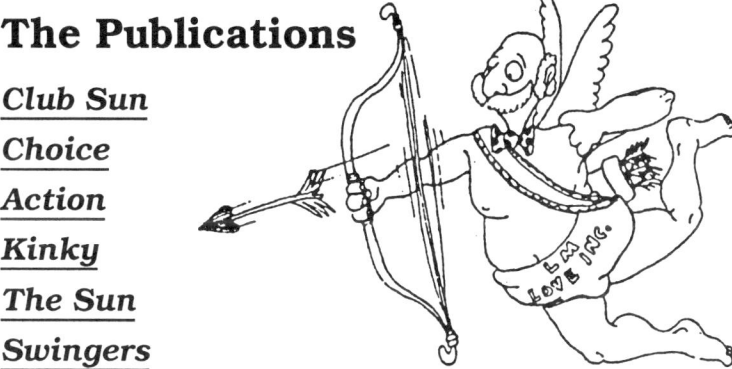

### Club Sun

### Choice

### Action

### Kinky

### The Sun

### Swingers

*1614 N. Cahuenga Blvd., Hollywood, CA 90028*  © 1995 DR TUPPER
*(213) 466-4020*

These publications have many commercial ads which feature many transsexuals. Club Sun and Swingers seem to have the most advertisements from real swingers. Swingers and Kinky are published every month while the others are published every two weeks. Also, there are many advertisements from phone sex operations and mail order companies.

# Swing

# Friends & Lovers

# Swingtime

*2801 Fourth Ave., San Diego, CA 92103*
*(619) 299-0500*

These publications are published in San Diego by Dawn Media, but all three magazines have many advertisements from swingers in the greater Los Angeles area, Orange County and the Inland Empire. There are also some commercial ads from transsexuals, escort services and individual working girls. Swing and Friends & Lovers are published every two weeks while Swingtime comes out about once a month.

## L.A. X Press

*1545 N. La Brea Avenue, Hollywood, CA 90028*
*(213) 969-8504 or (213) 969-8505*

This is published weekly and is loaded with advertisements from transsexuals, mistresses, masseuses, escorts, escort services and much more.

## Hollywood New Reality

## Hollywood Playmates

*Post Office Box 93398, Hollywood, CA 90093*
*(213) 878-0300*

These are published every two weeks and are quite similar. A multitude of hot, sexy ads from transsexuals, escorts, models, masseuses and more.

## West Coast Swingers

## Swingers Hotline

*105 Serra Way #403, Milpitas, CA 95035*
*(408) 956-5650*

These are high-quality publications published every month by Pathway Communications in Northern California. They have separate Southern California editions that have many personal advertisements from local swingers very few commercial ads.

## *TV Epic*

*105 Serra Way #403, Milpitas, CA 95035*
*(408) 956-5650*

Also published by *Pathway Communications*, this caters to the fetish crowd, with most of the advertisements from transvestites, transsexuals, cross-dressers. There are ads from all over California. If you're into a little gender-bending, pick up a copy of this publication.

## *Making Contact Magazine*

*Post Office Box 2006, Fullerton, CA 92633 (no phone)*

This is published monthly and has ads from swingers all over Southern California. I can't find it in the local bookstores very often, so you may have to write to the above address for a copy.

## *Swingers' News*

*P.O. Box 5019 #157, Upland, CA 91785*
*(no phone)*

Published by *On-Line Publications*, this is a monthly swing magazine with ads from local swingers.

## *Adam Magazine*

*Knight Publishing Corp., 8060 Melrose Avenue,*
*Los Angeles, CA 90046-7082*

This is a men's magazine with all the typical stories and photo spreads. They also have a great swingers' section with photo ads, listings, stories, and swingers' news and updates.

## *Amateurs in Action*

*256 S. Robertson Blvd. Suite 3901 Beverly Hills, CA 90211*

A glossy-cover magazine with ads from swingers and sellers of amateur videos and photos all over the United States.

## *Whips & Chains*

*(213) 878-0300*

A recent addition that is geared specifically to aficionados of B & D.

### Amateur Connexion
### Odyssey
### UnReal People
### Looking Glass

*Post Office Box 18796 Los Angeles, CA 90007 or*
*Post Office Box 77817 Los Angeles, CA 90007*
*(800) 397-5114*

These are all national publications, with glossy covers and hundreds of advertisements from swingers all over this great country of ours. Lots of hot action photos for your viewing pleasure. Lots of real, horny people!

### Loving Alternatives

*Omnific, Post Office Box 459, San Dimas, CA 91773*
*(909) 592-5217*

A monthly swingers magazine with loads of hot ads! Great place to meet new friends.

### B & D Pleasures
### Bizarre Erotic Fantasies

*Post Office Box 92889, Long Beach, CA 90809-2889*
*(310) 631-1600*

Published by *B & D Pleasures,* these publications cater to the dominance and submission crowd. Filled with personal and commercial ads from all over the country, hot stories and photos. If this is your scene, these are the papers for you.

### Adventure Line Newsletter

*Post Office Box 7683, Mission Hills, CA 91346-7683*

A small newsletter with ads and news for swingers and adventurous people.

# More Swinging Stuff . . .

### Lust Angeles

*Post Office Box 620219, San Diego, CA 92162-0219*

A fantastic book!!! But you must already know that.

## Lifestyles Convention

*Lifestyles, 2641 W. LaPalma, Suite A, Anaheim, CA 92801*
*(714) 821-9953 — http://www.gus.com/PlayCouples*

This is the major event on the swinging calendar. It is usually held sometime in August or September at a hotel in Las Vegas, San Diego or Los Angeles. In 1994, it was held at the Town & Country Hotel in San Diego. It will be there again in 1995. It consists of three days and nights of dances, pool-side socials, workshops, lectures, product booths and the culminating erotic ball. The erotic ball is a masquerade party like no other masquerade party. Swingers come from all over the country to attend and show their stuff. It's one of the wildest parties you'll ever attend!

## Lifestyles Tours

*Lifestyles Tours & Travel, 2641 W. LaPalma Suite A,*
*Anaheim, CA 92801 — (714) 821-9939*

This is a full-fledged travel agency which specializes in swingers tours. They have great vacations to places like Hedonism in Jamaica and other wild, exotic places. Even if you aren't interested in a swingers' tour, they can make any travel arrangements you need.

## *Pathway BBS*

*(714) 236-4247;*
*Northern California call (408) 956-5600 or (510) 790-3127.*

This is a computer BBS that caters to the swinging lifestyle and swingers. They have 16 lines, public and private chat, public and private message areas, adult GIF pictures, adult and public-domain software and much more. If you want to communicate with swingers through your modem . . . this is the BBS for you.

## L.A. Women

*c/o Omnific, 1037 N. Grand Ave., Suite 198,*
*Covina, CA 91724*

This is a network of bisexual women, most of whom are part of the swinging community. They have events from discussion groups to all-girl parties. Membership is $10.

# Home Lodging

*P.O. Box 3323, Newport Beach, CA 92659*
*(714) 646-7641 (9 am to Midnight); (800) 645-6853*
*(message); (714) 645-6854 (Fax)*

They offer "alternate bed and breakfast inns." There are overnight accommodations in private homes and other facilities for alternate lifestyle couples and, at certain places, singles. They also are a full-service agency that can book air travel, resorts, hotels, inns, yachts and tours for conventional and alternate lifestyles. Call for more information and a brochure.

# NASCA

*P.O. Box 7128, Buena Park, CA 90622*

This is the North American Swing Club Association and if you join you get membership cards, a newsletter, information on the swinging scene, the International Directory of Swing Clubs & Publications (see below) and more. The cost per year to join is $30.

# *International Directory of Swing Clubs & Periodicals*

*NASCA, P.O. Box 7128,*
*Buena Park, CA 90622*

This book has all the information you need on swing clubs and publications around the world.
The cost is $10.
(see back page)

© 1995 DR TUPPER

Pethouse Pet                                                    Taylor

# CHAPTER ELEVEN

# Personal Ads

> . . . she was a lovely girl. Our courtship was fast and furious
> – I was fast and she was furious.
> — *Max Kaufmann*

In the not too distant past, people who used personal ads as a means to meet friends, lovers or lifetime companions were viewed as either desperate, weird or way too bold and adventurous. If you did answer or place an ad, you kept that little secret to yourself to avoid the laughter and ridicule from your friends.

However, times have changed. My, how they have changed!! Personal ads are everywhere. Everyone is answering them!! Everyone is placing one!! Everyone is using them to meet that perfect friend, fantasy, lover or lifetime partner. The personals ads are no longer the private domain of the weirdos, the wackos, the wanna-bes, the sexually frustrated and the scam artists. Each year over 2,000,000 men and women place a personal advertisement and over 10,000,000 people answer those ads.

Why have they gained so much popularity?? Why is everyone doing it?? (Answering ads, that is).

First of all, even though the bars and nightclubs are still popular, fewer people are using them as a place to meet that perfect someone. Second, the pace of life seems so much more hectic and hurried, people need a quick and more efficient means of meeting dates. Thirdly, people are waking up to the fact that there are good quality singles in these ads. And lastly, with the advent of more sophisticated phone equipment and "900" numbers, entrepreneurs are realizing that there is a profit to be made in phone personals. With this great proliferation of "900" numbers, more people are utilizing them.

# Type of Personal Ad

There are basically two types of personal ad: the phone personal and the traditional written one. Phone personals are much easier and faster to use. With many of them you can hear the voice of the person who has placed the ad and, of course, the person running the ad can hear the respondent's voice on a voice mail message. Hearing a voice is much more personal, and sometimes more revealing, than a written response. However, there are some who still like to sit down and write a detailed letter and meet the "old-fashioned" way!

There are basically three negative aspects to phone personals. If you use your phone number when you respond to an ad, you are opening up your line to potential wackos. Though most people who use these ads are discreet and fairly responsible people, there are some weirdos out there in telephoneland. You may get calls at 3 am or heavy breathing or perverted talk. I recommend getting a second phone line just for ads . . . or a voice mail number or a pager. This way you don't have to give out your home phone number.

The second thing to watch out for is the cost! These "900" numbers can get rather expensive. On many of the lines you can leave an advertisement or listen to other advertisers for free, but if you want to pick up your messages or respond to an ad . . . it will cost you. That's how they make their profit!! The cost can be anywhere from 98 cents to $2.98 per minute. That may not sound like much – but it adds up very quickly!!! I have a friend who ran up a bill of over seven hundred dollars one month just answering ads! Since he was living at home, his mother saw the bill, and boy, was she pissed at him. She thought he was talking nasty on the phone sex lines, but he was just answering ads for fun and romance!!

You need to watch out for scam artists. Some phone lines are merely trying to make a quick profit. They fill their lines with bogus ads except for a few unsuspecting folks who never get any responses. Usually these phony lines are in business only a few months or so. I recommend using a line you know has been in business more than a few months. Also, there are scam artists and hookers operating on these lines. There are men who prey on naive women and all they want is your money.

If the man (or women) asks for money very early in the dating relationship, a warning flag should go up!! Watch out!! I know a woman who lent a guy two thousand dollars after the third date!! Do you think she ever saw or heard from him again?? And guys, there are call girls who advertise on these lines. If a girl starts using the word "generous" or other similar terms, she is probably a play-for-pay girl. That may be what you want . . . but if it isn't, stay away!!

# What To Say In Your Ad

Whether you are writing an ad or vocally recording one on a phone line, there are a few things you may want to consider including.

- **Physical features** . . . age, height, build, breast size (just a joke!!) or penis size to help the ladies (or guys) decide (I jest again!!).

- **Personality traits** . . . mellow, workaholic, loving, open-minded, shy, family- oriented, perverted . . . whatever!

- **Interests** . . . sports, theater, movies, books, hiking, beaches, pornography, rubber goods, whatever!

- **What you want** . . . and what you're looking for;  ath-letic, adventurous, educated, non-smoker, billionaire . . . marriage, fantasy, friendship, a quick screw (may be worth a try).

Remember, the keys to successful telephone dating are honesty and persistence. Keep trying!!

# Stories from Telephoneland

I have a friend who uses these phone personals on a regular basis. On almost any given week he has an ad running in some paper. He runs ads looking for everything from "just a friend" to "romance and relationship" to "submissive slave to satisfy me." And he has found women to meet every need.

He met a girl on the phone lines whom he chatted with several times. It turned out that her fantasy was to meet a guy in a parking lot, hop into his car and have wild sex in the backseat.

It sure sounded like he had a good time!! He also met a girl who desperately wanted to be a slave. So, she became his slave . . . not only did she satisfy him sexually, she also vacuumed and dusted his apartment – and she paid him for the pleasure!! She figured that a good slave should be financially subservient to her master, too!! Where do I find someone to pay me for the privilege of vacuuming my house???

# A Bedtime Story

I know another person (OK, it's me!) who met a girl over the phone who told me she had a fantasy of having a guy come over and read her nasty stories while she masturbated before she went to sleep. Which is what my friend did. I, oops, he went over to her apartment, read some of the letters out of Penthouse Forum while she played with herself.

After she came, she told him to lock up on his way out and then she drifted off to sleep. I guess she trusted him to leave without harassi. ̣ her. My friend saw her several times over the next few months and they eventually had sex before she drifted off to dreamland. She moved away soon after that and left him with a wonderful memory!!

# The Phone Lines

## L.A. Weekly

*Post Office Box 4315, Los Angeles, CA 90078-4315*
*(213) 465-4433 to answer an ad (900) 786-0033*

This weekly entertainment and information paper has plenty of ads to choose from. Women seeking men, men seeking women, men seeking men, women seeking women, either and more. You can find it all here, including fetishes like cross-dressers and dominants! The cost to listen to and answer ads is $1.49 per minute.

## L.A. Reader Call Dating

*5550 Wilshire Blvd. Suite 301, Los Angeles, CA 90036*
*to place a free ad (800) 275-5829*
*to listen to ads (900) 844-8880*

This weekly paper has all categories and advertisers. The cost of the call is $1.49 per minute. You can find The L.A. Reader all over the area . . . and it's free!

## Confidential Connection

*(310) 657-1515 or (818) 349-9477 or*
*(805) 257-9400 or (714) 539-5500*

Phone line where you can meet your choice of playmates . . . singles, couples, gay, bi, straight or whatever. Post and listen to ads free. The cost for listening to personal messages and sending personal messages is $1.98 per minute. Very popular line.

## Orange County Close Encounters

*(900) 844-2580; women free (714) 832-0322*

For dating, private phone secrets and "special requests." Cost is 98 cents per minute.

# Profile Systems

## Romantics line

*(900) 844-9797; women free (213) 625-4355 x. 123*

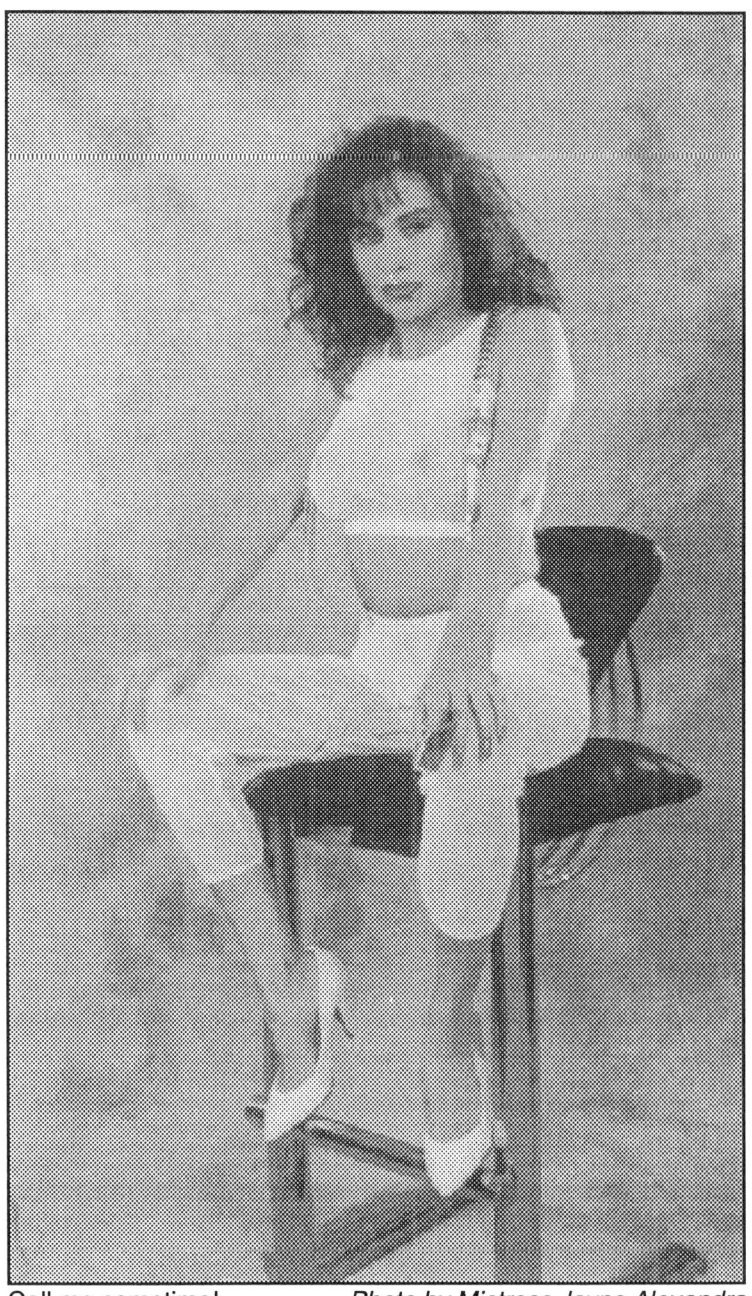

Call me sometime!                    *Photo by Mistress Jayne Alexandra*

## Nasty Adults

*(900) 844-9595; women free (213) 625-4355 x.123*

## Wild & Kinky

*(900) 844-9696; women free (213) 625-4355 x. 123*

These lines have men, women, singles, couples and adult services such as massage, escorts, models, strippers, swing clubs and more. Cost ranges from 98¢ to $1.98 per minute.

## The Nightline Service

*(900) 505-2275; to place ads (213) 613-4250*
*women call free (213) 613-4300*

The cost is $5 for 10 minutes. You will receive a membership number that is good for the next ten minutes of time.

## Elegant Connections

*(900) 844-8800; women free (213) 680-1753*

This line has ads from women, men, groups, bis, couples and more at 98¢ per minute ($2.98 for the first minute).

## *Hollywood Times*

*To place an ad (800) 278-1166*
*to answer ads (900) 562-1166*

A Hollywood area community paper that has ads for females, males and couples and swingers.

## *Whole Life Times*

*Post Office Box 1187, Malibu, CA 90265*
*(900) 680-3701*

Ads from singles who are into the new-age lifestyle. Calls cost $1.95 per minute.

## *Recycler*

*Post Office Box 27005, Los Angeles, CA 90027*
*(900) 844-1900 or (213) 668-1220 ext. 4331*

The *Recycler* publishes different editions in different areas. There are free ads, paid ads, or you can browse for $1.49 per minute. They also have a wide range of international ads in the paper.

## Telecompanions

*(213) 489-4646*

It's free to listen to ads. You need to become a member to do more. Call for more info.

## Telepersonals

*Men call (213) 782-4200; women call (213) 782-4300*

It's a free call with many men and women callers.

## Slaveline

*(900) 844-4404; women call free (213) 680-7728*

An adult dateline where slaves, mistresses and masters can meet. Cost is 98 cents per minute ($2.98 for the first minute).

## Voice Mail Bulletin Board

*(900) 844-TALK (8255); women free (213) 620-1852*

This line is a voice mail bulletin board for meeting adults who want free phone sex. It's not a professional phone sex line! The cost is 98 cents per minute ($2.98 for the first minute).

## Name Unknown (but who needs a name)

*(213) 976-6666; (213) 976-9999 or (213) 976-3333*

This line has swinging singles, couples, gay, bi and more. The cost for each of these lines is $2.00 per call plus any tolls. Don't get fooled . . . The calls are not of an unlimited duration; you only have a short time for each call.

## Los Angeles Love Connection

*(900) 844-2737; women call free at (213) 626-5117*

A very popular line that claims to have the best ratio of women to men callers. The only way to find out is to call!! It's 98 cents per minute.

## Large & Lovely Connection

*(900) 844-2525; women call free at (213) 626-2538*

A service exclusively for large and voluptuous women and the men who enjoy them. Cost is 98 cents per minute.

### B & D & S & M Hotline

*(900) 844-6239 (OBEY); women call free (213) 680-0329*

A connection line for those into fetish and fantasy. Cost is 98 cents per minute ($2.98 the first minute). .

# For Swingers Only

There are several publications that cater to swinging couples and singles in the greater Los Angeles area. If these are the type of personal ads you're looking for, you'll find them in the following papers. Look in the chapter SWINGING in this book for more detailed information.

*The Sun*

*Club Sun*

*Choice*

*Action*

*Kinky*

*Hollywood New Reality*

*West Coast Swingers*

*Swingers Hotline*

*Swing*

*Swingtime*

*Friends & Lovers*

*L.A. X-Press*

*Making Contact Magazine*

*Swingers News*

*Amateur Connection*

*Odyssey*

*UnReal People*

*Looking Glass*

*Adam Magazine*

# And More . . .

### Swingers' Club

*Post Office Box 2111, Orange, CA 92669-0111*

As a member you get a schedule of parties, dances, and other events. You also get a directory of other swingers. Membership is $75 or you can purchase the directory of swinging women and couples for $25.

# Gay, Lesbian or Bi

Most of the free gay periodicals have personal ads. Check out the following publications and look in the chapter THE GAY LIFE for more details.

*Frontiers*

*The Edge*

*Lesbian News*

*L.A. Girl Guide*

*Update*

# Other Dating Services . . .

There are other types of personals than phone lines and advertisements in periodicals. Following are a few of the other "personal" options in the area.

### P.I.C. (Pacific Island Connections)

*Box 461873, Los Angeles, CA 90046 — (213) 650-1994*

If you're interested in beautiful Oriental ladies, give this place a try. Penpals and more. Call for a free color brochure.

### Adult Exchange

*1626 N. Wilcox Ave. Suite 591, Hollywood, CA 90028-6273*

This is a meeting service mostly for swingers. For $10 you can get a current computer listing without photos of their members. For $20, they will send out information of each new and renewal member each month. Write for more details.

# Perfect Match Dating Service

*(805) 964-7055*

If you're a single living anywhere from the San Fernando Valley to Santa Barbara, this may be the dating service for you. Ventura and Santa Barbara County singles especially.

# Great Expectations

- *17207 Ventura Blvd., Encino — (818) 788-7878*
- *1640 S. Sepulveda, West Los Angeles — (310) 477-5566*
- *450 N. Mountain, Upland — (909) 985-2733*

This is one of the oldest and largest video introduction services in the country. This isn't a swingers' service, but if you're interested in meeting quality singles who are looking for romance and love . . . this may be for you.

# Russian Romance

*Post Office Box 610 Rancho Mirage, CA 92270*
*(619) 770-1848*

An agency that places together American men and Russian women. They also offer tours to Russia. Call for more details.

# Beverly Hills Matchmaker

*(310) 273-5557*

An upscale dating service for gentlemen with discriminating tastes.

# Orange County Social Club

*4533 MacArthur Blvd. #226-A, Newport Beach, CA 92660*
*(714) 997-8455*

A dating club that publishes a monthly newsletter containing lists of club members of the opposite sex. You can contact others directly or through the club. Membership rates are $125 for a year, $75 for 6 months and $40 for 3 months.

"The Gay Caballero"                    *Photo by Emilio Velasquez*

## FRONTERA GAY
From cover of Tijuana's Spanish Language Gay Newspaper

# CHAPTER TWELVE

# The Gay/Bi Life

... I'd rather be black than gay because when you're black
you don't have to tell your mother.
— *Charles Pierce*

... bisexuality immediately doubles your chances
for a date on Saturday night.
— *Woody Allen*

If you're gay in L.A., you can find lots of places to play. Bad poetry aside, Los Angeles has a large and diverse gay and lesbian community. The center of the community is the city of West Hollywood, with other concentrations in Hollywood, Laguna Beach, Long Beach and Palm Springs. There are numerous bars, events, publications, phone lines and businesses catering to gays and lesbians all over the area.

If you're out or still in the closet or curious or bisexual, or a friend to the community, you will find plenty of action and plenty of fun.

## Bars & Clubs

Want to meet "Mr. Right" or maybe just "Mr. Right Now?" Gay bars and clubs have always been a way of meeting guys or just socializing. The following will give you a selection to choose from. Not being one to "walk on the wild side" I had to get help from some of my gay friends to gather all this information.

# West Hollywood & Hollywood

## Asylum

*8531 Santa Monica Blvd. — (310) 917-8124*

Popular dance club with go-go boys for your voyeuristic pleasure.

## Axis

*652 N. LaPeer — (310) 659-0471*

This location used to be Studio One, a very popular club and it's still a happening dance place with a good young crowd.

## Capones

*8277-79 Santa Monica Blvd.*
*(213) 654-7224*

An upscale bar and restaurant and piano bar with a friendly crowd.

## Arena

*6655 Santa Monica Blvd., Hollywood*
*(213) 462-4221*

A 22,000 square-foot nightclub with various theme nights. Sometimes gay, sometimes not, sometimes mixed. A young crowd with lots of alternative types. Great dance club.

## Circus Disco

*6655 Santa Monica Blvd., Hollywood*
*(213) 462-1291*

Located right behind the Arena. A very popular disco that plays dance music, rock & roll and Latin. They also have drag shows and special events. Also has a young mixed gay/straight crowd. In addition, they have a pool table and outside patio. Call to see what's hot and when.

## Girl Bar

*(213) 460-2531*

Hot club for lesbians with special events and dances all over the city on various dates. Look for them at The Love Lounge Saturday nights. Call for upcoming events and clubs.

## Entre Nous

*2214 Stoner Ave., West Los Angeles*
*(310) 477-1485*

Fun dance club for lesbians.

## Love Lounge

*657 N. Robertson*
*(310) 659-0472*

Popular dance club featuring  go-go boys. It's a hot spot for lesbians on Saturdays.

## Mahogany's Unlimited Productions

*(310) 493-9063*

Sponsors special events and clubs for lesbians.

## The Palms

*8572 Santa Monica Blvd.*
*(310) 652-6188*

Very popular lesbian dance and social bar.

## Probe

*836 N. Highland*
*(213) 461-8301*

Popular after-hours club with dancing.

## Rage

*8911 Santa Monica Blvd.*
*(310) 652-7055*

Very popular club that draws a young, hip crowd out on the prowl.

## 7969

*7969 Santa Monica Blvd.*
*(213) 654-0280*

Popular dance bar with entertainment and more. Sometimes popular with the fetish crowd such as transvestites and S & M aficionados.

## Spike

*7746 Santa Monica Blvd.*
*(213) 656-9343*

Cruise bar for the Levi and leather crowd. Pool tables and video games.

## Trunks

*8809 Santa Monica Blvd.*
*(310) 652-1015*

Sports and video bar with pool tables.

# Other Los Angeles City Bars

## Catch One

*4067 Pico Blvd. — (213) 734-8849*

Dance club with large dance floor, ethnically diverse crowd and an after-hours club on weekends.

## The Connection

*4363 Sepulveda Blvd., Culver City*
*(310) 391-6817*

A lesbian bar that has dancing, pool tables and big-screen television for your entertainment pleasure.

© 1995 DR TUPPER

## Cuffs

*1941 Hyperion — (213) 660-2649*

A Levi and leather bar for cruisers located in the Silver Lake area.

## Faultline

*4216 Melrose — (213) 660-0889*

Popular leather bar where you'll see all your favorite leather duds and uniforms.

## Hyperion

*2810 Hyperion — (213) 660-1503*

Popular neighborhood bar located in Silver Lake with dancing and entertainment.

## J.J.'s Pub

*2692 S. La Cienega Blvd. — (310) 837-7443*

Friendly neighborhood bar with a mixture of all genders and sexual persuasions.

## The Redhead Bar

*2218 E. First St. — (213) 263-2995*

A lesbian bar that was once primarily popular with Latinas; it is now popular with a diverse ethnic crowd.

# San Fernando Valley

## Apache

*11608 Ventura Blvd., Studio City — (818) 506-0404*

Popular Valley dance club that is also an after-hours club on weekends.

## Club 22

*4882 Lankershim Blvd. — (818) 760-9792*

Lesbian bar with quiet lounge and small dance floor.

## Oil Can Harry's

*11502 Ventura Blvd., Studio City*
*(818) 760-9749*

If you like country & western music, here's your place. DJs play those shit-kicking tunes all night long.

## Queen Mary

*12449 Ventura Blvd., Studio City*
*(818) 506-5619*

Appropriately named bar where you can see strip shows and female impersonators.

## Rawhide

*10937 Burbank Blvd., North Hollywood*
*(818) 760-9798*

Western bar with lots of hot men in Levis. And if you find the right one, you can step out on their dance floor.

## Rumors

*10622 Magnolia, North Hollywood*
*(818) 506-9651*

Lesbian bar with dancing and a patio area.

# Long Beach Area

## The Broadway

*1100 E. Broadway — (310) 432-3646*

Piano bar with pool tables, darts and other games.

## Bulldogs

*5935 Cherry — (310) 423-8228*

A Levi and leather bar with pool table and patio.

## Executive Suite

*3428 E. Pacific Coast Hwy. — (310) 597-3884*

A very popular lesbian bar with a big dance floor, pool tables, and nude strippers on occasion.

## Mineshaft

*1720 E. Broadway — (310) 436-2433*

A Levi and cruising bar with DJ and pool table.

## Que Sera Sera

*1923 E. 7th Street — (310) 599-6170*

Popular lesbian bar with DJ, live music, pool table, etc..

## Ripples

*5101 E. Ocean Blvd.— (310) 433-0357*

A popular place with two levels, dancing, pool tables, a piano bar and more.

## Wolf's

*2020 Artesia Blvd. — (310) 422-1928*

Another leather and Levi bar where you can cruise for your favorite hunk.

# Other Greater Los Angeles Area Bars

## Club 3772

*3772 E. Foothill Blvd., Pasadena — (818) 578-9359*

A popular and friendly place with live music, DJ and more.

## Encounters

*203 N. Sierra Madre Blvd., Pasadena — (818) 792-3735*

A popular place with dancing, a patio, pool tables and much more.

## JR Brians

*2105 Artesia Blvd., Redondo Beach — (310) 371-7859*

Has dancing, entertainment, live shows, go-go boys, pool tables and more.

# Inland Empire

## Alibi East

225 S. San Antonio Ave , Pomona — (909) 623-9422

Mixed dance place with a good lively crowd.

## Grand Central

*345 W. 7th Street, San Bernardino — (909) 889-5204*

Dancing and more.

## Menagerie

*3581 University, Riverside — (909) 788-8000*

Dancing, pool tables and more in a friendly atmosphere.

## Robbie's

*390 College, Pomona — (909) 620-4371*

Popular dance club that caters to both lesbians and gays.

© 1995 DR TUPPER

# North Counties

## The Backdoor

*1285 W. Avenue I, Lancaster*
*(805) 945-2566*

The place to go in the Antelope Valley. Crowd is a mix of gay men and lesbians.

## Lipstix

*577 E. Main St., Ventura*
*(805) 652-1071*

Dance bar in downtown Ventura. The only place around.

# Orange County (central)

Yes, conservative Orange County does have gay bars. Of course, most of the closeted Republicans go to L.A. for their fun and games.

## Happy Hour

*12081 Garden Grove Blvd., Garden Grove*
*(714) 537-9079*

A very busy lesbian dancing and cruising bar.

## Huntress

*8122 Bolsa Ave., Midway City*
*(714) 892-0048*

A friendly lesbian bar with dancing and occasional live entertainment.

## Newport Station

*1945 Placentia, Costa Mesa*
*(714) 631-0031*

A very popular club with dancing, videos, dancers and more. Has ladies' night on Fridays.

### Ozz Supper Club

*6231 Manchester, Buena Park*
*(714) 522-1542*

A popular restaurant, cabaret and nightclub.

# Laguna Beach

Laguna is known as the home of the "Swish Alps" and is one of the few cities where gays have real political power.

### Boom-Boom Room

*1401 S. Coast Hwy.*
*(714) 494-7588*

Popular with the after-beach crowd. Work on your tan and then work on your love life. Dancing nightly.

### Little Shrimp

*1305 S. Coast Hwy.*
*(714) 494-4111*

A piano bar and restaurant with entertainment.

### Main Street

*1460 S. Coast Hwy*
*(714) 494-0056*

A popular piano bar with nightly entertainment.

# Palm Springs Area

### CC Construction

*68-449 Perez Road, Cathedral City*
*(619) 324-4241*

A hot dance bar in a hot area. Gays and lesbians are found here in abundance. Look for their country & western nights.

### Choices

*68-352 Perez Road, Cathedral City*
*(619) 321-1145*

Cabaret bar with dancing.

## Spurs

*36-737 Cathedral Canyon Road, Cathedral City*
*(619) 321-1233*

Country & western bar. Get out those spurs and chaps and mosey on down, partner!

## Wolf's

*67-625 Highway 111, Cathedral City*
*(619) 321-9688*

Check out the leather and Levi crowd and they'll check you out, too!

# Book & Video Stores

## Adult Stores . . .

Most adult book stores carry at least some gay material, but the following carry more than most.

## Andy's Adult World

*4624 Whittier Blvd., East Los Angeles*
*(213) 269-4123*

Adult store with huge selection of gay material and a 63 channel video arcade.

## Circus of Books

- *8230 Santa Monica Blvd. West Hollywood*
  *(213) 656-6533*

- *4001 Sunset Blvd., Silverlake*
  *(213) 666-1304*

Adult erotica stores with huge selections of gay videos and magazines, toys, lubricants and gay fiction.

## Videoactive Annex

*2522 Hyperion*
*l(213) 669-8544*

A great erotica store to buy your favorite items and cruise for your favorite guys.

## Diamond Adult World

*6406 Van Nuys Blvd. Van Nuys*
*(818) 997-3665*

Typical adult store with many gay related items and a 100 channel video arcade.

# General Interest Bookstores

Interested in more than just pornography? Want a little more plot than just boy meets boy, boy hops in bed with boy? Then try one of these shops.

## A Different Light

*8853 Santa Monica Blvd., West Hollywood*
*(310) 854-6601*

Great selection of gay and lesbian literature, cards, calendars, gifts and much more.

## Book Soup

*8818 Sunset Blvd., West Hollywood*
*(310) 659-3110*

Books of all types with lots of gay and lesbian items.

## Page One Books

*1196 E. Walnut, Pasadena*
*(818) 796-8418*

Books by and for women. Lots of feminist and lesbian literature.

## Sisterhood Bookstore

*1351 Westwood Blvd., Los Angeles*
*(310) 477-7300*

Books, music, videos, jewelry and more for women.

# Baths

The gay bathhouses have been a controversial issue since the AIDS crisis changed the way people think about sex. Conservative politicians made it a crusade to close them down, thinking they were one of the reasons for the AIDS epidemic. The bathhouses have cleaned up their act a bit and appear more concerned with preventing the spread of STDs and promoting the use of condoms and safe sex. Things are a bit quieter out there on the political and legal front right now, and a few more bathhouses have opened up in recent years.

Most of these places offer a membership and a daily rate. They usually have a sauna, jacuzzi, lockers and rooms. The

Most of these places offer a membership and a daily rate. They usually have a sauna, jacuzzi, lockers and rooms. The prices vary but they are all competitive. Call the individual places for their current rates and prices.

## Basic Plumbing

*1924 Hyperion Ave., Silverlake — (213) 953-6731*

## Flex Complex

*4424 Melrose Ave. — (213) 663-5858*

## Melrose Baths

*7269 Melrose Ave., Hollywood — (213) 937-2122*

## Midtowne Spa

*615 S. Kohler St. — (213) 680-1838*

## Roman Holiday Health Spas

*12814 Venice Blvd., Mar Vista — (310) 391-0200*

## Roman Holiday Health Spas

*14435 Victory Blvd., Van Nuys — (818) 780-1320*

## 1350 Club

*510 W. Anaheim, Wilmington — (310) 830-4784*

## Zone Club

*1230 E. 223rd Street #206 — (310) 518-HOMO*

## King of Hearts

*1800 Hyperion — (213) 661-9417*

# Phone Lines and Personals

There are several phone lines catering to the gay and lesbian community. Some of these phone lines are basically hot sex lines, offering talk with other callers and party lines. Other lines are voice messages from people looking for others, or personals. Some lines offer both services.

The cost for these lines varies from number to number. Find out all the costs and phone charges before you dial. At the beginning of each call, you should be informed of the cost for the call; however, there may be additional phone tolls. You can find these out by calling an operator and giving him or her the prefix and asking for the charge for that particular prefix.

These lines can be a good way to meet people with similar interests. I know several friends who have met sex partners, lovers, friends, and long-term companions through the phone lines. Of course, there is plenty of phoniness and bullshit on the lines too; some people just don't like telling the truth about themselves. Be skeptical but open, and you may find that Mister or Miss Right . . . or Mister or Miss Right-For-Now.

## The Confidential Connection

- *(310) 854-6666 — Los Angeles*
- *(818) 349-9477 — West San Fernando Valley*
- *(714) 539-7000 — Orange County*
- *(714) 537-1000 — Garden Grove*
- *(805) 257-9400 — Santa Clarita*
- *(619) 322-9200 — Palm Springs*
- *(619) 692-1200 — San Diego*

This is an excellent line on which to meet new friends and lovers. It's for gay, straight and bi . . . and everything else. You can listen to messages or leave your own phone personal. The cost is 98 cents per minute.

## The Gay Connection

*(900) 505-6339*

Cost is 98¢ per minute and you can meet others for fun.

## *Edge* **Male Call**

*(900) 844-3343*

Pick up a copy of *Edge*, one of the area's gay papers, and you'll see the personals. You can respond to these ads by calling this number. The cost is $1.45 per minute with the first minute costing $1.95. You can call their customer service number at (213) 962-7040.

## The Wolfline

*976-9653 (WOLF)*

You can call this line from the 213, 310, and 818 area codes. The cost is $2 per call. It's all gay and offers introductions and personals, leather and S & M and hot phone talk.

## Faces

*(900) 844-3223 (FACES)*

Meet gay men of all races 24 hours a day. Owned and operated by Concept St. James, their customer service number is (213) 871-0755.

## 976-CREW

*976-2739 (good in all L.A. County areas)*

Hot talk for hot men. It's $2 to call and get a code number and telephone number that is good for 24 hours of talk. Watch out for any extra phone charges.

## 976-MUSCLE

*976-6872 (good in all L.A. County areas)*

On this line you can find hot talk, voice personals, bulletin board and masseur ads. The cost is $2 per call. You can record a free message by calling (213) 613-1416.

## First Date

*(213) 656-3283 (DATE)*
*(900) 844-4844*

This line is owned by Frontiers, a popular gay periodical in the area, and has phone classifieds with lots of hot men to choose from. You can look for phone ads in the paper. Call (900) 844-4844 in the 213, 310, 818, and 714 area codes to listen and respond to ads. The cost is $1.50 for the first minute and 98 cents for each extra minute. Call (900) 370-4844 to listen and respond anywhere else in the nation. The cost for this is $2.50 for the first minute and 98 cents for each additional one. To place an ad call (213) 656-DATE.

## 976-HUNK

*976-4865 (good in all L.A. County areas)*

This is a one-on-one service, a party line and a message center. The cost is only $2 for 12 hours of fun.

## Integrity

*(900) 844-7587 (PLUS)*

Telephone introductions for HIV-positive persons. HIV-negative callers very welcome. Part of the proceeds is contributed to local AIDS charities.

## Studline

*(800) 574-7883 (STUD) or (900) 745-1631*

Lots of hot action to choose from on this line. Groups, fantasies, dates and more.

## The Call Guys

*(900) 505-5646 pass code 6969*

You can find one-on-one, date line and a model and masseur line. The cost is $1.50 per minute. Models and masseurs advertise free by calling (213) 931-4930.

## CHUMS

*(213) 461-5664 or (800) 231-2487*

This is not a phone personal line, but an introduction network for gays, lesbians and bisexuals looking for that certain someone. Call for more details.

# Gay Tourism

Gay tourism has really been taking off in the last few years. By now, most people know that gay men and women without children have a lot of money to spend on luxuries such as travel. There are many all gay tours from luxury ocean cruises to adventure tours such as white-water rafting. Some countries, such as Australia, even have special tourist bureaux to promote gay travel. There are gay travel magazines, such as *Our World*, and even an *International Gay and Lesbian Travel Association*.

There are too many gay/lesbian travel agencies to list them here, but you can find them in your local gay newspaper or directory.

Even my editor/publisher, who is gay as a goose, has gotten in the act and promotes an annual All Gay Copper Canyon and Guaymas Rail Cruise (see ad for more details). I guess I had better give him a plug. His travel company is —

## Happy People Tours*

*Post Office Box 620219, San Diego, CA 92163*
*(619) 236-0984. Email: warren@cyberheads.com*

In addition to the Copper Canyon rail tour, they give private tours of northern Baja border cities including gay bars, discos and an all day tour of the Baja wine country.

# Publications

There are a few excellent publications serving the Los Angeles area's gay and lesbian community. They contain a wealth of information about the gay lifestyle and gay news and views. You can find out about events, businesses, clubs, meeting places, personals and much more in these papers. In fact, if you pick up the papers you probably won't need this book. But please, buy it anyway . . . I need the money!!

## The Lesbian News

*P.O. Box 5128, Santa Monica, CA 90405*
*(310) 392-8224 or (800) 458-9888*

As the title suggests, this periodical covers news, views, clubs, events and much more in the local lesbian community. Very informative and entertaining. Published monthly and found all over the city in bookstores and other gay-friendly places.

---

\* The name, Happy People, was derived when a young Mexican lad with limited English came upon a group of flamboyant gay tourist in a small Mexican railroad town and said to them, "I know, I know — you happy people!"

# L.A. Girl Guide

*2531 Sawtelle Blvd. #175, Los Angeles, CA 90064*
*(310) 390-3979*

Monthly publication that covers the lesbian scene in the L.A. area.

## Female FYI

*8033 Sunset Blvd. Suite 2013, Los Angeles, CA 90046*
*(310) 657-5592*

Monthly publication for lesbians.

## Edge Magazine

*6434 Santa Monica Blvd., Hollywood, CA 90038*
*(213) 962-6994*

Bi-weekly publication that covers the gay men's scene in the area. Lots of personals, lots of club and event news, and much more.

## Frontiers

*Post Office Box 46367, 7985 Santa Monica Blvd.,*
*Suite 109, West Hollywood, CA 90046*
*(213) 848-2222*

Bi-weekly publication in which you will find lots of information, articles, plus a hot "yellow pages" section of personals and ads.

## Planet Homo

*8380 Santa Monica Blvd., #200, W. Hollywood, CA 90069*
*(213) 848-2220*

Published bi-weekly; it's a small paper with personals and information on events, clubs, restaurants and more.

## Think Pink Publications

*2101 S. Standard, Suite C, Santa Ana, CA 92707*
*(800) 844-6574*

They publish a "pink pages" guide to gay-friendly businesses and organizations in the Southern California area. You can pick it up in many gay and lesbian businesses or call them to get your copy.

# Update

*Dawn Media Publications, 2801 Fourth Ave.,*
*San Diego, CA 92103*
*(619) 299-0500; Email: GayEditor@AOL.com*

A weekly publication from San Diego that extensively covers the greater San Diego area, with some good coverage of the L.A. area.

# Gay & Lesbian Times

*P.O. Box 34624, San Diego, CA 92163*
*(619) 299-6397; Email: GayLT@AOL.com*

Another San Diego publication with some coverage of the L.A. area.

# Frontera Gay

*Post Office Box 620219, San Diego, CA 92162*
*(619) 231-8557 or from the U.S. to Tijuana (011-5266)*
*88-02-67; warren@cyberheads.com*

A monthly Spanish language gay newspaper edited by Max Mejía and published by *F.I.G.H.T.* (a Mexican gay civil rights group) in Tijuana. Represented in the U.S. by Warren Communications. Also has personal ads. Send $1 for sample copy.

# Naked Magazine

*7985 Santa Monica Blvd. #109-232,*
*West Hollywood, CA 90046*

Has information on gay male nude club news, male nudity in the media, group events and anything to do with male nudity. Write for subscription information.

# Celebrities

*Chuck Thompson, Post Office Box 691024,*
*Hollywood, CA 90024*

Ever wonder if your favorite Hollywood stud has been clipped or not? Ever wonder about Ronnie or Clinton? Well, you don't have to ask Jennifer Flowers as Chuck's hobby is to find out and he has been checking for years. He has a list of over 2,000 celibrities. (Now that I'm a famous author, I wonder if I'm listed.)

# Community Support

## Gay & Lesbian Community Centers

- *Los Angeles . . . (213) 993-7600*
- *Long Beach . . . (310) 434-4455*
- *Orange County . . . (714) 534-0961*
- *South Bay . . . (310) 379-2850*
- *Inland Empire . . . (909) 884-5447*
- *Camarillo . . . 805-389-1530*
- *San Diego . . . (619) 692-4297*

At these centers you can find information about all types of activities, resources, groups and support organizations in the gay and lesbian community.

### National AIDS Hotline

*(800) 922-2437 (AIDS);*
*Espanol (800) 222-7432 (SIDA)*

### Los Angeles AIDS Hotline

*(213) 876-2437 (AIDS)*

© 1995 DR TUPPER

### Stop AIDS L.A.
*(213) 659-4778*

### AIDS Walk (Orange County)
*(714) 786-2601*

### Orange County Cultural Pride
*(714) 534-0961*

### Christopher Street West
*(213) 656-6553*

### Long Beach Lesbian & Gay Pride
*(310) 987-9191 or (310) 987-6742*

### Men's Activities Hotline
*(213) 993-7445*

### ACLU- Lesbian & Gay Rights Chapter
*(213) 977-9500 ext. 237*

### Bi-Sexual Support Services
*(310) 434-4455 (Long Beach)*

### AIDS Health Care Foundation
*(213) 463-2273*

If you are HIV-positive, you may qualify for free AIDS drugs at several area clinics. For more support and resource groups and organizations call one of the above for information or look in the *Pink Pages*.

# Gay Computer BBS's

In addition to the numbers listed below, most of the large national servers, such as *America OnLine, Prodigy, CompuServe*, etc. have a large gay section where you can "chat" or read gay notices and news items. You can also get email (messages sent from one computer to another) through them. Most of them cost around $10 a month for five hours on-line with a nominal charge for additional time.

By the time this book comes out, all of the national boards will offer InterNet connections. With InterNet connections, you have the world at your fingertips (see *COMPUTER SEX*). By-the-way, if you have any information you would like to contribute to the next revision of *Lust Angeles*, send it via email to: warren@cyberheads.com.

Lecher McRich, our cartoon curmungeon mascot, has his own homepage where you can purchase books (including this one), leave messages and cruise the personal ads. His address is: http://www.electriciti.com/~warren/index.htm.

## Modem Boy

*(310) 659-7000*

## Alternate Lifestyles

*(818) 457-6325*

## GLAAD/LA

*(213) 463-9257*

## Joystick BBS

*(818) 952-1311*

## Butch's BBS

*(213) 560-6548*

## Power House BBS

*(310) 763-5201*

## Taboo Topics

*(714) 240-8480*

# Other Resources

## Best Buddies

*Box 461135,*
*West Hollywood, CA 90046*

Local masturbation club for men. They have bi-monthly parties and their members also love phone sex. Sounds like a city version of the "circle jerks" we ex-farm boys had. Write for more details. Tell them that Jocelyn Elders sent you.

## Personal Photography

*(213) 469-4993*

This photographer offers a photo session that is discreet and private. Photos are processed while you wait. The cost for 30 shots, proofsheet, negatives and one 8" x 10" is $30. Sounds like a great deal to me!

## Tom of Finland Co.

*Post Office Box 26716,*
*Los Angeles, CA 90026*
*(213) 250-4736*

They sell prints, videos and more, featuring the work of the well known gay artist, Tom of Finland.

## Nude Maids

*(310) 391-0169*

Have a sexy nude male clean your place. What next!! A nude plumber . . . a nude car mechanic??? I don't care what they wear, just as long as they do the job.

## BFI Publications

*Post Office Box 3884,*
*Orange, CA 92665-0884*
*(714) 974-0995*

They put out a newsletter and host parties. Into butt fun and fantasies?? This may be the group for you.

# Gay Desert Resorts

There are many hotels, inns, resorts, restaurants, bars, etc., in the Palm Springs area that are a great getaway for a week or a weekend. We we have included a few, however, we don't have space to list them all. For more detailed information, pick up a copy of a gay guide book from one of the adult book stores listed in this book, a gay newspaper or the Pink Directory.

## Harlow Club Hotel

*175 E. El Alameda, Palm Springs*
*(619) 323-3977*

## Triangle Inn

*555 San Lorenzo Road*
*(619) 322-7993*

## Canyon Boys Club

*960 N. Palm Canyon, Palm Springs*
*(619) 322-4024*

## The Villa

*67-670 Carey Road, Cathedral City*
*(619) 328-7211*

## 550 Resort

*550 Warm Sands Drive, Palm Springs*
*(619) 320-7144*

## The Columns Resort

*537 Grenfall Road, Palm Springs*
*(800) 798-0655*

## Inntrique

*526 Warm Sands Drive, Palm Springs*
*(619) 323-7505*

## Avanti

*715 San Lorenzo Road, Palm Springs*
*(619) 325-9723*

## Camp Palm Springs

*722 San Lorenzo Road, Palm Springs*
*(800) 793-0063*

## El Mirasol Villas

*525 Warm Sands Drive, Palm Springs*
*(619) 327-5913*

## Circle P Ranch

*(909) 360-5584*

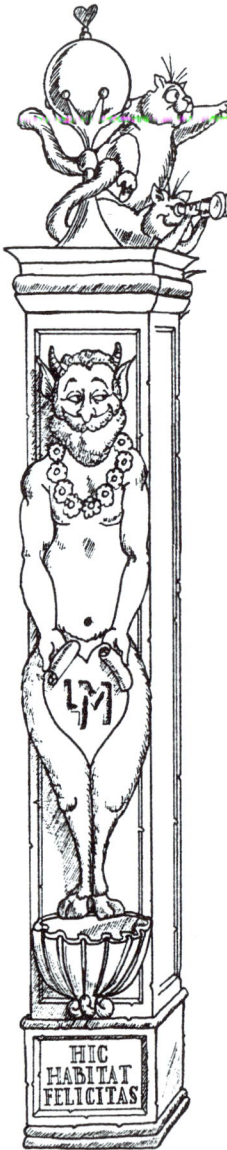

A place for TVs, crossdressers and others interested in that aspect of sexuality. They have parties, makeovers, private boutique and much more.

# Gay Mail Order Videos

The important thing to remember when writing to a gay porn video company is to always include a signed statement attesting to your age. No company will send you information without a signed age statement in their files.

## Adam & Company

*10640 Burbank Blvd., N. Hollywood, CA 91501*
*(818) 752-9769*

Send $5 for a catalog (refundable).

## Avalon Video International

*Post Office Box 91257, Los Angeles, CA 90009*
*(800) 222-9622*

In addition to their own lines, they are the exclusive distributor for Jean Daniel Cadinot Videos.

## BG Enterprises

*Post Office Box 5291*
*Huntington Beach, CA 92615-5291*
*(714) 964-0871*

They have a line of erotic wrestling, male stripping and solo masturbation tapes. Catalog: $5.

## Caballero Direct

*7920 Alabama Ave., Canoga Park, CA 91304*
*(800) 451-9666 or (818) 992-0288*

They produce a number of lines of videos. For their complete catalog, send $5.

## Catalina Video Direct

*7985 Santa Monica Blvd., #109-R,*
*West Hollywood, CA 90046*
*(818) 708-9200*

For their catalog, send $15 to the attention of Rusty James.

## Champions Video of America

*8721 Santa Monica Blvd., #37, West Hollywood, CA 90069*
*(800) 726-1610 or (310) 854-3540*

They are the distribution arm of Planet Video Group. They have a large line of male videos.

## Cinderella/CDI Video

*8021 Remmett Ave., Canoga Park, CA 91304*
*(818) 884-6681.*

Five bucks for their catalog.

## Colt Studios

*Post Office Box 1608-AG, Studio City, CA 91614*
*(818)985-5786*

They will not ship to certain states. If you are in the U.S. their catalog is $10.00, otherwise send $17.50.

## Frat House Boys

*7985 Santa Monica Blvd. #109-300, Los Angeles, CA 90046*
*(800) 423-0496*

## HIS Video

*9650 DeSoto Ave., Chatsworth, CA 91311-5012*
*(818) 718-0404*

A division of VCA Pictures with many lines. Send for catalog.

## Insider Video Club

*Post Office Box 93399, Hollywood, CA 90093*
*(800) 634-2242*

They carry feature length, youth-oriented, motion pictures from around the world

## International Wavelength

*2215-R Market Street #829, San Francisco, CA 94114*
*(415) 864-6500*

If you like brown sugar, this is the company for you. They cary a line of Asian, Latin, and other foreign country, youth-oriented features. Their catalog is $5.00.

## Leisure Time Entertainment

*20725 Praire Street, Chatsworth, CA 91311*
*(818) 407-5050*

Formerly Video Exclusives.

## Mack Releasing

*6709 La Tijera Blvd., Suite 242, Los Angeles, CA 90045*
*(800) 497-2967*

## Sierra Pacific Productions

*Post Office Box 12109, Marina del Rey, CA 90295*
*(800) 828-4336*

## Stryker Productions

*7985 Santa Monica Blvd., Suite 109,*
*West Hollywood, CA 90046*
*(800) 542-2131 or (213) 655-3531*

This company has only one product and that is Jeff Stryker himself. It's not only the movie stars that have their own production companies.

## U.S. Male

*15904 Strathern Street #14, Van Nuys, CA 91406(800)*
*748-6155 or (818) 902-9697*

They carry all the lines and their catalog is free — one-stop shopping.

## Varsity Productions

*100 S. Sunrise Way #100, Palm Springs, CA 92262-67737*
*(800) 748-5625 or (619) 325-3457*

Send $5.00 for their catalog of many lines.

## Vivid Video

*15127 Califa Street, Van Nuys, CA 91411-3033*
*(800) 423-4227 for mail orders or (818) 908-0481*

Send for their free catalog.

192 pages of information on Mexican Gays & Lesbians in an easy to read form with alphabetized cities. Includes 32 pictures of interest and city maps for ease of travel. Includes a Bonus chapter on Gay travel in Cuba.  Only $16.95 plus tax and shipping.

**See Appendix B on page 323 for details**

### Zeus Collection
*Post Office Box 64250, Los Angeles CA 90064-0250*
*FAX: (310) 474-9645*

Their catalog is free but they don't ship to 14 states. Must be some hot stuff!!

### Zone Films/Zone Video Club
*Post Office Box 461300, Los Angeles, CA 90048-9300*
*(213) 878-0800 or (800) 934-1254*

Their catalog is $5.00.

# Gender Bender Goodies

### JMPG
*Post Office Box 7217 Burbank, 91510-7217*

Publishes the *Crossdresser's Quarterly* and the *Crossdresser's International Shopping Guide.*

### Waxing by Mistress Gloria
*14021 Ventura Blvd., Sherman Oaks*
*(818) 907-1196*

Tired of looking like a truck driver in drag?? TVs & TSs – get your unwanted hair removed.

## Gay/Lesbian/Bi/ Gender Bender Social Clubs

The gay, etc., community has has an organization for about anything you can think about — from Dikes on Bikes to Transvestite stamp collectors (I made that one up). Joining a club is a great way to meet and network with other people with the same interests — sex!! To find the group that fits your lifestyle, scan the gay rags, guide books, directories, community centers, gay churches, etc.

"Wana party?"  *Photo by Jack Messick Photography*

# CHAPTER FOURTEEN

# Nightlife

> . . . wasted away again in Margaritaville.
> — *Jimmy Buffett*

> . . . I may be drunk, but you're ugly
> and tomorrow I'll be sober.
> — *Winston Churchill*

**L**os Angeles has a cornucopia of nightlife to choose from. From down-home pubs to dive bars to fancy discos to world famous original music venues, Los Angeles has it all. If you can't find some action in the City of Angels, you might as well stop looking and check yourself into a rest home! From mild to wild, from straight to gay, from the worldly to the weird, from jeans and tee-shirts to leather and chains, from middle-class suburban to upscale urban to fetish kink . . . L.A. rocks and jams and raps and pulsates and dances and glitters and rolls.

Much of the scene caters to the young, but the young at heart can fit right in. And the women!! Oh, the women!!! Again . . . oh, the women!!! There are women all over the place. Short women, tall women, skinny women, fat women, slender women, voluptuous women . . . you want women, L.A. has them. Of course, ladies, there are plenty of men out there in Lust Angeles, too!! In fact, there are usually more men than women in most nightclubs.

This section will tell you about a few of the bars and clubs in town. Be warned that bars start up and go out of business all the time; some of those listed here may be closed or renamed by the time you get this book. Some may have changed their format or the type of music they feature. Call before you go so you know! Or look in publications such as *The L.A. Weekly* or *The L.A. Reader* for more information and nightclub listings.

Also, some of the clubs listed are roving dance clubs that happen at specific nightclubs. A particular club may have a different theme every night of the week. Call to find out what's happening on a particular night.

Ok . . . here's the bars and the clubs and the moving dance clubs. The lisT is very brief and only intended to get you going in the right direction. Cover charges vary widely in the clubs and they can change from month to month and week to week. Different admission charges apply on different nights of the week. The average charge at a happening dance club seems to be about $10-$15 on weekends and $5 - $10 on week nights.

However, many clubs are free or only a few dollars on week nights and many also let you in free before a certain time. This chapter would be two hundred pages if I mentioned all the cover charges . . . I'll leave it up to you to find up how much a night of fun will cost you! For more specific and detailed information, call the clubs directly.

# Remember!!!

Responsible drinking is the key to fun. Alcohol messes with your love life, your sex life, your life, if you don't drink in moderation. And never, never drink and drive. Never!! Call a cab, call a friend, call your mom, call my mom, take a bus, beg a lonesome lady (or man) for a ride, just don't get behind the wheel after drinking!

# The Bars and Clubs

## Los Angeles Area

### Abyss

*2735 Beverly Blvd.*
*(213) 388-8166*

Happening after-hours club that rocks every night.

### Al's Bar

*305 S. Hewitt St.*
*(213) 625-9703*

Live original music . . . sometimes good . . . sometimes, well . . . bad! But, always interesting!

### Anti-club

*4658 Melrose*
*(213) 661-3913*

A long-established club that features up and coming alternative bands. Full bar, but minors allowed.

### Arena

*6655 Santa Monica Blvd., Hollywood*
*(213) 462-4221*

A 22,000 square-foot nightclub with various theme nights. Sometimes gay, sometimes not, sometimes mixed. Great dance club.

### Circus Disco

*6655 Santa Monica Blvd., Hollywood*
*(213) 462-1291*

Located right behind the Arena. A very popular disco that plays dance music, rock & roll and Latin. They also have drag shows and special events. Also has a mixed gay/straight crowd. In addition, they have a pool table and outside patio. Call to see what's hot and when.

## Bourbon Square

*15322 Victory Blvd., Van Nuys*
*(818) 997-8562*

Live music every night in the Valley. Maybe you'll meet some "Valley girls"!!

## Brent Bolthouse Productions

*Info line: (213) 848-9300*

A moving dance party that always draws a crowd. Call their info line for upcoming events.

## Checca

*7323 Santa Monica Blvd.*
*(213) 850-7471*

It's a French-Italian restaurant and a happening disco. Gay, lesbian and mixed.

## Club Exposure

*Info line: (310) 858-3976*

An erotic and fetish nightclub for couples and singles. Come dressed in your sexiest and most risque attire. In fact, you must wear risque or fetish or formal attire, or they won't let you in!! Wild crowd, wild music, wild erotic entertainment. At the time of publication, they are without a location – but they are looking for a new one and will have one soon.

## Club Lingerie

*6507 Sunset Blvd., Hollywood*
*(213) 466-8557*

No, this isn't one of those lingerie strip places . . . it's a happening Sunset Strip live music venue with local and national bands.

## Coconut Teaszer

*8117 Sunset Blvd., West Hollywood*
*(213) 654-4773*

Lots of live hard rock and alternative music here.

# Dragonfly

*6506 Santa Monica Blvd., Hollywood*
*(213) 466-6111*

A large club with three different rooms. Several different dance parties make this place happen most nights of the week.

# Foothill Club

*1922 Cherry Ave., Signal Hill*
*(310) 984-8349*

A large club that features rock and country music Thursdays, Fridays and Saturdays.

# Glam Slam

*333 S. Boylston, Downtown*
*(213) 482-6626*

A club owned by funk rocker Prince (or whatever he is called now). It has concerts, special events and dancing and a sensuous dance cabaret.

# Hell's Gate

*6423 Yucca St.*
*(213) 463-9661*

Yes, you may think you have passed through "Hell's gate" when you enter this club . . . it's a little weird and a little wild, but it's fun.

# House of Blues

*8430 Sunset Blvd., West Hollywood*
*(213) 650-0247*

Doesn't look like much on the outside, but inside it rocks. Blues, rock and more.

# Jack's Sugar Shack

*8751 W. Pico Blvd*
*(310) 271-7887*

Pool tables, outdoor patio, food and live music . . . what more could you ask for???

The Whisky in L.A.                    *Photo by F.M. Philips*

## L.A. Tower

*11434 W. Pico, West L.A.*
*(310) 473-9921*

A Los Angeles landmark, this place hosts a variety of different clubs and caters to many musical tastes.

## Malibu Inn

*22969 Pacific Coast Highway, Malibu*
*(310) 456-6060*

About the only club located in Malibu, it's a good restaurant and has live music.

## Mancini's Club

*20923 Roscoe Blvd., Canoga Park*
*(818) 341-8503*

Lots of live, original music.

## Pelican's Retreat

*24454 Calabasas Rd., Calabasas*
*(818) 222-1155*

Located way out there, but it's got live music seven nights a week, outdoor dining and dancing.

## Mayan

*1038 S. Hill St., Downtown*
*(213) 746-4287*

This former movie palace has a huge dance floor and hops on weekends. The F.O.X.E. adult movie awards are held here, and it used to host special swingers dances monthly, but alas, they are no more.

## Moose McGillycuddy's

*13535 Mindanao Way, Marina Del Rey*
*(310) 574-3932*

Dancing, drinking and eating. Young crowd on the prowl in the Marina.

## The Palace

*1735 Vine St., Hollywood*
*(213) 462-3000*

A historical landmark, this place has two dance floors and many promotional specials.

# Renaissance

*1212 Third Street Promenade, Santa Monica*
*(310) 587-0766*

A very large club with restaurant, dance club, bar and live performance space. Happening spot for the Santa Monica crowd.

# Roxbury

*8225 Sunset Blvd., West Hollywood*
*(213) 656-1750*

An upscale club on the Sunset Strip, it has three levels of fun, several bars and plenty of attractive women.

# The Roxy

*9009 Sunset Blvd., West Hollywood*
*(310) 276-2222*

Live music venue that hosts a variety of national rock and jazz acts.

# Sin-a-matic At 7969

*7969 Santa Monica Blvd., West Hollywood*
*(213) 654-0280*

On Saturdays, Club Fetish and Fuck! presents Sin-a-matic at 7969. Industrial drone, interesting people, mixed crowd. Every Saturday is Halloween at the *Sin-a-matic.*

# Toe's Tavern

*732 N. Catalina Ave, Redondo Beach*
*310) 374-4628*

*37 N. Catalina, Pasadena*
*818) 577-6675*

These could be called typical "Southern California beach bars" How they managed to have the same street name in both locations is a miracle to me. They have darts, pool, ping-pong, live music and more.

## Sinners Repent
*3772 E. Foothill Blvd., Pasadena*
*Info line: (818) 403-1169*

Dance to rap, industrial and alternative music.

## Troubadour
*9081 Santa Monica Blvd., West Hollywood*
*(310) 276-6168*

It's been around for well over 30 years and it has featured some top names in music. Food, drink and live music by some big and little names.

## The Viper Room
*8852 Sunset Blvd. West Hollywood*
*(310) 358-1880*

This popular club is owned by actor Johnny Depp (of *Edward Scissorhands* fame). Live music with some national artists. A lot of celebrities and "want-a-bees" hang out here (This is also where the actor River Phoenix died of a mixture of alcohol and drugs}.

## Whisky a Go Go
*8901 Sunset Blvd.,*
*West Hollywood*
*(310) 652-4205*

The most well-known club on the Sunset Strip, it's not quite as popular as it was in the sixties when groups like The Doors took the stage and warmed up for future fame. Mostly heavy metal and hard rock.

© 1995 DR TUPPER

# And Still More Popular Spots . . .

The following clubs and bars are favorite meeting places, hangouts or good places to hear live music. Call for information about cover charges, type of music, etc.

### Carlos O'Brien's

*3667 De Anza, Riverside*
*(714) 686-5860*

### Chillers

*239 N. Harbor Dr.,*
*Redondo Beach*
*(310) 798-3170*

### Club Paradise

*995 E. Los Angeles Ave.,*
*Simi Valley*
*(805) 583-2582*

### Fashions Niteclub

*1005 Fisherman's Wharf,*
*Redondo Beach*
*(310) 376-6455*

### FM Station

*11700 Victory Blvd., North*
*Hollywood*
*(818) 769-2220*

### Hennessey's Tavern

*8 Pier Ave., Hermosa Beach*
*(310) 546-4813*

### Ice House

*112 E. Walnut, Fullerton*
*(714) 525-3648*

### Indigo Jazz Club

*111 E. Artesia Blvd.,*
*Compton*
*(310) 632-1234 ext. 251*

### Lighthouse Cafe

*30 Pier Ave., Hermosa*
*Beach*
*(310) 372-6911*

### The Palomino

*6907 Lankershim Blvd.,*
*North Hollywood*
*(818) 764-4010*

### Picasso's

*1276 Seventh St., Upland*
*(909) 982-8712*

### Pier 52

*52 Pier Ave., Hermosa*
*Beach*
*(310) 376-1629*

### Rude Dog

*1114 N. Citrus Ave., Covina*
*(818) 332-8922*

### The Strand

*1700 S. Pacific Coast*
*Hwy., Redondo Beach*
*(310) 316-1700*

# Orange County

## Harry and David's Goat Hill Tavern

*Where Harbor Blvd. meets Newport Blvd. in Costa Mesa*
*(714) 548-8428*

This popular Orange County bar is owned by an old curmudgeon by the name of Zeb O'Brean, personal friend of the publisher of this book. It's a beach-type of bar (but not near the beach) with lots of games and odd collectables hanging everywhere. They were in the *Guinness Book of Records* for having the most brands of beer on tap.

Zeb is quoted as once grousing, "I designed this bar for myself, but if someone else wants to come in and have a good time, that's alright too." The "Harry" comes from Harry Truman, "David" comes from Eisenhower and "Goat Hill" comes from the former name of the city of Costa Mesa. This plug ought to at least be worth a free beer.

© 1993 DR TUPPER

## Club 369

*1641 N. Placentia, Fullerton*
*(714) 572-1816*

Some great original-music bands get loud and nasty here. Pool tables, dancing and more.

## The Coach House

*33157 Camino Capistrano, San Juan Capistrano*
*(714) 496-8927*

The place in southern Orange County to see local and national acts. Lots of big names here. Great place for some great music and to see some great girls.

## The White House

*340 S. Coast Hwy., Laguna Beach*
*(714) 494-8088*

Laguna Beach tradition. Draws a mixed crowd from the mixed residents of Laguna.

# Meeting In The Meat Market

What's it take to score with the women (or men) in the clubs? That age-old question has been debated by lounge lizard philosophers for decades. A million dollars in your pocket, a penis the size of the Washington Monument (or breasts the size of the Grand Tetons), a Rolls Royce key dangling from your pocket or a quick wit and a pick up line as smooth as honey-colored tequila. Don't look to me for advice. Though I had my share of successes . . . I would have to say, in all honesty, that my winning percentage would make the Clippers look good!

The bars aren't quite the Bacchanalian meeting places they once were . . . but people still meet, and people still have sex, and lust and love are still found in the nightclubs. People are more cautious now (especially the women – men can still be dogs!!). One night stands, though not entirely eliminated as a pastime, are mostly a thing of the past, and there are many other alternatives where people can meet . . . coffee shops and phone personal ads to name just two.

But the bars and clubs can still be fun. Even though many social philosophers and experts have said that the bar scene is dead in the age of AIDS, I find that to be far from the truth. The night spots are crowded and happening. They are places to see and be seen. They are places to hear music, laugh with friends and meet someone special. People still like to party! And L.A.'s scene is one of the best around. Enjoy it . . . but be responsible!!

# More Nightlife

There is so much to do in the Los Angeles area . . . socially and culterally. There are movie houses, theaters, comedy clubs and coffeehouses. People meet and date at all of these. Good sources to find out what's happening or other places to go are *The L.A. Weekly* and The *L.A. Reader.* Nightlife in L.A. is a kaliedoscopic of events and clubs and music; there should be something for everyone!!

© 1995 DR TUPPER

Deep Creek Hot Sprints          *Photo by Roger Warren*

# "Let's all go skinny dipping!"

# CHAPTER FIFTEEN

# Nude Beaches & Resorts

. . . what a man enjoys about a women's clothes are his
fantasies of how she would look without them.
— *Brendan Francis*

Clothes make the man . . . naked people
have little or no influence on society.
— *Mark Twain*

**W**elcome to the world of nudism and naturism. This is
where you let it all hang out. Expose yourself and be free.
That is, expose yourself in designated spots where it is
accepted, not in the grocery store or walking down the street!

Nude sunbathing and recreation are much more acceptable than they were not too many years ago. There are
hundreds of locations all the through the great state of
California where you can strip to your birthday suit and
enjoy the fun and sun.

There are also nude beaches and resorts all over the world.
From the exotic beaches of the Greek Islands where you can
strip and dip and drink ouzo to the palm-fringed beaches of
the Caribbean where you sit back on a beach chair and take
in the serenity of the turquoise sea and the sensuality of the
naked bodies. There is even a nude city on the Riviera in the

south of France. Yep, a fully-functional nude city where you can buy groceries, do your banking and shop for the kids . . . all in the buff! This true "naked city" is Cap d'Agde and is a definite visit if you are in that part of the world.

Of course, we Americans haven't totally shed our inhibitions and Puritanical roots; there are forces working against those who want to be free and naked. Law enforcement officials sometimes crack down on established nude areas and those of us who practice nudity or nudism are usually seen as living on the fringes of society or involved in something that is not socially acceptable. Oh well, there are enough nudists around to support a thriving industry in nude sun clubs, nude resorts, nude bed-&-breakfasts and nude hotels. And all these people, your neighbors and friends and family, don't care what the cops or the conservatives think . . . they like to be naked!!

The managers of Domino's Pizza Home Delivery reports that the percentage of people ordering pizza who come to the door nude increased by 23% in 1994. Were these people nude and decided not to dress . . . or did they purposely undress to greet the delivery person??

Unfortunately, Los Angeles, home of Hollyweird, sin city to the stars, is not the nude beach paradise that it should be. With all the beautiful beaches lining the Los Angeles area coastline, nude beach areas should be a dime a dozen . . .

---

# IMPORTANT NOTICE

A sweeping anti-nudity bill was introduced to the California Legislature by assemblyman Jim (Anally Retentive) Morrissey. If passed, it would make any form of public nudity illegal. It would make it illegal to strip at any of the many California nude beaches and may even make it illegal to get nude at nudist resorts.

The bill, AB1200 has so far stalled in an Assembly Committee, but it's still a potential threat to our freedom. Write to your political representatives about it!

but they're not. Law enforcement officials have cracked down on those who dare to bathe in the buff. Nonetheless, a few areas have established themselves as clothing-optional. I have also listed a few nude beaches in the Santa Barbara area that are beautiful and hassle-free.

There are also several nude resorts and hotels in the Los Angeles and Palm Springs areas that offer the uninhibited a nice, naked weekend getaway. They are not exactly Motel 6!!

# Etiquette

Yes, there is nude beach etiquette. No, it's not in Miss Manners' book. Most etiquette is just basic common sense and respect for others, but since some people lack those qualities or may be from another planet, here are some basics about nude beach and resort behavior.

- **First of all** . . . you go to a nude beach or resort to be nude, not to have sex! Some people who are nudists are swingers, but many are not. Nude beaches are no different than regular beaches . . . except people can take off their clothes if they want to. If the beautiful woman on the towel next to yours is naked, that is not an invitation!

- **Second**, overt sexual behavior is a no-no. I have certainly seen my share of subtle and overt sexual play at a variety of nude beaches . . . but this behavior is frowned upon and could only lead to complaints against the area and possible closure of the site as clothes optional.

- **Third,** excessive looking or staring (gawking!!!) is rude behavior. Look but don't drool! Enjoy the sight of that beautiful naked body but don't burn holes through it with your beady little eyes! No excessive heavy breathing, either!

- **Fourth,** do not litter. Take away from the beach what you brought to it. Or put it in any trash cans you can find.

- **Fifth,** don't take glass bottles to the beach. A nasty cut on your foot can ruin a pleasant day at the beach.

- **Sixth,** don't stray from the designated or established nude areas. Doing this will only cause complaints and lead to law enforcement action against the area. Respect the right of those who don't want to see your naked flesh!

- **And lastly** . . . do not be a dick! And don't always think with that part of your anatomy. Treat people nicely and they will usually treat you the same. If you see a gorgeous naked woman whom you'd love to meet, go over and talk with her – don't gawk at her or sit in a position to look up her crotch. And if she says no . . . she means **NO!**

# The Problem of Gawkers

As mentioned above, it is impolite and downright disgusting to gawk. However, many men still feel the need to do this. It ruins the nude beach experience for many women who would otherwise enjoy sunbathing and playing frisbee in their birthday suits. Most clothing-optional beaches have at least a few gawkers. Some beaches are better than others. Don't let the terminally stupid ruin your nude beach fun. Unfortunately they exist, like rats and snakes and mildew; you should just try and stay clear of them and discourage them whenever they bother you. If you are a single woman or a couple, sit near other couples and use them as a barrier against unwanted invasions by the gawkers. Or, just point and laugh and remark how small their weenies are . . . that is sure to send them running away!

© 1995 DR TUPPER

# Nude Beaches

Here we go boys and girls. Pack your sunscreens, your shades, your frisbee, and forget that bathing suit. Following is a listing of the nude beaches in the greater Los Angeles area, including a few from the Santa Barbara and San Diego areas. Have fun and get naked!!

## Smuggler's Cove

This is an exceptionally beautiful beach located on the exceptionally beautiful Palos Verdes peninsula. It is a very easy climb down to a pretty cove. It is called "Sacred Beach" by those in the know and was once relatively hassle-free. However, the City of Palos Verdes recently outlawed nudity here. I'm not sure what the future will hold. Nude sunbathers should rebel and demand their beach back!!

The beach is located just off Palos Verdes Drive South between Portuguese Point and Inspiration Point and you'll have to park at Abalone Cove where they'll charge you some cash (was $4). Walk along the road past Wayfarer's Chapel and look for the trail down.

## Point Dume Beach/Paradise Cove

Located along the beautiful Malibu coast, this used to be a safe spot to strip and dip, but law enforcement has cracked down on those evil nudists. Park at Paradise Cove parking lot and walk west for awhile. Be careful and keep your clothes at arm's reach!

## Pirate's Cove

Also located in Malibu, this is another area that sees some law enforcement activity, but you can still find some naked bodies here. Pirate's Cove is located just south of Zuma Beach.

## Venice Beach

For a brief period of time around the late sixties and early seventies, Venice Beach was a popular and crowded nude beach. But, having a nude beach in such a popular area was too much for law enforcement . . . and nudity was no more. You may still see some topless or nude activity, but one goes to

Venice to watch the roller skaters, the weight lifters, the girls in g-strings, the freaks, the weirdos . . . the sights and sounds of L.A.. - not to get naked in the sun.

# San Bernardino County

## Deep Creek Hot Springs

Located in the Apple Valley area, this spot is administered under the U.S. Forest Service. As there is no federal law against nudity and this place is accepted as a nude spot . . . you can take it all off and commune with nature!! After a rugged 2-mile trek, you'll find the springs and pools at the bottom of a canyon. It's a gorgeous spot and well worth the hike. You'll find others here enjoying the beauty and• sun *au naturel.* It is a bit confusing getting here . . . so listen closely.

Exit Interstate 15 at Lucerne Valley, turn right on Bear Valley Cutoff Rd., go for 9 1/2 miles and turn right on Central Ave., go 3 miles and turn left on Ocotillo Way. Soon the pavement ends and 2.2 miles after turning on Ocotillo, turn right on Bowen Ranch Rd. Go 5.8 miles until you come to a fork in the road; take the right fork and in 1/2 mile turn into Bowen Ranch. You pay a fee to enter and drive about a mile to park. Look for the trail and follow it down the canyon.

# Santa Barbara County

## More Mesa

This is one of my favorite beaches, and though it has had police problems in the past, it seems fairly safe now. And popular. Very friendly, very fun beach. It's located north of Santa Barbara. Exit off Highway 101 at Turnpike Road south, left on Hollister, right on Puente, right on Viejas, then turn on Mockingbird Lane which ends at the path to the water.

## Carpinteria Beach          ## Gaviota Beach

## Summerland Beach          ## Cemetery Beach

## Rincon Beach

You can find descriptions and directions for these beaches in a great book, *California's Nude Beaches,* by Dave Patrick. You can buy this at your local adult bookstore, in the back of this book or on *Lecher McRich's Mansion* on the InterNet.

## Big & Little Caliente Hot Springs

This has been a popular spot with local skinny-dippers throughout the years. There is a specific law against nudity here, but law enforcement is erratic. To get there, take Gibraltar Road which climbs the Santa Ynez Mountains behind Santa Barbara. Turn right on Camino Cielo. At Romero Saddle, the road turns rough and it's all dirt and dips and holes from there.

To get to Big Caliente, take the right fork at the Pendola Ranger station and go 3 miles. To get to Little Caliente, go straight on the road at the ranger station for 5 miles to Mono Campground. Park the car and hike past the gate. Take the right fork past the gate, follow the trail until it makes a horseshoe bend, turn off at the bend and follow a narrow trail to the spring. This spring is more isolated and generally more hassle-free.

# San Diego County

For additional information on San Diego County, pick up a copy of *Sin Diego*, (see the back of this book to order your copy or on *Lecher McRich's Mansion* on the InterNet).

## Black's Beach

This is one of the most famous nude beaches in the world. It's popular, crowded, enjoyable, beautiful and sometimes has too many gawkers. It is hassle-free and you'll find all sorts of people swimming, socializing, jogging, playing frisbee, playing volleyball and enjoying life . . . in the nude!

The unofficial mayor of Blacks' Beach is Al Spencer, who is there everyday (weather permitting). He also puts out a newsletter for the Blacks' Beach Bares (see page 201).

There are several trails down the three-hundred foot cliffs, but the one just south of the glider port, called the goat trail, is the safest; it is basically a switch-back trail and there are spots with handrails and steps. At this time, after the severe winter storms, the trail is quite difficult to walk down, so be sure you are in good shape before you try.

To get there, exit Interstate 5 at Genesee and go west. You'll merge with North Torrey Pines Road as you bear right. Turn right at the light and go until the road ends in a parking lot. You will see the hang glider port. Follow the people to the start of the trail just south of the port.

## San Onofre Beach

If you ever thought of swimming and tanning in the shadows of a nuclear power plant, here's your chance. This beach is adjacent to the San Onofre nuclear power facility, which is comprised of two reactors that look like giant tits sticking up in the air. It is located at the southern end of San Onofre State Beach and adjacent to Camp Pendleton Marine base. Jagged cliffs and white sand, it is a beautiful beach with friendly people and a minimum of gawkers. And I don't think the Marines on patrol mind staring at all the nude bodies on the beach below!

Recently, officials controlling San Onofre say that they will bar nude use. Since this beach has been nude off and on for awhile, I'm not certain how effective this new crackdown will be. But, check it out before you disrobe because I can't guarantee it will be a nude beach when you go.

To get there, exit I5 at Basilone Road and head toward the water. Follow the road to the entrance to the park and pay the fee ($4 or $6 depending on the season), and then follow the park road to the very end. Park your car and follow the people or look for trail #6. It's an easy hike down, and once on the beach, head to the left until you see the naked bodies.

# Nude Resorts & Hotels

There are many nude resorts and hotels within easy driving distance of Los Angeles. Nude resorts have facilities such as a swimming pool, jacuzzi, tennis courts, snack bar, and places to tan your butt. Nude hotels are hotels that offer clothing-optional sunbathing. The hotels are generally small places with a limited number of rooms . . . so book your reservations in advance as they tend to sell out on the weekends.

Nude resorts usually have cabins or rooms to rent or have spaces for R.V. or camping. Both types of places cater to nudists of all ages and nude resorts or clubs are usually family-oriented. These places are not swingers' clubs!! Though you may meet some swingers . . . don't expect any sexual activity. Most nudist resorts and clubs have a day usage fee. So, if the fog is settling over the coast, head to one of the clubs for some hot, inland sunshine.

Following is a list of some of the clubs in close proximity to the greater L.A. area. The clubs and resorts are listed alphabetically . . . you'll have to find the one nearest you. And remember, some of these places are nudist clubs while others are nudist inns.

## Desert Shadows Inn
*Palm Springs — (619) 325-6410 or (800) 292-9298*

A beautiful nudist resort with two pools, tennis, volleyball, exercise room, giant covered spa and luxury rooms and suites. Bring the kids, too

## Happy Tanner Inn
*1466 N. Palm Canyon Drive, Palm Springs, CA 92262*
*(619) 320-5984*

They have a large pool and jacuzzi, beautiful gardens, a barbecue area and friendly hospitality. Rooms are $68 during the week and $89 on the weekends.

## Elysium Fields
*(310) 455-1000*

Located in Topanga Canyon, this place is a center for New Age and alternative lifestyles. In a beautiful setting, it has a swimming pool, sauna, jacuzzi, volleyball and tennis courts.

They also have New Age and alternative lifestyles workshops. It will cost you $20 or $25 for a couple the first and second times you visit. After that you will need to get a membership, which costs $200 for the year.

Founded by Ed Lange, photographer-nudist, in 1967. Mr. Lange, who died recently, regularly contributed to Vogue and Life. Daring in its day, the in-the-raw retreat is now such a community fixture that Lange was named citizen of the year by the local chamber of commerce.

## Glen Eden Sun Club

*25999 Glen Eden Rd., Corona, CA 91719*
*(714) 277-4650 or 800) 843-6833*

This club encompasses a very large area and has indoor and outdoor swimming pools, a sauna, camping facilities and hiking trails where you can trek around in the nude. This is a very family-oriented club and does not allow any sexual activity. They have frequent special and social events, so call for more information on upcoming happenings.

## Le Petit Chateau

*1491 Via Soledad, Palm Springs, CA 92264*
*(619) 325-2686*

A charming bed-&-breakfast inn tucked away in a quiet residential area. They have beautiful rooms, swimming pool and a great breakfast. Perfect place to take off your clothes and relax for the weekend. Room rates range from $80 to $130, which includes a wonderful breakfast buffet in the buff and afternoon snacks.

## McConville

*Post Office Box 477, Lake Elsinore, CA 92531*
*(909) 678-2333*

This resort is located in the heart of the Cleveland National Forest and offers cabins, camping areas, hiking trails, R.V. spaces, swimming, volleyball, tennis, horseshoes, badminton, shuffleboard and more. They claim to be California's oldest nudist camp; they've been around for 61 years! That's a long time!!

## Morningside Inn

*888 N. Indian Canyon, Palm Springs, CA 92262*
*(619) 325-2668*

This couples only bed and breakfast has lots of amenities.

# Naked City

*Post Office Box 2000, Homeland, CA 92348*
*(909) 926-BANG*

This is not your usual nudist sun club. Not for the entire family as there seem to be many swingers who go here. They host nude beauty pageants and other special events during the year. It will cost you $20 during the week and $30 on the weekends. There can be an abundance of single men here.

# Olive Dell Ranch

*26520 Keissel Road, Colton, CA 92324*
*(909) 825-6619*

It is not the largest nudist club in the area, but it has all the amenities you need: swimming pool, jacuzzi, sauna, tennis, badminton, table tennis and more. A very friendly and fun club!

# Raffles

*(619) 320-3949*

A very beautiful hotel with pool, jacuzzi, barbecue pits, and your choice of a studio room, a suite with kitchen, or a patio suite with kitchen. Prices range from $95 to $135. Take off your clothes and stay awhile.

# Swallows

*1631 Harbison Canyon Rd., El Cajon, CA 92019*
*(619) 445-3754*

If you're down in the San Diego area, check this place out. It is a sun club with pool, jacuzzi, tennis, volleyball, basketball, ping-pong, and campsites. It's $15 admission for the day. When I went there in the late afternoon, they only charged me $5.

# Treehouse Too Hotel & Resort

*1466 N. Palm Canyon Dr., Palm Springs*
*(619) 322-9431*

A clothing-optional hotel with 27 luxury rooms. Pool, jacuzzi, recreation room and more. Day use is available.

## Silver Valley Sun Club

*48382 Silver Valley Rd., Newberry Springs, CA 92365*
*(619) 257-4239*

This is California's only clothing-optional lake resort, and has all the amenities. It is $12 to visit for the day and $7 for a camping site A very beautiful spot. Located 25 miles east of Barstow; it's a long drive . . . but worth it!!

## Treehouse Fun Ranch

*(909) 887-7056*

This place has all the good stuff: tennis, basketball, volleyball, pools, sauna, ping-pong, horseshoes and more. They also have many special events throughout the year. They have room for R.V.s, so you can stay awhile. They do not offer daily rates; you have to buy a membership for $50, then you can visit any day for $25.

## Garbo Inn

*(619) 325-6737*

A small intimate clothing optional desert retreat for couples and select singles. Rooms are $65-$100. Day use is $20.

# Other Nude Stuff

## Age of Travel

*18010 S. Crenshaw Blvd., Torrance, CA 90504-5196*
*(213) 516-1253*

They make travel arrangements for clothing-optional vacations all over the globe.

## Air-A-Tans

*P.O. Box 1053, Gardena, CA 90249*

This is a family social travel club that visits various nudist resorts. They have camping outings, parties and more.

## *Scannin: Southern California Area Nudist Information Network*

*(619) 581-9262*

A computer BBS for those interested in the nude lifestyle.

# Camping Bares

*Post Office Box 81589, San Diego, CA 92138-1589*

An organization in San Diego that promotes nude recreation and sponsors nude hiking and camping activities. They hike on federal land where there are no specific laws against nudity. This is definitely not a swingers group . . . just a fun group that enjoys the great outdoors in the altogether.

# Canyon Sun Club

*Post Office Box 5053, San Bernardino, CA 92412*

A social nudist club that travels to various resorts around the area.

# Lifestyles

*Post Office Box 661268, Los Angeles, CA 90066*

They sell videos, publications, directories and lore about the nudist lifestyle.

# Friends of Deep Creek

*c/o The Bowen Ranch 6221 Bowen Ranch Rd. Apple Valley, CA 92308*

Concerned with the use of Deep Creek Hot Springs. Write for information.

# Golden Bares

*Post Office. Box 2896, Anaheim, CA 92814*

A family-oriented travel club that holds parties. meetings and other outings.

# Hot Springs SIG

*5322 S. Centinela Ave., Los Angeles, CA 90066*

This is a special interest group (SIG) that concerns itself with matters of hot spring activities and usage. Write for more information.

## *Hot Springs World*
*5322 Centinela Ave., Los Angeles, CA 90066-6908*

A quarterly newsletter about hot springs, nude and otherwise, throughout the west and elsewhere. Subscriptions are $18 per year.

## The Olympian Club
*P.O. Box 15277, North Hollywood, CA 91615*

A travel nudist club that holds and sponsors many events during the year.

## Pacificans
*P.O. Box 7842, Van Nuys, CA 91409*

Another travel club that sponsors various events throughout the year.

## Sun-Air
*Box 122, Corona, CA 91718*

They sell old nudist magazines and new publications from all over the world. Send for their price list.

## Blacks' Beach Bares
*Post Office Box 12255, La Jolla, CA 92039-0620*

Headed up by Al Spencer, a retired journalist and the unofficial "mayor" of Blacks' Beach. He publishes a monthly newsletter for the members. Membership is $15 a year.

## Naturist Penpal Club
*Post Office Box 182, Canoga Park, CA 91305-0182*

You can meet naturist from all over the country and the world. Not for swingers . . . just those who love to frolic *au natural.*

## Nude Weddings
*(213) 848-9903*

This minister advertises that he will perform nude weddings at a nude beach. If you want to get married without the gown and tux (or anything else!) . . . check this out. (I should have thought of this before I got married. Just think of all the money I would have saved on tux and gown rentals.)

# Guides To Nude Recreation

## California's Nude Beaches

*by Dave Patrick*

A great book with maps, outstanding photos and detailed information on where to get that all-over tan in California, Oregon, Washington, Hawaii and Nevada.

## World Guide To Nude Beaches & Recreation
## Nude & Natural

*By Lee Baxandall*
*The Naturists Inc., P.O. Box 132, Oshkosh, WI 54902*

The bible and the magazine of nude recreation. They covers the entire world. Great photos, detailed descriptions and directions. On trips to Europe I found some great spots!

Normandie Casino                                    *Photo by F.M. Philips*

# CHAPTER SIXTEEN

# Gambling

> . . . the only man who makes money following the races
> is one who does it with a broom and shovel.
> — *Elbert Hubbard*

Gambling is alive and well in this country despite those moral do-gooders who attempt to take all the sin, lust and greed out of our lives. Las Vegas is thriving, Atlantic City is luring gamblers, and other areas are opening up or considering opening up gambling.

Gambling has been a major source of fun and profit ever since colonial times. The Puritans of Massachusetts were the first to enact a law against gambling in 1638. Did you know that our freedom is a direct result of gambling profits? The colonies raised money to pay the Continental Army and fight the Revolutionary War by sponsoring a lottery. Even our prized Statue of Liberty was paid for by a series of lotteries in France. Just as today, the colonies relied on lotteries as a respectable financial tool to raise money for schools and public works.

Many independent operators began running their own lotteries or raffles. However, our government bowed to pressure from the evangelicals and by 1830, lotteries were banned throughout America. This lasted until 1860 when legalized gambling reemerged as a form of fun and entertainment. But, by the early 1900's, the tide had once again turned against the sin of gambling.

However, there was one place you were sure to find a good game of chance – at church! Yes, many of our churches used gambling throughout the twentieth century to raise money; they had raffles, bingo and "Monte Carlo" nights. In fact, one church representative during the Depression years stated, "there is no eleventh commandment against gambling", in an effort to explain why the church was using such a "sinful" activity to raise money.

During the 40's Las Vegas began building casinos and through the fifties and sixties it blossomed into a gamblers' paradise. However, the fifties in general were bad for gamblers as lawyers, members of Congress, reporters and district attorneys all fought the forces of illegal gambling everywhere.

In 1964 New Hampshire held a lottery; by selling $3 tickets and offering a $100,000 first prize, the state raised $2.5 million. Now there are lotteries in over thirty states. It seems that gambling isn't such a bad idea after all, is it, Big Brother?? Of course, the government doesn't really consider the lottery to be gambling.

Atlantic City legalized gambling in 1978. Deadwood, South Dakota began casino operations in 1989 and earned $90 million on betting revenues the first year. Certain areas of Louisiana are opening up gambling places, Indian reservations all over the country are operating or considering the possibility of operating gaming establishments, and off-track betting is riding a wave of popularity.

Gambling is part of our national scene, it's part of human nature. Sure, it's a bit sinful and many more people lose than win, but it is a form of adult entertainment for which there is a major demand. Just as long as you don't lose the rent money and your wife and kids are out on the street.

In Los Angeles you will find horse tracks, card rooms, Indian reservations only a short drive away, the state lottery and its various games, and of course, just a short plane flight away over the parched California desert to the gamblers' mecca: Las Vegas. You can find a little action in LA, and if that's not enough, head east to the bright lights of Las Vegas.

# Card Rooms

There are over 200 card rooms in the greater Los Angeles area; many of them are just smoke-filled rooms with only a few tables for poker. However, some of them have been transformed into large poker palaces that almost make you feel as if you are in Las Vegas. They are large, luxurious and have plenty of tables and a variety of game and limit options.

There was a spurt of growth in the card room industry during the 1980s which corresponds to the increase in Asian immigration during those same years. The Asian games of pai gow and super pan nine are very popular in many card rooms now. California is the only state where the local governments have primary control of card clubs and pseudo casinos. In this budget-conscious and recession era, the taxes these establishments pay are economic godsends to financially strapped small city governments.

The state supervision by the Attorney General's office, the Gaming Registration Program and the Gaming Registration Act are quite inadequate and create a feeling of powerlessness in big government. And you know what happens when big government feels powerless? They create more laws and more regulations and more supervisory positions.

There are moves in the state government to keep an eye on the card rooms and casinos; so who knows what will happen to these poker palaces in the near future? But, right now they are operating and waiting to take your money . . . or hand out some if you win!

## Bicycle Club

*7301 Eastern Avenue,*
*Bell Gardens*
*(310) 806-4646*

This place is open 24 hours and has close to 200 tables and many limits for all types of spenders, big and small. It has two restaurants in case you get hungry while losing . . . er, winning all that cash!

"I don't gamble on men!"     *©1995 Mistress Jayne Alexander*

## Hollywood Park Casino

*1050 S. Prairie, Inglewood*
*(310) 330-2800*

This is the nation's only card club next to a race track and it is a beauty. It is a $25 million Art Deco casino where you can play cards, bet on certain horse races, watch sports on a vast number of televisions (but not bet on the games), work out in a health club, get a massage, get a haircut and more. It has approximately 70 tables for your gambling pleasure.

## Normandie Club

*1045 W. Rosecrans, Gardena*
*(310) 352-3400 or (310) 715-7400*

This club has around 80 tables, is open 24 hours and has a variety of games including poker and pai gow.

## Huntington Park Casino

*6611 S. Alameda, Huntington Park*
*(213) 585-3050*

This club has over 70 tables and you can play all your favorite games here.

## Commerce Casino

*6131 E. Telegraph Road, City of Commerce*
*(213) 721-2100*

A large club with 200 tables and plenty of action.

## El Dorado Club

*15401 S. Vermont, Gardena*
*(310) 323-2800*

They have over 40 tables for your gambling satisfaction.

## Lake Elsinore Casino

*20930 Malaga Road, Lake Elsinore*
*(909) 674-3101*

If you are down Lake Elsinore way and you have some money burning a hole in your pocket, check this place out. There are nearly 40 tables for your gambling convenience.

# Indian Reservations

Native Americans have been getting the shaft from the white man for so long, they finally said enough is enough. They figured out a way to get his money while he was enjoying it. Open up casinos all over the country; let the white man (or any color man or woman) come and enjoy throwing their money away.

The Indians then put it to use on the reservation by providing for education, public services and employment. Indian tribes in Connecticut, Illinois, Colorado, Michigan and California have been raking in the money in their mini-Las Vegas's.

The Indian reservations are viewed as legal sovereign territories within the United States, and are thus responsible for many of their own laws and regulations. The Native American gaming places follow in the tradition of the churches in the 1930's which used bingo and casino nights to raise money. In many states the law allowed churches to run these gaming operations . . . so, Indians picked up on these laws and embraced them.

Of course, the federal and state government didn't want the Native Americans to do this, but they never want the Indians to do anything. The Indians created these casinos as a way to elevate their standard of living (i.e., make a lot of cash!!) and they, just as the churches did in the thirties, have done just that.

The government is constantly bothering the Indians with new proposals and regulations and broken promises (remember those treaties), but nonetheless, Indian gambling has prospered. The fighting has been going on since the first white man set foot on the "new land" and it will probably go on forever.

I say, let the Indians do what they want . . . as long as human sacrifices aren't being performed, let them be. Give them the power to create their own world, make their own money, educate their own people if that is what they want. I'm sure that not all Indian leaders are thrilled with the idea of casinos and gambling as a savior for their children, but if good comes from some people taking risks, having some fun, and throwing their cash on the table, then let it be!

Big Brother is always worried about organized crime infiltrating any gambling operations, but I would imagine that the Indian casinos are far "cleaner" than any of the Las Vegas or Atlantic City ones. The Indians proclaim their cleanliness . . . and I believe them!

## Casino Morongo

*49750 Seminole Drive,. Cabazon*
*(800) 252-4499*

They have a card room where you can play poker, Morongo 21 and more. They have bingo in the evening, machine from 5 cents to $1. They are open 24 hours, seven days a week.

## Cabazon Casino

*84-245 Indio Springs Drive, Indio*
*(619) 342-2593*

They have slots, video games, poker, cards, 21, keno, off-track betting, a good restaurant and are open 24 hours every day. What more could you ask for? A money tree, perhaps??

## Fantasy Springs Casino

*84245 Indians Springs Drive, Indio*
*(800) 827-2946*

Bingo!! They have cards, pull-tab machines, off-track betting and lots of other ways to lose your money.

## Spotlight 29 Casino

*Call (619) 775-5566 for address and directions in Coachella*

Haven't had time to check them out yet, but I hear that they also have bingo, card and much more.

## Agua Caliente Palm Springs

*Just off Indian Canyon Drive in Palm Springs*

The Agua Caliente band of Cahuilla Indians are planning a new casino, possibly opening sometime in 1995. Watch for more information on this new casino.

# Reservations Casinos in San Diego County

There are a few excellent casinos on Indian reservations in the greater San Diego area that are within two or three hours' drive from Los Angeles. For more information about these casinos, call them or pick up a copy of the book: Sin Diego, by F.M. Philips (that's me!), which is available from Warren Communications. There is an order form in the back of this book.

### Sycuan Indian Reservation

*(619) 445-6002*

### Viejas Indian Reservation

*(619) 445-5400*

### Barona Indian Reservation

*(619) 433-2300*

### Rincon Indian Reservation

*(619) 749-2100 in Valley Center*

© 1995 DR TUPPER

# Race Tracks

## Santa Anita Race Track

*285 W. Huntington Drive, Arcadia*
*(818) 574-7223*

The horses run here in autumn and they have off-track betting facilities during most of the year, except when there is a fair or special event. Call for more information and details.

## Hollywood Park

*1050 S. Prairie, Inglewood*
*(310) 419-1500*

The horses race in autumn. The place is near the Forum . . . so you can catch the races and then go to a Lakers game afterwards.

## Los Alamitos Race Track

*4961 Katella Avenue, Los Alamitos*
*(714) 995-1234*

The horses race in autumn here, too. It costs $3 for general admission and $4.50 for clubhouse. There is also off-track betting.

# The Lottery

Yes . . . the state does sponsor gambling. They will not exactly call it gambling . . . but that's what it is. You take a chance to win . . . and you usually lose!! The state . . . in an attempt to make a profit just like the casinos, happily takes your money to spend on useless social programs, an endless, mind-boggling bureaucracy and other money-wasting efforts that the common voter is helpless to stop. Hey . . . Big Brother . . . gambling is a sin . . . and you sponsor and operate places of gambling!!! Remember that the next time you attempt to legislate morality!!

The state lottery was created in an attempt to get more money to the public school system, which it so desperately needs. Gambling profits were supposed to pay for education . . . hmmmm . . . I think that is what the Native Americans are attempting to do with their casinos. Why are they being hassled . . . hmmm . . . how ironic . . . and hypocritical.

There has been plenty of debate since the inception of the lottery as to whether it has contributed much money to the schools, but regardless, the lottery exists and you can play it. There are several different games and the state continually creates new ones to keep interest high. Like any gambling, partake at your own risk. It can be fun . . . and profitable. But remember, there are more losers than winners!!!

# Your Odds of Winning . . .

The odds of the house (or the track or the state) winning are greater than your odds of winning. That's how they make money. According to Consumer's Research magazine, different games vary in how much they pay out in comparison to how much they take in. Craps has the highest payout at 98%. Roulette is next with 95%, followed by slots at 75% - 95%, jai alai at 85% -87%, the race track at 83% -87% and guess what ends up last . . . yep, the good old state lottery with an average payout of 49%. And, your odds of winning depend on which state lottery you're playing. Guess which state is the worst? Right again . . . California!

**EDITOR'S QUESTION:** I wonder if it is worth risking the cost of a stamp to win the Publisher's Clearing House sweepstake?

# Got a Gambling Problem?

Before you gamble away the kids' college fund or your vacation money or retirement savings . . . get help!

Gambling on the horses or at the casinos, card rooms or on the government-sponsored lottery can be a great form of entertainment, but for some people it can be a problem. For some, it is very addictive. Every place that offers any form of gambling (including our state-run lottery) is designed to make a profit for them . . . not for you. That means there will be more losers than winners. And some of those losers keep on losing and losing and losing. An occasional win keeps them salivating for that huge payoff that never comes.

If you think you have a problem, or if you're asking yourself whether or not you have a problem . . . you probably have one; get help!

I have a friend who has a regular middle management job, a family and a good life. But that life was almost threatened because of his gambling addiction. The lure of Vegas and its bright lights and promises of a big payoff lured him into throwing away most of his money. Luckily for him and his family, he got help before he went too deeply into debt. He was able to consolidate his losses and get back on his feet.

Gambling even effects the rich. One man who kept making millions and kept losing it all was Chico Marx of the famous Marx Brothers. This brothers had to keep bailing him out of trouble, but he went to his grave a compulsive gambler and his family suffered for it.

Get help if you need it!!!!! Take a chance and give one of these help groups a call!

## Gamblers Anonymous

*(213) 260-4657,*
*(818) 591-7850,*
*(818) 581-6266*

## Gamblers Anonymous National Service Office

*3255 Wilshire Blvd.*
*(213) 386-8789*

## California Council on Compulsive Gambling

*(800) 322-8748*

I'll give you odds that one of them can help you kick the gambling habit.

# CHAPTER SEVENTEEN

# Drugs

## Aphrodisiacs, Recreational & Smart Drugs

> . . . if we're looking for the source of our troubles, we shouldn't test people for drugs, we should test them for stupidity, ignorance, greed and love of power.
> — *P.J. O'Rourke,* Give War A Chance

> . . . religion is the opiate of the masses.
> — *Karl Marx*

In this chapter we will take a look at those substances you introduce into your body for pleasure, performance, or prowess. Aphrodisiacs may or may not increase your sexual performance, prowess and pleasure. Smart drugs may or may not stimulate your mental performance and prowess. And recreational drugs, though some users claim that they experience an increase in either performance, prowess or pleasure, or all three, generally only cause long-term harm to your body. Many of the recreational drugs that are popular today have glowing endorsements from users (addicts?) as aphrodisiacs. Don't believe the claims!!

# Aphrodisiacs

Do you believe there are such things as aphrodisiacs? Do you believe that a food substance, a drug, an herb, or some other ingredient or chemical can increase your potency or your vitality? Do you think that something you ingest can actually help get it up???

Named after the Greek goddess, Aphrodite, many substances have been touted as sex enhancers down through the years. Some of them include oysters, powdered rhinoceros horn, Spanish fly, hashish, cocaine, amphetamine, ginseng, and many more. Do any of these substances work? Well, no one has ever scientifically proven that there is a direct link between a substance and sexual vitality.

But some of these substances do have a scientific basis as to why they are considered aphrodisiacs, while others have no effect on the well-being of the body, and in fact can cause considerable damage. Following is a list of various substances that have been promoted as aphrodisiacs and our feelings about them based on experts' opinions and scientific research.

## Willis

*1317 North San Fernando Blvd., Suite 310*
*Burbank, CA 91504*

They are a mail order company that sells herbal aphrodisiacs in addition to a variety of books, gifts and more.


## Herbs

**Ginseng Root** – This ancient Chinese herb has been used for 3000 years as a revitalizer and an aphrodisiac. It is not some quick-acting stimulant, but a long-term revitalizer for the body. Its botanical name, Panax, is derived from the Greek word for panacea.

Its effect as an aphrodisiac has never been studied, but if it increases general energy and stamina, there is undoubtedly some sexual benefit to be derived.

**Yohimbine** – Yohimbine is a tree bark and supposedly has a stimulating effect on the spinal ganglia which can help to produce an erection. I haven't found any studies that prove this, but many users claim it to be a true aphrodisiac. The drug yohimbine, an extract from the herb, is recognized as a treatment for impotency in the U.S. Yohimbine can be toxic to the liver and should only be taken under supervision of a qualified specialist.

**Damiana** – Its botanical name is *turnera aphrodisiaca,* and as its name suggests, it is considered an aphrodisiac by some. It also may produce a high similar to that of marijuana. It is sometimes smoked or drunk as a tea. It seems safe to take and is used mainly as an overall tonic for the body's well-being.

**Schizandra** – This is another prized Chinese herb similar to ginseng. It is reputed to increase stamina, fight fatigue, slow aging and enhance sexual vitality in both men and women. It is now widely available and seems safe to take.

**Betel Nuts** – This is one of the most popular stimulants in Asia. This is the fruit of the areca tree and is utilized as a stimulant. It elevates a person's mood, stimulates the nervous system and, according to many, acts as an aphrodisiac. I don't know if it works, but there are millions of Asians who will attest to its powers.

**Herbal Ecstasy** – A blend of herbs that is supposed to give the user a high that lasts for about eight hours. As its name suggests, it is supposed to simulate the effects of the designer drug ecstasy. You can order it from the following Venice company:

## Global World Media

*(800) 365-0000*

The cost is $10 per dose and one dose is five pills. The company often runs half-price specials and they take credit cards.

# Drugs

The following is a list of drugs and their effects. Some are legal, while others are illegal. Never, never buy drugs off street. You don't know what you are getting. You could be poisoning yourself big time. That means either your local liquor store, pharmacy or neighborhood drug dealer — or better yet, abstention.

**Alcohol** – Mainly a depressant; however, used in small amounts, champagne, beer and wine can lower inhibitions and not cause too many problems, including addiction. Heavy use may lead to impotence (and no one wants that!!).

**Amphetamines** – These drugs stimulate the nervous system and speed up the cardiovascular system, possibly having some small effect on stimulating the sex drive. They can be habit-forming and dangerous in the long run. Some people even say that they tend to reduce penis size (and no one wants that!!!!!).

**Amyl Nitrite** – Called poppers, this drug decreases blood pressure and causes lightheadedness. The low blood pressure may make an orgasm seem longer in some people. Very popular in the gay community.

**Barbiturates** – These are downers and can cause your sex life and your penis to go down! Very addictive in the long term.

**Cocaine** – This drug stimulates the nervous system and increases the heart rate. Some people report feelings of contentment and exhilaration. It is also used in other forms such as crack. It is highly psychologically addictive and can be fatal. It can slow down the onset of orgasm; this may seem like a good thing at first, but nothing is a good thing with cocaine for very long.

Some people apply it directly to the genitals; it has a numbing effect. I know too many people who have turned from fun-loving, enthusiastic people to lazy bums without much of a life because of cocaine. Stay away!!!! Many people tout coke as an aphrodisiac, but it's merely a "snow" job.

**Heroin** – For some reason, heroin is making a comeback. For your sexual performance, it's a real downer. Why it's making a comeback is a mystery to me.

**LSD** – A hallucinogen that is very unpredictable. Accounts of people jumping out of windows and attempting to fly in the 60's were extremely exaggerated, but it is still a dangerous drug. It intensifies the mood of the user; perhaps the reason some people use it for sex. Stay away!!

**Marijuana** – It first stimulates, then depresses; somewhat like alcohol. I see marijuana on a par with alcohol and therefore, I prefer to see it legalized, but I don't believe it has much effect on your sex life. It may cause you to eat too many Doritos; whether that affects your sex life is open to debate.

**MDMA** – Methylene Dioxy Meth Amphetamine, is also known as *Ecstasy,* and is an amphetamine-like drug with hallucinogenic properties, currently popular on the rave scene. It is so unique that is in a class by itself and is known as the "hug" or "love" drug because it is reported to induce the desire to give or receive affection or to caress someone. As with any amphetamine, it can be dangerous and addictive. Patented as long ago as 1913 by a German company, it was legal in the U.S. until mid 1980's. As soon as something becomes popular the government has to either control or outlaw it.

**Ecstasy** - See above.

**Mescaline** – This is derived from the peyote cactus and is like a high dose of marijuana. It is not thought to be addictive, but it is difficult to get pure mescaline on the street; it is usually mixed with other substances which can be addictive. Again, like marijuana, it doesn't have much effect on your sex life.

**Nitrous oxide** – Also known as laughing gas, this can cause brain and liver damage. Since its effect on your sex drive is an illusion, stay away from this dangerous high!

**Quaaludes** – These are depressants which some users say offer a sense of euphoria. Stay away as they are highly addictive and can be fatal!

# Aphrodisiacs

Though I cannot vouch for the effectiveness of any of these substances as "aphrodisiacs" (I would never need such things!), I do know that the herbs and vitamins mentioned in this chapter contribute to one's overall well-being and health. And if you are healthy, you are usually horny!! As for the drugs, some of them may increase the heart rate or stimulate the central nervous system or lower your inhibitions, but I do not recommend the use of drugs or alcohol to increase your sexual arousal. The use of drugs can be extremely dangerous and destructive.

Sex is so wonderful on its own . . . who needs drugs to improve it? Just give me a beautiful woman and a hot tub and that's all I need. Hell, just give me the beautiful woman and I'd be happy!

**Spanish Fly** – True Spanish fly is made from the wings of the *Cantharis vesicatoria* beetle and can cause intense itching in the genitals due to its irritation of the urethra. I suppose that this itch drove some people to have sex (to satisfy that itch!!). It can be fatal and is very dangerous. Yes, it did cause erection, but it sometimes caused insanity and death, which tended to slow sales considerably. The Spanish fly you see sold in stores and through mail order is actually made with cayenne pepper and has no effect on the sex drive.

**Testicles** – Yes, balls, nuts, huevos, whatever you want to call them. Some cultures think that by eating the testicles of a species of animal, you can increase your potency and virility. Perhaps, due to the testosterone in testes, there may be some truth to this, but no research has ever shown this to be true. Bulls' balls is a favorite of some cultures. The Romans and Greeks both thought that eating chopped up testicles or swallowing sperm, preferably human, increased potency. Maybe that is the reason my gay friends seem so horny!!

**Rhinoceros Horn** – Another exotic sex enhancer which some cultures swear by. It is usually ingested in powdered form, and I have no idea if it has any effect.

**Mandrake** – This one is touted in the Bible for all you God-fearing sinners. In the book of Genesis when Jacob and his wife failed at having more children, she got him to try mandrake. It must have gotten Jacob in the mood because they eventually had thirteen children.

**Vitamin E** – Since a high concentration of this vitamin is found in the testicles, it has been assumed that it was good for your sex life. It may be, as it is certainly good for your overall well-being, though I doubt you can pop in a few vitamin E pills in the afternoon and be a stud by evening.

**Oysters** – A favorite dish for the sexual appetite. Oysters do have an effect on the libido, but it is not the quick reaction most people are looking for. Oysters contain a high amount of zinc, and semen contains a high amount of zinc. Every time you lose some semen ( i.e. get your rocks off!!), you lose zinc. Zinc is also necessary for normally functioning sexual glands and for a normal sex life. Eat your oysters; they may not give you an immediate erection, but . . . you never know.

If you visit some of the "zones of tolerances" in Mexico, you will quite often see an oyster and clam cart, piled with shells, parked in front doing a good business. A Mexican husler friend of mine in Tijuana used to always order something called "pata de mula," a mixture of raw clams, lime juice and salsa. It looked terrible but he swore by it.

**Musk oil & Ambergris** – No, you don't ingest them, you rub them on your penis. These are externally applied aphrodisiacs. About an hour before sex, wash your penis (or have someone else wash it!) with warm water and milk, dry it and then apply some oil of musk or ambergris. These ingredients cause a contractile reaction in the muscles of the penis and allow it to remain stiff. I don't know if this works . . . so if any of you horny readers out there try this, let us know how it works.

**Celery Seeds** – Another externally applied aphrodisiac. You wash your penis with an infusion of celery seeds and then follow that by rubbing in some oil of purslane (maybe it's just all that rubbing that gets you aroused).

**Lilly-of-the-Valley Oil** – Another oil that is rubbed on the penis before sex which is supposed to get you "up and going."

## Try This Cure For Impotence

The Romans developed this hideous cure which seems worse than the problem. The impotent man should eat foods ouch ao oniono and pray to the godo (thcir godo or ouro?). Ncxt, he is told to grab a dildo, cover it with oil, pepper and nettleseed and insert it in his anus. Then, he is to beat himself on the butt and legs with a bunch of stinging nettles. Modern medicine has come a long way!!

# Recreational Drugs

... the only reason that cocaine is such a rage today is that people are too dumb and lazy to get themselves together to roll a joint.
— *Jack Nicholson*

I have already mentioned many of the drugs popular today in the aphrodisiacs section. Cocaine, crystal, ice, methamphetamine, MDMA, DMT, LSD, quaaludes, peyote; these and many more are all available on the street today. Though I understand that drugs are inextricably linked with the underground and many subcultures including the adult entertainment industry, I do not recommend the use of any of these drugs.

They are illegal, in most cases highly addictive, in some cases they can be fatal, and they are generally all downers in the long term. Just saying no to drugs sounds like a good idea to me.

Of course, alcohol and marijuana are also drugs. And they both have serious side effects. Since alcohol is legal, millions of people enjoy (and regret) these side effects every day. And even though marijuana is illegal, millions more enjoy the high from that drug every day also. And I tend to believe that marijuana should be legalized, especially for medical use. Its effects are mild, though driving while stoned is definitely a hazard and there are long-term effects. Everyone should be careful when using these drugs. Never, never, never drive while under the influence of alcohol or marijuana – or any drug! It is a crime and it's dangerous. It is a stupid thing to do!!

# Marijuana

Or pot, or reefer, or Mary Jane, hemp, or a million other names. Marijuana is the term used for the flowering tops and the leaves of the plant *cannabis sativa*. It was brought to the new world by the Spaniards in the sixteenth century. The word "marijuana" comes from the Spanish word for "intoxication." Pot is probably the most widely used illicit drug in the world. At one time, the stems were used to make rope, paper and fabric. If we could legally grow the stuff, think of all the beautiful trees we could save!!

Many of our founding fathers smoked it and it was required that everyone grow hemp so that the Navy would have a supply of rope during wars. Our Declaration of Independence and our Constitution were written on hemp paper and are still in good shape today. If they were printed on the paper we have today, they would have turned yellow and started to fall apart, as many of our books are doing today.

The campaign to outlaw hemp was sponsored by William Randolph Hearst (the newspaper tycoon), who owned large tracks of timber. After hemp was outlawed, the value of his holdings skyrocketed. The liquor industry was also against hemp. I wonder why? Maybe it's because you can't grow a six-pack.

The main ingredient in pot that gets you high is THC (delta-9-tetrahydrocannabinol, for you chemistry geeks). The most potent preparation from this plant is hashish (or hash, for all you stoners). Hash is perhaps 5 to 15 times stronger than pot.

The use of pot seems to be on the rise again after a period of declining use. Pot leaf designs and pot leaf fashions are all around, just like in the seventies (my high school yearbook had pot leaves strategically hidden in the coverartwork).

# Hemp Products

Hemp cloth makes very good durable clothing, back packs, paper, oils, etc. For a catalog of hemp products see *Lecher McRich's Mansion* on the InterNet or contact —

## Sunsports Hemp

*2091 Las Palmas, #C, Carlsbad, CA 92009*
*(619) 438-7810*

# The Effects

Pot usage does carry some risks. It has been speculated that the smoke, just as with cigarettes, can cause cancer. It can decrease hormone production in both sexes. It can impair the immune system, it can cause short-term memory loss, it . . . er . . . it can . . . ah . . . um . . . what was I talking about? Oh yeah, marijuana.

Pot does seem to have some medicinal use; glaucoma and epilepsy are two afflictions that marijuana seems to affect positively. It also takes the pain and discomfort away for cancer patients undergoing chemotherapy. AIDS patients sometimes use it to make their lives more tolerable. It can relieve the symptoms of multiple sclerosis.

There presently is a debate about legalizing marijuana for medicinal use. The Bush administration totally rejected the idea of marijuana for medicinal purposes, but the Clinton administration is looking into it. Perhaps if we don't inhale, the President will let us use it as a medicine or a painkiller!!

A recent case down in San Diego concerned a person living with AIDS who was arrested for growing his own pot in his backyard for his use. He swore that the pot alleviated his aches and pains and made life just a bit more bearable. Of course, the local authorities stepped in and saved the general public from this evil man!! The court sympathized with his plight and placed him on probation if he would refrain from growing any more pot. He continued to grow his own and was jailed for violating the conditions of his probation.

If you do smoke pot, never have more than one ounce around at a time. Possession of only one ounce is a misdemeanor. Also, if you have too much around, the police will think you are intending to sell it and that would mean a much harsher sentence. Buying in bulk may save you money, but it could cost you dearly in the long run.

An older friend of mine used to be totally against the use of pot in any form. However, he was under medication for heart trouble and his medication had many negative side effects including insomnia and impotence. A friend of his induced him to try marijuana. Now he saves a small fortune on heart medication and sleeps like a baby and has a personal ad in *Swing* magazine. In addition, to save money, he became a small time dealer to friends, many who were suffering from AIDS related deseases.

# Smoke if You Got 'em

### Prissy's High Society

*12136 Beach Blvd., Stanton, CA 90680*
*(714) 893-0066*

A toke shop with pipes, papers and more. What happened to the good 'ol days when there was a head shop on every block.

# My Opinion . . .

We do have a major drug problem in this country, but I do not feel that the legalization of marijuana would do any more damage. Drugs and drug-related crime are eroding many of our neighborhoods and destroying many of our children's lives before they even have a chance. This is a tragedy and a travesty on both an individual and a societal level.

Would marijuana make all this worse?? I sincerely doubt it. A large body of evidence shows that in the 1970s marijuana usage rates did not increase more in the 11 states where pot was decriminalized than in the states where marijuana remained a criminal offense.

If you are interested in the legalization of marijuana, pick up a copy of *High Times* at your local bookstore or newsstand, or write to NORML.

## NORML (National Organization for the Reform of Marijuana Laws)

*1636 "R" Street NW #3, Washington D.C.20009*
*(202) 483-5500*

### California NORML

*2215 A Market Street #278, San Francisco, CA 94114*
*(415) 563-5858*

Another organization that may be of interest is:

### The Drug Policy Foundation

*4455 Connecticut Avenue, NW Suite B-500,*
*Washington D.C. 20008*
*(800) 388-DRUG (3784)*

They are a non-profit organization that promotes an open debate on the issue of drug policy. They are not a legalization group, but many of their members are involved in the legalization struggle. They are interested in discovering alternatives to our current drug policy and finding solutions to the problems that our current policies have caused.

# Get High on Life

Stay away from hard drugs!! Get high on life!! Drugs can be dangerous!! There is too much life to enjoy to let drugs get in the way!!

**PUBLISHER'S NOTE:** I agree fully with the author, but would go further. Although I don't recommend using most drugs, I do recommend legalizing and controling them as has been done successfully in more enlightened European countries. Drug abusers should be given medical attention, not police attention – and the profit motive should be eliminated.

My European friends think Americans are crazy. We promote violence but repress pleasure. We legalize guns and outlaw sex, drugs and gambling. We picked up the idea of pleasure being evil originally from Europe, but they progressed past this idea a long time ago.

Some people can handle drugs and others can't – just like some people can drive a car and some can't. We should not make something illegal for all just because a minority abuse it. We have more people in jails that any other industrialized country – mostly for drug related crimes. Let's educate and help them – not lock them up and make them into criminals.

# Drunk (or Stoned) Driving

. . . alcohol is like love: the first kiss is magic, the second is intimate, the third is routine. After that you just take the girl's clothes off.
— *Raymond Chandler*

**D**runk drivers deserve what they get. If you are going to use substances to alter your reactions or moods, be responsible!! Be extremely responsible and never, never, never drink and drive! Get someone to drive you home, call your mom, get a taxi, walk, ride the bus, crawl, have a designated driver . . . do anything but get behind the wheel of a motorized vehicle when you drink.

If you are stopped while driving with alcohol in your system, there are a few things you should know which may help you avoid jail and fines and the basic nightmare that is DUI!! You are under no obligation to answer the law enforcement officer's questions. Be polite and courteous and respond by saying, "I don't wish to answer any questions right now."

It is also better to refuse any field coordination tests as they can sometimes be rather tricky even when you are sober. However, you cannot refuse a chemical test; if you do so, you automatically lose your driver's license.

If you are instructed to take a chemical sobriety test, choose the breath test. The blood test is the most accurate, the urine test is second best, and the breath test is the least accurate. If you think you are over the limit, choose inaccuracy! Also, refuse to consent to a search of your car. Always exercise your rights under the 4th and 5th Amendments by remaining silent and having an attorney present during any questioning.

Remember, you can be charged with DUI if your blood alcohol level registers .08 and above. You may be charged even if it is lower. For the average-sized person, .08 can be reached by having three drinks. Your body burns off approximately one drink per hour.

Field sobriety tests currently in use include the one-legged stand, counting backwards, touching your nose with your fingers, standing with your feet together and tilting your head and closing your eyes and counting to thirty. These tests can be quite confusing . . . if you're uncoordinated to begin with, you may want to practice these so the cops won't think you're wasted when you're completely sober!!

Nothing works to mask the level of alcohol in your system. Don't use Certs or mouthwash. The cops may catch a whiff of a breath mint or a sweet-smelling mouthwash and instantly think DUI. Forget about coffee; it does nothing to hide the fact that your bloodstream is loaded with alcohol and it doesn't help to sober you up!

I know a highway patrolman who pulled over a suspected drunk driver and found him to be over the legal limit. Too bad he was also well over the legal limit for motor oil. That's right: motor oil!! It seems the driver had ingested nearly a quart of motor oil in hopes that it would mask his blood alcohol level. Not only was he a drunk driver . . . he was a moron, too!!

> I've got some beer and the hightway's free . . .
> — *Bruce Springstein*

Drunk driving is moronic. You can face jail time, heavy fines, greatly increased auto insurance (if you can even get it!), but most moronic of all, you endanger your life and the lives of innocent others!!

# If You Have a Problem . . .

## Alcoholics Anonymous

- *9604 S. Figueroa — (213) 777-9740*
- *767 S. Harvard Blvd. — (213) 936-4343*

## Alcoholics Anonymous For Spanish Speakers

*(213) 384-2449*

## Alcoholics Anonymous For Deaf Callers

*(213) 735-2922*

## Alcoholism Center For Women

*(213) 381-8500*

## California Self-Help Center

*(800) 222-5465*

Makes referrals to support groups.

## Marijuana Anonymous

*(213) 964-2370*

## Narcotics Anonymous

*(213) 850-1624 (Hollywood area)*

## Los Angeles Center For Alcohol & Drug Abuse

*901 E 6th Street*
*(213) 624-2911*

## Drugbusters International

*(213) 935-7647*

## Partnership For A Drug-Free America (National Institute on Drug Abuse Help Line)

*(800) 662-HELP (4357)*

## National Council on Alcoholism and Drug Dependency

*(213) 384-0403*

### Al-Anon

*(213) 387-3158 (English) or (310) 948-2190 (Spanish)*

Or, if you want (and can afford) to go where the stars go and get some of the best treatment around:

### Betty Ford Center

*(800) 854-9211*

# Secular Saviors

Most of the "Anonymous" groups rely on the 12-step program modeled after the one that AA uses which is religion based. If you don't need the power of a god to cure you of your addiction, you might try:

### Rational Recovery Self Help Network

*Post Office Box 800, Lotus, CA 95651*
*(916) 621-4374*

The founder and director of Rational Recovery is Jack Trimpey. This is the address for the national headquarters. There are many chapters in the Greater L.A. area, so contact them to find a chapter nearest to you. I heard him speak once and know that they have a very effective organization.

# Cops and the Law and You . . .

Even though there are a few bad apples, most police officers are hard-working men and women who are just doing their jobs. They are enforcing the laws which we live by, whether or not you, or they, for that matter, agree with those laws. They have a job to do and deserve your respect. If you get caught with illegal substances or with alcohol in your blood while behind the wheel of your car, it's your fault, not theirs!!

Cops love to play word games when questioning someone and are very adept at keeping you off your guard. Remember that you have the right to remain silent thanks to the 5th Amendment.

If the cops attempt to search your house, they need a warrant and you can demand that your lawyer be present during the search. You have the right to refuse admittance to your home thanks to the 4th Amendment. Don't physically attempt to stop them if they burst in your door, don't sign any statements, and don't offer any verbal comments.

Your rights on the highway are extremely limited. The cop has the right to peer into your car from the outside. He can search closed containers in your car and he or she may conduct a full search if they have probable cause. If the officer asks to search your car, refuse politely. He or she may search anyway, but at least you have exercised your rights.

The cops may throw around such fancy terms as "reasonable suspicion" or "probable cause." Reasonable suspicion allows them to look briefly, but not make an all-out search. Probable cause, such as an aromatic cloud of pot smoke or a joint lying on the floor, gives them more rights to search. Refusal to allow a search does not in itself constitute probable cause.

If you get arrested, the cops must tell you why you have been arrested, you get two phone calls, and you must be formally charged within 48 hours. If you cannot afford an attorney, demand that one be provided for you. There are many other things you should know about the law. You should contact an attorney who specializes in drug or alcohol cases for more information.

Remember that cops are people just like you and me. They are charged with upholding the laws as they are made by our elected officials. If you don't agree with the laws, work in the system to change them, don't get mad at the cops!!

# Smart and Life Extension Drugs

> . . . drugs are a one-man birthday party.
> — *P.J. O'Rourke*
> *(Republican Party Reptile)*

**T**o paraphrase an old saying . . . you are what you ingest. And that is what this chapter is all about: Ingesting the right drugs and nutrients that will increase your cognitive ability and extend your life. The longer you live, the more sinful pleasures you can enjoy . . . and the more sinful books you can buy . . . and the more money I can make!!

What are smart drugs?? Why, smart drugs are drugs that make you smart! To be more specific, they increase your cognitive power, concentration, memory, mental energy, alertness, mental clarity and creativity. What are life extension drugs?? Why, they are drugs that extend your life!!! To be more precise, they promote wellness, increase resistance to disease, slow the aging process and provide protection against free radicals in your system (which some say causes diseases such as cancer).

It sounds as if these drugs should be in every home, on every store shelf . . . everywhere. But such is not the case. It seems that many of these drugs are new, unproven and a thorn in the FDA's side. The government wants to protect you from getting smart and living longer!! To be fair, the FDA sometimes does a good job in protecting the public and is very concerned with fraud and false claims, but other times it is over zealous in its regulation and control.

Therefore, the "smart and life extension drug culture" has been pushed underground just like illicit drugs. These drugs have created a subculture of pill poppers, smart drink pushers and shadowy figures trying to reach mental nirvana. It's a little taste of the sixties here in the nineties . . .

Timothy Leary talks about them, the government is against them and kids are doing them. Sound familiar??

Smart and life extension drugs range from basic nutrients to ancient herbs to prescription drugs to experimental drugs for troublesome afflictions. Some are readily available, some have been tested and deemed safe, others are untested, and others have been shown to be dangerous. Some of these you can get on the shelves, some with a prescription, some you can get in Mexico or other countries and some you just can't get your greedy hands on. Some are even considered to be aphrodisiacs; many porn stars swear by them!

If you are contemplating the use of any smart drugs or nutrients, it is wise to consult an expert in the field or a physician. Even with readily available herbs and nutrients, you should begin taking any new substance gradually and slowly. Everyone is different and some people may experience reactions to substances that are otherwise safe. Neither I, nor my crack research staff claim to be experts on smart and life extension drugs (lust and sin are our fields of endeavor) . . . we merely provide the following information as a guideline in your search for intelligence and immortality. So . . . don't get "high" in the traditional sitting-around-the-room-passing-a-joint-or-a-bong sense . . . get high by increasing your IQ a few points.

# The Drugs

## The Nootropics

These drugs are not approved in the U.S., but they include several exciting substances. Nootropic comes from a Greek word meaning "acting on the mind." The following are reported to be cerebroactive:

**Hydergine** – the once popular king of nootropics, it is available by prescription and over the counter in Mexico.

**Vinopocetine** – it is the current darling of the subculture. It was developed in Hungary and was widely tested in Japan. It increases blood flow and glucose uptake in the brain.

**Piracetam** – This is one of the most popular smart drugs and can be purchased in Mexico. In some studies it has helped dyslexic children.

**Oxiracetam** – A promising drug that is available outside the U.S.

**Eldepryl** – This drug is known as Deprenyl all over the world, except in North America. It shows promise as an anti-aging substance, aphrodisiac (you get smart and you get horny!!) and as a weapon against Alzheimer's Disease. There has been a number of things on TV about this drug, all positive. It is available in the U.S. by prescription. It does not appear to be cheaper South of the Border and you still need a prescription.

**PUBLISHER'S NOTE**: I use this one myself. It made me smart enough to get the author to write this book for me. Being a sexy senior citizen, it even helps me get it up again. Before using this drug, get a liver and kidney checkup as Eldepryl/ Deprenyl can be harmful on a weak organ. Another negative factor is that this drug is expensive (about $2 per tiny tablet; half a tablet per day). So get your friends to buy this book so I can afford to get a refill.

**Choline** – This is a nutrient available everywhere. Many users combine it with vitamin B5. It works by raising your brain's acetylcholine, the neurotransmitter moving your thoughts from synapse to synapse. Choline is a major ingredient of the various smart drinks.

**DMAE** – Its effect on the brain is basically the same as choline and it is found in health food stores all over.

**Phosphatidylserine** – another substance you can take without breaking the law. It shows promise against Alzheimer's.

**Centrophenoxine** (Lucidril) – Another promising anti-aging substance. Available over the counter in Mexico.

**Pyroglutamate** (PCA) – A naturally occurring amino acid that can be bought in the U.S.

**Ginkgo** Biloba – It comes from the oldest species of tree. A herb that reportedly helps memory and cognition. Available everywhere.

**Ginseng** – Another herb available everywhere. Good for both physical and mental well-being.

**Phenylalanine** – it is naturally occurring in some foods like bananas. It is a restorative nutrient. and can be bought from vitamin sellers. It is considered a neurotransmitter precursor.

**Vasopressin** (Diapid) – Available by prescription and over the counter in Mexico. One of my friends considers this his favorite smart drug, but he warns: use sparingly as it can cause cardiovascular problems. But, he says it gives him a real thought rush!

**Catovit** – A stimulant comprised of vitamins, nicotine and a mild steroid. Available over the counter in Mexico.

**Gerovital** (G –3) - Can be purchased in Nevada and over the counter in Mexico.

**Acety** –L-Carnitine (ALC) - A naturally occurring substance that is sold in the U.S.

# Get Smart
# and Live Longer

For more information on smart drugs, pick up a copy of one or both of the following books:

### *Smart Drugs & Nutrients*

### *Smart Drugs II.*

Both are available from Lecher McRich's Bookstore at the back of this book. You might also want to subscribe to:

### Smart Drug News

*Smart Publications, Post Office Box 4667,*
*Petaluma, CA 94955*

This is a newsletter of cognition enhancement and how to get smart!!. It keeps you informed on all the latest smart drugs, research, laws, availabilities and more. Tell them you saw it in Lust Angeles.

# Stay Smart!!!

Some of the drugs and nutrients are legal; many you can find in your local supermarket. Some you need a prescription for, while others are illegal in this country. Just because they are prohibited here in the U.S. doesn't mean they can't be found. There is a thriving black market for all the illegal smart drugs. We can't tell you where to get them on the black market, but they are out there.

Smart drugs are available in many foreign countries and we are lucky to be relatively close to one of those foreign countries. Pharmacies in Mexico often stock many of the drugs listed here and U.S. Customs has traditionally allowed importation of drugs for personal use. However, I would learn more about the law before I brought some over . . . and that doesn't mean you can bring over a truckload. You are only allowed to bring enough for personal use).

Remember, the use of many of these smart drugs is against the law. You could be fined or imprisoned just as if you were using cocaine or heroin. Know the consequences before you take the risks. Also, before you ingest, learn all you can about the physical risks and side effects. Many substances are beneficial at certain dosages, but harmful at other levels.

Be smart and get smart! . . . this book is not ment for dummies who take risks with their bodies.

© 1995 DR Tupper

© 1995 DR TUPPER

# CHAPTER EIGHTEEN

# Oddities & Ends

> . . . there are a number of mechanical devices which increase sexual arousal, particularly in women. Chief among these is the Mercedes Benz 380SL convertible.
> — *P.J. O'Rourke*

**I**n this chapter we include a wide assortment of services and products that are sexual, sinful or seriously sensual. There are plenty of oddities and ends for you to choose from . . . so read on . . . and enjoy!

# Carnal Clothing . . .

> . . . you'd be surprised how much it costs to look this cheap.
> — *Dolly Parton*

## Body Shock
*14522 1/2 Ventura Blvd., Sherman Oaks, CA 91403*
*(818) 789-3204*

If you're a fetish freak, this may be the place for you. As their motto says, "good things for naughty girls and naughty things for good girls." They offer fetish clothing, leather, PVC, lingerie, g-strings, chain g-strings, thigh-high boots, open-breast design outfits and many European designs. Also has imported fetish magazines and books. Send $3 for their latest full-color mail order catalog.

## Fit To Be Tied

*222 Main Street Suite D, Seal Beach CA 90740*
*(310) 597-1234*

This quiet seaside community seems like an odd place for a fetish store, but there it is . . . right on Main Street. They have a variety of men's and women's items. The hours of operation vary, so call for details.

## Fantasy Lingerie

*16112 Harbor Blvd., Fountain Valley*

They have an excellent stock of lingerie, boots, shoes, dresses, fetish gear and other sexy clothing. Located in Orange County, a conservative Republican stomping ground.

## Frederick's of Hollywood

*6608 Hollywood Blvd., Hollywood, CA 90028*
*(213) 466-8506*

It's the king (or queen) of lingerie stores. The venerable Frederick's has been around for a long time. They have all the hottest lingerie fashions for women and men. You can also visit their lingerie museum. It's free to enter and you can take a nostalgic look back at lingerie fashions dating to the 1940's.

## Playmates

*6438 Hollywood Blvd., Hollywood, CA 90028*
*(213) 464-7636*

Great place to locate some of those special items of lingerie, costumes for special events, and wildly provocative clothes for going out or staying in. They have a wide selection of hot items and there is even a bargain basement. I've seen some great-looking girls trying on clothes here. In fact, once when my girlfriend was browsing, there was a knockout girl and her almost knockout friend trying on lingerie. They kept coming out of their dressing rooms to look in the mirror or check each other out. I got to see them in g-strings, see-through tops and more. They even forgot to close their doors on occasion and I got to see it all. Boy, did I feel like a perverted voyeur . . . but was it fun!

## The Pleasure Chest

*7733 Santa Monica Blvd. — (213) 650-1022*

This store has much more than lingerie, but they do carry a good selection of sexy attire. Lots of other fun things too such as magazines, cards, toys and more.

## Trashies Lingerie

*402 N. LaCienega Blvd.*
*(310) 652-4543*

Looking for that perfect slutty attire . . . you may be able to find it here. Lots of lingerie and other sexy, seductive wear.

## Versatile Fashions

*1925 East Lincoln Blvd., Anaheim, CA 92667*
*(714) 776-1510 or (714) 538-7950 or (714) 538-6498*

A great store for the fetish crowd. Whether you are a dominant or a submissive or just a role-player, you can find the perfect piece of clothing. Mistress Antoinette, owner and principal designer, is the queen of PVC and she has a wide array of corsets, shoes, boots, lingerie, fantasy costumes and clothes for TVs. They have both custom and off-the-rack styles.

## High Strung By Jolie

*P.O. Box 1289, Helendale, CA 92342*

Jolie creates and sells a wide array of corsets and waist cinchers. Nasty creations for mistresses, Tvs and everyone. Rubber, latex, leather, whatever! Write for catalog.

## Rubber & Rivets

*2750 Associated Road, D-70, Fullerton, CA 92635*
*(714) 671-1402*

They offer original designs in rubber wear, heavy bondage gear, accessories for latex freaks, and more. You can get an illustrated brochure for $2, which is deductible from your first order.

## Syren

*7225 Beverly Boulevard, Los Angeles, CA 90036*
*(213) 936-6693*

If you are into the "latex couture," check this place out. Order a brochure for $3.

## J. Heartwood Corsets of Desire

*412 N. Coast Hwy. #210, Laguna Beach, CA 92651*
*(714) 376-9558*

Janette, former creator of Heartwood Whips of Passion, is focusing her attention on creating beautiful corsets for your wearing pleasure. For a copy of her 16-page corset booklet, send $5. She creates some beautiful fashions.

## XXXtreme Fashions

*11138 Magnolia Blvd., North Hollywood, CA 91601*
*(818) 763-8228*

They offer all the hot fashions and lingerie you could want. Give them a call for more details.

## Especially For Me

*113 North First Ave., Upland, CA 91785*
*(909) 946-6251*

Great store for the guy who wants to be a girl. Lingerie, leather, PVC, large-size dresses, wigs, shoes, and more. Complete workshops available. Mail order also offered.

## Sally J

*Box 1683, Santa Ynez, CA 93460*
*1-(800) 4-SALLY J (1-(800) 472-5595)*

A mail order company that sells "lingerie for lovers." Call or write for their new catalog.

## Women of Size

*(800) 808-9883*

Mail order company that offers lingerie for both men and women. Call for their latest catalogs.

# Erotic Events . . .

> . . . so little time and so little to do.
> — *Oscar Levant*

## American Sunbathing Annual Convention

*1703 N. Main St. Kissimmee, FL 34744-3396*
*(800) 879-6833*

In 1994, this event was held during August at the Glen Eden Sun Club. There were nudists from all over the country. Call to find out when and where their next event is.

## The Ball Bizarre

*(213) 463-7868*

An annual and unusual ball usually held somewhere in Los Angeles in the summer. There are fashion shows, contests and plenty of other entertainment. The fetish crowd is out in full force here. The most recent ball attracted around 1000 wildly dressed fetish freaks and their friends. The last ball cost $15.00. Call for more details.

## Couples Lifestyles Organization

*2641 W. LaPalma Ave. Suite A Anaheim, CA 92801-2602*
*(714) 821-9953*

A springtime convention of sexuality workshops, discussions, couples dances and the Couple Costume Ball. It's a spring warmup for the Lifestyles Convention.

## Dressed To Thrill Versatile Fashions

*Box 1051, Tustin, CA 92681*
*(714) 538-0257*

Sponsored by the fetish clothing store, Versatile Fashions, this event was held for the first time in May, 1994, in Long Beach. It should become an annual event. It was a very well organized event with some great guests and fashions.

## F.O.X.E.

### (Fans of X-Rated Entertainment) Awards

*8231 DeLongpre Ave., Suite #1, West Hollywood, CA 90046*
*(213) 650-7121*

This is an annual awards show for adult videos and movies. It's basically the "People's Choice Awards" for the porno business. Come out and see your favorite adult actors and actresses. It's a fun and fascinating event where you get to mingle with your favorite stars. For you X-rated fans – this show's for you!!

## Lifestyles Convention

*2641 W. LaPalma Ave., Suite A, Anaheim, CA 92801-2602*
*(714) 821-9953*

This is the major event of the year for swingers. There are workshops, discussion groups, exhibits, socials and of course, the famous Erotic Masquerade Ball. Couples from all over the world come to this special event. Sometimes it is held in Las Vegas, sometimes in San Diego and sometimes in Los Angeles. For 1995, it will be held in San Diego in the late summer.

## AVN (Adult Video News) Awards

*8599 Venice Blvd., Suite J, Los Angeles, CA 90034*
*(310) 842-7450*

A yearly event sponsored by AVN. There's music, comedy, dancing girls, and you can meet the stars. Held in Las Vegas last year. Tickets are around $100. Proceeds from the event go to several charities including The Free Speech Coalition, AIDS Project L.A. and others.

## AVN Presents Deep Inside
## The Adult Video Industry

*8599 Venice Blvd., Suite J, Los Angeles, CA 90034*
*(310) 842-7450*

A one day seminar where you can interact with some of the hottest stars in the industry. The event was held in December last year. I'm not sure if they are sponsoring another one, but it's worth a call to find out.

## Miss Exotic World
## Exotic World Burlesque Museum

*29053 Wild Rd., Helendale, CA 92342*
*(619) 243-5261*

Come see who will be crowned Miss Exotic World. Also, enjoy the "Reunion of the Diamonds of Burlesque." Come see the strippers of yesteryear.

### Naked City L.A.

*P.O. Box 2000, Homeland, CA 92548-2000*
*(909) 926-2264*

This is a swingers' nudist resort which hosts several contests throughout the year. Ms. Nude America, Ms. Nude Hollywood and many more sex-citing contests. Traditional nudists will probably feel somewhat out of place here.

### Tattoo Mania's Annual Inkslippers Ball

*P.O. Box 2208, Redondo Beach, CA 90278*
*(800) 824-8046*

The special event of the year for all you body art aficionados. If you have, want, like or want to see tattoos, this is the event for you.

### Topless Dancer
### World Championships

*Five Star Entertainment Inc.*
*(800) 695-5745*

It's only a short flight from Los Angeles to Las Vegas to see the best topless dancers in the world strut and shake their stuff. Held at the Stardust Hotel.

© 1995 DR TUPPER

# Jaded Jewelry

> . . . a woman is always buying something.
> — *Ovid (Roman poet)*

### Club Fantasy

*c/o Barbara, 11012 Ventura Blvd., Suite #210, Studio City, CA 91604*

Want some pretty jewelry to adorn your nipples? They have nipple jewelry for any size nipples. No piercing. Each piece sells for about $17.

### Judy Kirk Design

*13428 Maxella Ave., Suite 314, Marina Del Rey, CA 90292*

She designs and creates jewelry for your clitoris. Don't pierce it, clip it on!! And if it gets in the way . . . it's easy to unclip!! Also, new from Judy is the Titti-Twinkler. Send $5 for catalog and get $5 credit towards purchase.

### The Good Art Company

*218 Pier Ave., Santa Monica*
*(310) 452-7602*

This is one of the largest manufacturers of body jewelry in the world. You can visit their showroom or order by mail. They have everything you can imagine for every imaginable part of your body. For mail order catalog send $1 to P.O. Box 5605, Santa Monica, CA 90409.

### Mild to Wild

*P.O. Box 271, San Luis Rey, CA 92068*
*(619) 941-7552*

Located in northern San Diego County, they offer a variety of adult jewelry in silver, gold and vermeil. As the name says . . . from mild to wild. They do custom designs and offer wholesale and retail.

# Tantalizing Toys

> . . . it's been so long since I made love I can't even
> remember who gets tied up.
> — *Joan Rivers*

Here are a few places to buy those adult toys through the mail. We know you use them, we know you want them . . . so order them!!

## B & D Enterprises

*P.O. Box 107, Westminster, CA 92683*

They sell dildos, vibrators and other toys. Also sell swing magazines for you wild swingers out there.

## KIKS

*11684 Ventura Blvd. #783, Studio City, CA 91607*

They offer vibrators, toys, novelties, condoms, lotions, lubricants and much more. Write for more details.

## B & D Vending & Distributing

*3450 W. Orange Ave. #1806, Anaheim, CA 92804*

They sell "The Zapper," an erotic toy that will send mini shock waves through you or your partner. It's battery-operated, so you can keep it in your purse. I'm not sure if I want zaps of current going through my erogenous zones . . . but you may.

## Knick Knacks 'N More

*2060 Emery Avenue, Suite 205, La Habra, CA 90631*

A mail order company with lingerie, toys, gifts and more.

## MOR Enterprises, Inc.

*Post Office Box 1007, Malibu, CA 90265*
*(310) 456-9353*

Creator of sexual aids including an electrically powered male genital stimulation device. It's quite expensive, but it is state of the art.

*Photo by F.M. Philips*

## Oasis Latex

*3202 Factory Drive, Pomona, CA 91768*
*(909) 595-5423*

Makers of latex products including the *Oradam*, a facial dam that fits over your head, providing a barrier between you and any bodily fluids.

## Doc Johnson Products

*Post Office Box 9908, North Hollywood, CA 91609*

Makers of a variety of toys, sex devices and novelties. Very popular brand of sex toys sold in all the stores.

## Pleasure Products

*Post Office Box 5973-379, Sherman Oaks, CA 91413*

Mail order company that sells toys, lubricants, condoms, novelties, etc., etc., etc.

## Centurian-Spartacus Distributors

*13331 Garden Grove Blvd., Suite H,*
*Garden Grove, CA 92643*
*(714) 971-9877*

A major distributor of fetish supplies. They sell only to retailers, but you can find their products all over. One place to find a full line of their stuff is at Fantasy Lingerie in Fountain Valley. They will send out various catalogs for a price ranging from $4 -$22.

## Discount Dolls

*P.O. Box 32, North Hollywood, CA 91603*

OK guys, here's your chance to buy those blow up dolls you always wanted at discount prices. They offer a few models that and are life-like in every detail. If you want a love doll that will obey your every command and submit to your kinkiest desires, this may be the place for you. Write for more details and current prices.

## Secret Pleasures

*1800 So. Robertson Blvd., Suite 69, Los Angeles, CA 90035*

A mail order company selling toys, lingerie, lotions, etc.

# Let's Hear It for the
# Lawyers

**Q:** *Why are lawyers like enemas?*

**A:** *You hate them before you need them. When you need them, you still hate them.*

If you've been arrested for soliciting a prostitute or for any other sexual misconduct offense, you will need an experienced lawyer. You will need someone familiar with the law as it relates to sexual matters. I know that lawyers are easy targets for jokes and humorous gags, but a good lawyer just may be the difference between jail and freedom.

### Chase & Associates

*(800) 459-2500*

This team of lawyers is experienced in a variety of sexual misconduct cases including rape, prostitution, solicitation of prostitution, pimping and pandering, indecent exposure, and lewd and lascivious acts. If you are in trouble with the law because of your overactive hormones or if you feel you have been wronged in a sexual misconduct matter, give this group of attorneys a call.

# Raunchy Radio

### The Howard Stern Show

*KLSX-FM 97.1, 6 to 10 am.*

If you like your radio raunchy and a bit rowdy with a comic edge, listen to the Howard Stern Show. He certainly doesn't need me to publicize his show as it has a tremendously large and loyal following from coast to coast. He broadcasts from New York and is syndicated all over the country. He always says whatever is on his mind, consequently, he has amassed quite a sum of fines from the FCC. Damn the FCC and listen to Howard!!

# Private Mail Boxes

If you are thinking of placing an advertisement or answering an ad in a swingers' or singles' publication, you may need a mail box. You may be answering ads behind your lover's back or you may be looking for an extra playmate as a surprise for him or her, and discretion is an important consideration. You certainly don't want to give out your home address, and the post office may be inconvenient. There are scores of mail box places in the greater Los Angeles area where you can receive mail discreetly. The ones listed here offer very discreet and private service and would be perfect for your needs.

### Blix Mail & Answering Service

*11325 Blix, North Hollywood, CA 91602*
*(818) 762-2082 or (213) 877-3124*

They run advertisements in swingers' papers and specialize in the mail needs of swingers. They offer mail box rentals, answering service, expert ad analysis and writing. They will also take a free nude photo of you if you need one in your advertisement.

### The Mail Box Place

*3450 W. Orange Ave., Anaheim, CA 92804*
*(714) 827-4881*

They offer mail box rentals, 24-hour access, voice mail and more. They are private, discreet and confidential.

# Carnal Cakes

Looking for some erotic edibles and phallic pastries? . . . check out the following places.

### Cake And Art

*8709 Santa Monica Blvd.*
*(310) 657-8694*

### Exotic Cakes

*8490 Santa Monica Blvd.*
*(310) 273-0237*

# Maids in the Buff

If you would like to employ nude maid service for your house or business or would like some naked bar and party workers, the following place can help you out. They have gay, straight, male and female workers. So sit back, open a beer and watch the maid clean your kitchen . . . in the nude!!

### Maid In LA

*(310) 202-6469*

# Pubic Hair Salon

## Pubic Hair Salon

*8344 Beverly Boulevard*
*(213) 656-0913*

My pubic hair is not public, but if you want just that right style, that certain look, that specific sexy something . . . but you just can't do a damn thing with your hair . . . your hair down there. Here's the place to go. They will cut, shave, bleach or straighten your pubic hair and get you ready for that very special date.

# Penis Power!!

> . . . generally speaking, it is in love as it is in war, where the
> longest weapon carries it.
> — *John Leland (Fanny Hill)*

We're not going to answer that age-old question for you: "Is bigger better?" I suppose it's a matter of personal choice. Whatever gets you through the night! But, for the owner of the magic wand, it's always been, "make the most of what you were given." Until now, that is.

In this day of modern miracles and advanced technology, great minds have developed methods and surgery that will lengthen and thicken your penis. Now, any guy can become the new John Holmes! Well, maybe. I'll leave that for you to find out. Since the fear of some mad doctor cutting into my penis outweighs the desire for a "monster penis," and since I already have a monumental phallus, (I hope my girlfriend doesn't laugh too hard when she reads this!), I am leaving any further research on the following procedures to the readers.

Hmmm, I wonder if I can get mine shortened a bit. If you have any testimonials that you would like included in the next edition of this book, send us your penis enlargement story.

The following is merely a list of a few of the places that offer some sort of penis enlargement, and is not a recommendation of the procedure or of those performing the procedure. Be careful about who handles your prized possession and find out **ALL** the details before undergoing any operation or procedure.

## The Center For Men

*9201 Sunset Blvd., Los Angeles, CA 90069*
*(800) 347-1999*

You can get a new penis at The Clinic For Male Cosmetic & Sexual-Medical Needs. Well, not exactly a new penis, but they do offer "penile expansion." It's a confidential procedure done on an outpatient basis. It is a surgical procedure and requires some time for recovery. They take Master Card and Visa and also offer financing. (I wonder how they handle repossessions?) Call for more information.

## Best Care Medical Clinic

*9100 Wilshire Blvd., #605E, Beverly Hills, CA 90210*
*(310) 858-5090 (800) 773-3771*

They offer penile enlargement on an outpatient basis, performed by board-certified urologists. They can make it longer or thicker or both. If you want to be the biggest stud in town . . . call for more information.

## Dr. Saks

*(310) 547-5278*

Dr. Saks has specialized in liposuction for both men and women and now also offers penile enlargement. He has offices in San Pedro or Redondo Beach. Also offers laser removal of tattoos, nose, eye and face lifts, and more.

## Dr. Rodney Brown

*(310) 288-1918*

Has all the newest techniques and is known as a worldwide pioneer in penis enlargement surgery. I wonder, does he get introduced at parties as "the penis pioneer?"

# The Male Clinic

*P.O. Box 2218, Beverly Hills, CA 90213*
*(800) 787-4366 (SURGEON)*

More penis enlargement specialists. Find out if bigger is better!

# Success Motivation & Healing Institute

*15840 Ventura Blvd., Suite 318, Encino, CA 91436*
*(818) 503-3303*

This is the "Iron Man Personal Workout" – a weight training system for your most prized possession. Gives new meaning to "pumping iron." Supposedly, this system will add length and strength to your penis. There are no pumps, no artificial extensions, and no surgery. Just weights!! If you're interested, you can send $3 for more information.

# Dr. Joel Kaplan

*2336 Market Street, Suite #1, San Francisco, CA 94114*
*(415) 739-5847 or (800) 987-7867*

Dr. Kaplan offers a vacuum pump system for penis enlargement. If you believe that these pumps work, Dr. Kaplan's pump is one of the best on the market. It's not a cheap toy, but a scientifically engineered device. He also offers nipple enlargement pumps. If you're interested, write or call for more detailed information.

# MIDN

*Post Office Box 27833, Santa Ana, CA 92799*

This company advertised in a local gay paper offering facts about penis enlargement. If you sent $5, you receive confidential and detailed information. If I were you, I would write first without sending a dime. May be worth your while if they can help you measure up!!

# Global International, Inc.

*Post Office Box 662, Garden Grove, CA 92642*

This company doesn't offer a way to make your penis larger, but they do claim to have something that will increase your sexual vitality, stamina, endurance, energy and muscle tone. It's called *Prolong SX* and it costs $29.95 per bottle.

## Added Dimensions Publishing

- *Box 208, 2000 W. Magnolia, Burbank, CA 91506*
- *100 S. Sunrise Way, Suite 484, Palm Springs, CA 92263*

They publish Penis Power Quarterly. It has the latest news on penis and scrotal enlargement, erection enhancement, vacuum pumps, aphrodisiacs and more. Subscribe now if you want to know everything there is to know about penis power. Annual subscription is $19.95.

## The Hung Jury

*P.O. Box 417, Los Angeles, CA 90078*

No, we're not talking about the pathetic state of our justice system . . . this is a group for well-hung men and the women who love them. If this is for you, check it out!

# And for those Vast Vaginas . . .

## David Matlock, M.D.

*436 N. Bedford Dr., Beverly Hills, CA 90210*
*(310) 859-9052*

Here's a doctor who specializes in laser vaginal reconstruction . . . that's "tightening the vagina" in medicalspeak. The operation is done on an outpatient basis and costs anywhere from $1,800 to $3,000. It's sort of like a tummy tuck – but for a different part of the anatomy!

# Tantalizing Tours

## The Player's Club

*8721 Santa Monica Blvd., #35, West Hollywood, CA 90069*
*(310) 289-0320*

This company offers sex tours to exotic Thailand. They offer a complete tour package; air fare, land transportation, luxury hotel accommodations, meals, drinks and more. The complete packages start at $3,950. They show you where all the action is; where to see sex shows, get a fabulous Thai massage from an exotic Thai beauty, and have all the hot steamy sex you want.

It's a non-stop tour of the sex industry in Thailand, taking you to the high-quality spots while avoiding the rip-off places. The tours take you to Bangkok and Pattaya, the two hottest spots in Thailand. It sounds like a very hot tour. Call or write for more information. And if you book a reservation, don't forget to bring along plenty of rubbers. Though the Thai government has a difficult time admitting it, AIDS does exist in Thailand.

# Photography

## Phantasy Photos

> . . . a picture is worth a thousand words.
> — *Famous quotation*

You just took that special photo of your special lover . . . or someone just took that special action shot of you and your special lover . . . or you just took a nasty naked snapshot of yourself in the mirror, and you don't know where to take that roll of film for uncensored processing. Well, the following places will take your film and develop all those clever carnal

shots and they won't even sell the negatives on the side (though we can't promise that they won't point and laugh!). Happy photography . . . and send any extra hot shots of your wife or girlfriend to me care of the publisher. I'd be happy to check them out and critique your photographic talents.

## 1 Hour Photo Plus

*7962 Knott Ave., Buena Park, CA 90620*
*(714) 523-5470*

They offer discreet one-hour photo processing. They also offer all the usual reprints, enlargement and they will transfer your movies, slides and prints to video (hmmmm, enlargements).

## FilmeXpert

*Post Office Box 46667, Los Angeles, CA 90046*

Custom photo finishing for all your erotic snapshots. They do color, black & white, enlargements and video duplication and transfer. Write for price information.

## T.C.E.

*18107 Sherman Way, #108, Reseda, CA 91335*

A mail order place that will print your nasty shots. Fast and discreet. 24 exposures cost $14.00 and 36 exposures cost $19.00. Send for more information.

## Image Experts

- *7095 Hollywood Blvd.*
  *(213) 874-0624*

- *11207 National Blvd., West Los Angeles*
  *(310) 473-1202*

They will discreetly process your sexual shenanigans expertly.

## Quicksilver Photo

*10048 Rosecrans Avenue, Bellflower, CA 90706*

Mail order for color and B & W film processing.

## Bill & Debbie Majors Enterprises

*Post Office Box 92889, Long Beach, CA 90809*
*(310) 631-1600.*

They offer reasonably priced processing, enlargements and reprints. Call or write for more information.

## J. Wink Pleck

*7011 Warner Avenue, Suite L-170,*
*Huntington Beach, CA 92647*

This is where all the conservative Orange County Republicans get their confidential B & W film processed.

## Playtime Kopies

*211 S. State College, Suite 317, Anaheim, CA 92806*
*(714) 778-6126*

They offer a unique service for you uninhibited people. They will make a calendar from your nude photos. A twelve month calendar is $14.95 and a twenty-four month calendar is only $19.95.

# Girls Who Sell Their
# Nasty Photos

There are many girls around who will sell you their nasty or nude photos for a price. Look in men's magazines or swingers' periodicals for their advertisements or personal ads. There are also a few girls in our chapter on Mail Order Videos, who along with selling videos, also offer still photos.

The following is a list of a few that were advertising at the time this book went to print.

## Golden California Girls

*Post Office Box 5633, Pasadena, CA 91117*

Sells videos and photo sets of sexy girls.

*Photo by F.M. Philips*

## Starfire

*Post Office Box 5363, Sherman Oaks, CA 91403*

Sells photos, slides and tapes of sexy girls. Also has nudes from 50s, 60s and 70s.

## Sandy's Modeling

*P.O. Box 3892, Thousand Oaks, CA 91360*

Many different male or female models to choose from. Explicit or nude or custom. Photo and video catalog is $4.

## D.T.

*19425-B Soledad Canyon, #152,*
*Canyon Country, CA 91351*

She offers "pictures of me naked in public". Ten 4x6 photos are $20 and twenty-five sell for $40.

## Vicky

*1626 N. Wilcox Ave., Suite 591, Hollywood, CA 90028*

She is a busty lady who sells photos. Color sample $1.

# Phantasy Photography

If you are interested in photography, you may want to pick up the following magazines. They are published by the same company and are aimed at amateur photographers interested in nude, lingerie and glamour photography. You can find ads from models, listings of major photo shoots, listings of photography groups, articles, personal stories, and much more.

If you're looking for some pretty models to focus on, you may find what you're looking for in the following periodicals. You can find these fine publications at various newsstands throughout the area, or call to order your subscriptions.

I have a friend who goes to many of these photo shoots around Southern California. Through his devotion to nude and glamour photography he has met dozens of sexy models. And the best part is - he has dated a few of them. Hey, it could happen to you. Get out that camera, unfold your, er, tripod, and focus on those models!

## Western Photographer
## Glamour Photographer

*Bearwithme Productions, Inc.,*
*2031 Via Burton Unit C,*
*Anaheim, CA 92806-1202*
*(714) 535-1166;*
*Fax (714) 535-7546*

*Western Photographer Magazine* comes out monthly and *Glamour Photographer Magazine* comes out on a semi-regular basis. They are both edited by Bear (that his complete name), a friend of the publisher who has use Bear's photographic talent many times in many of his publications. Bear looks like Smokey the Bear personified.

# Phantasy Photographic Models

The following are studios which offer models for your private use and individual girls who allow you to practice your nude or glamour photography technique. These are not call girls or escort operations . . . just models and studios for all you amateur photographers out there. So, strap that big lens on and shoot!

## Golden California Girls

*P.O. Box 5633, Pasadena, CA 91117*
*(818) 351-5239*

They offer professional lighting, sets and professional models. Prices start at $55. Call for more details.

## Kiser Models

*37348 Laramie St., Palmdale, CA 93552*
*(805) 274-9432*

It's a modeling agency and a fully-equipped rental studio.

## Alejandro Photo Studio

*13737 Inglewood Ave., Hawthorne, CA 90250*
*(310) 978-1331*

They have many glamourous models available and offer good rates and a convenient location.

## Miad Productions

*3220 S. Susan St., Santa Ana, CA 92704*
*(714) 549-4101*

They offer studio figure shoots at various times. The cost is around $50. Call for more details. They also sell photos of their young nude or semi-nude models.

## Foto Forge

*403 C Gardena Blvd.*
*(310) 327-9850*

An affordable members-only studio where you can improve and practice your photographic skills. Call for membership information.

### Photo Image Club

*P.O. Box 2714, Huntington Beach, CA 92647*
*(714) 557-1588 or (310) 836-4463*

This is not a studio or a group of models, but a club for amateur photographers. They have many shoots and gatherings. Call for information and prices.

# Photographers

The following is a list of a few of the area photographers who create erotic images and would properly be called artists. Some of them exhibited art at the erotic art show at the Lifestyles Convention last year.

### Imagers

*940 E. 2nd Street, Studio, 12, Los Angeles, CA 90012*
*(213) 625-0753*

Photographers: Jim Tobak and Ace Dawson Tobak

### Anthony Yazzolino

*12113 Emelita Street, North Hollywood, CA 91607*
*(818) 508-8963*

### Jack Messick

*105 Copperwood, Suite J, Oceanside, CA 92054*
*(619) 434-1182*

A photographer who works out of the North County area of San Diego. He works with many Los Angeles area models and is available to work on a wide variety of subjects, especially in portfolios. Many of the outstanding photos in this book were taken by Jack — professional, experienced and excellent.

### Image King

*(619) 721-1459*

Another photographer in the North County area of San Diego, Catherine will take those erotic photos of you. Males, females or couples. She will shoot anything legal. Be a star! Professional and discreet.

# Stimulating Stationery

## No! No! Greetings

*P.O. Box 221, Norco, CA 91760 — (714) 734-0594*

They offer high-quality adult greeting cards . . . romantic, risque and X-rated, with a variety of drawings and sayings. Write for more information or send $2 for their catalog.

# Provocative Piercing

. . . he promised me earrings, but he only pierced my ears.
— *Arabian saying*

## Gauntlet

*Santa Monica Blvd. & Huntley Drive — (310) 657-6677*

They offer all sorts of provocative body piercing. It's $25 for the first hole, $20 for the second and $15 for the third. Their jewelry starts at $30.

## Earring Collection

*7353 Melrose Ave. — (213) 653-6358*

They offer body piercing by appointment or walk-in. They also have earrings from all over the world. Open 11 am to 7 pm (12-5 on Sunday).

# You Be the Director

## D.O.M. Corporation

*Box 9786, Marina Del Rey, CA 90295*

Tell them what you want: you want a beautiful girl talking to you while she touches herself, you want people having sex, you want a threesome? You write the script and they will do the filming just for you. They also have access to your favorite X-rated film stars. Imagine your favorite video vixen talking to you and doing exactly what you want . . . stop imagining and send for more information.

*Photo by F.M. Philips*

# Amazing Audio

### Ecstasy Audio

*P.O. Box 2617,*
*Gardena, CA 90247*

Heather sells 45-minute audio cassettes that are very hot. Her tapes; *The Adventures of Heather,* Volume I, II, or III, sell for $21.65 each. I haven't heard them . . . but if you do, let me know how hot they are. Of course, you could always send me a sample, too!

### Bill & Debbie Majors Enterprises

*P.O. Box 92889,*
*Long Beach, CA 90809-2889*

They sell audio cassettes for fetish freaks. Lots of spankings and whippings. Tapes cost around $15.

# Torrid Tattoos

## Sunset Strip Tattoo

*8418 W. Sunset Blvd.*
*(213) 650-6530*

Located in the heart of the Sunset Strip, tattoos start at $25. They have all types of designs and creations. Open 10 am to midnight.

## Purple Panther Designs

*7560 W. Sunset Blvd.*
*(213) 882-8165*

Tattoos start at $40 with any type of custom design. Open noon to midnight. Look for the purple neon signs.

## Hollywood Tattoo

*6317 Hollywood Blvd., Hollywood*
*(213) 464-9938*

Tattoos start at $15 and they do custom designs.

## Easyriders

*7450 Melrose*
*(213) 658-8817*

Tattoos start at $40 and they specialize in custom work. Open 11 to 9.

## L.A. Tattoo

*6700 Hollywood Blvd.*
*(213) 463-3919*

Tattoos start at $40, and they will do anything you want. Open 12 to 12.

## Dr. John's Tattoo American

*6636 Lankershim Blvd., North Hollywood*
*(818) 764-7775*

Prices start at $50 and their custom work starts at $200. They're open 10 to 10.

### Melrose Tattoo

*7661 1/2 Melrose*
*(213) 655-4345*

Located upstairs, they have many designs to choose from, or they'll do custom work.

### Joker's Wild Tattoo Studio

*1605 Pacific Coast Hwy., Harbor City*
*(310) 534-4532*

Open every day 2 pm to 10 pm except Tuesday. You can choose from a set design or they do custom work.

### Body Shop Tattoo

*216 1/2 Broadway, Glendale*
*(818) 956-8288*

Their motto is "your design or mine?"

# and one more . . .

### *Tattoo Directory*

*P.O. Box 15893, Newport Beach, CA 92659*
*(714) 836-0572*

They publish a directory of tattoo artists located all across the country. If you are into body art . . . this is a great publication.

© 1995 DR TUPPER

# Passionate Products

## D.O.M. Corporation

*Box 9786, Marina Del Rey, CA 90295*

Company owned by a Bill Wilson, sells many videos, rubber goods, magazines and much more. They offer phone sex and customized videos. You tell them what you want . . . they'll film it for you. Bill has access to most of your favorite X-rated stars in case you want them in your custom video. Write for their 32-page color catalog.

## Kiss

*P.O. Box 789, Downey, CA 90241*
*(310) 923-8960*

They sell products designed to enhance loving relationships and to add a little spice in your sex life. They have a variety of romantic games and gifts.

# Bawdy Books

> . . . I'm going to introduce a resolution to have the Postmaster General stop reading dirty books and deliver the mail.
> — *Gail McGee*

### *The Porn Star Handbook*

*Bearly Decent Enterprises, 8033 Sunset Blvd., #851, Los Angeles, CA 90046*

Also titled; Breaking Into XXX or Everything You Always Wanted To Know About The X-Rated Industry. It is written by Bill Margold and gives all you potential studs the inside tips on becoming a porno star. It's from someone who has done it all in the business. It's $15 and worth it for potential studs!

## Infonet Publications

*Post Office Box 91, Topanga, CA 90290*
*(310) 572-4125*

Sells a variety of adult how-to-guides and other books.

## *Secrets of Attracting Beautiful Women*

*Wynning Publications, Post Office Box 570141, Tarzana, CA 91357*

Miracles do happen. Maybe this book will work for you.

## *Adult Coupon Book*

*Omnific, Post Office Box 459, San Dimas, CA 91773*

Over $900 in adult coupons on toys, books, videos and more. Send $14.95 + $2.00 shipping.

## *Cathouse Guide Royal*

*Post Office Box 99, Woodland Hills, CA 91365*

For $10 you will receive a 48-page book detailing the Nevada brothels. With prices and ratings! Write for information before sending your cash.

## *Robert Rimmer's X-Rated Video Tape Guide*

*P.O. Box 18709, Los Angeles, CA 90007*
*(800) 397-5114*

It has over 600 pages and over 300 reviews of professional and amateur videos.

## *Nude Models Directory*

*Model Media, 9852 W. Katella Ave., #204,*
*Anaheim, CA 92804*

This is a directory of models who pose for photos in person or send photos by mail.

## *International Directory of Swing Clubs & Publications*

*NASCA, P.O. Box 7128, Buena Park, CA 90622*

Has international information for swingers. Cost is $10.

# Other Oddities

> . . . how did sex come to be thought of as
> dirty in the first place? God must
> have been a Republican.
> — *Will Durst*

## Motel Meetings

### Movieland Motel

*19335 Ventura Blvd., Tarzana*
*(818) 344-5886*

### Cinema Motel

*6242 Sepulveda Blvd., Van Nuys*
*(818) 786-1719*

Two motels with three channels of X-rated movies in the privacy of your room. For a sexy rendezvous, check these places out!

### Royal Roman Motel

*1504 First St., Santa Ana*
*(714) 547-8411*

They have regular rooms, rooms with X-rated movies. and rooms with jacuzzis. Overnight rates range from $35 - $65. They also have a 9 - 5 day rate that ranges from $30 -$50.

## Sensuous Spa Sessions

### SPLASH

*10932 Santa Monica Blvd. — (310) 479-4657*

You can rent private jacuzzi suites with shower, steam or sauna. They are open 7 days, 10 am to midnight. It's $30 per hour for two people and $20 for singles.

## SPLASH

*8054 West Third Street*
*(213) 653-4410*

This location also has some luxurious jacuzzi suites. You can get waterfalls, fireplaces, eucalyptus steam, video and more. Rates begin at $30 for couples and range up to $100. Open 11:30 am to midnight.

## Waxing by Mistress Gloria

*14021 Ventura Blvd., Sherman Oaks*
*(818) 907-1196*

Tired of looking like a truck driver in drag?? Girl! get your unwanted hair removed. I know of a lot of guys who wish they had more.

# Getting It Up on High

## The Mile-High Club

*Kern Charter Service*
*(805) 765-5744*

If you want to become a member of the Mile-High Club, this charter company can help you out. They supply the pilot, the plane and the champagne. You get a willing partner. Couples or groups welcome. You can go to them or they can take off from an airport near you.

# Get Paid to Get Off

## National Research Group

*Post Office Box 266, Mendocino, CA 95460*
*In L.A. call: (213) 960-7782*

They publish a booklet for those interested in being paid sperm donors. There are many doctors, clinics and facilities located in the greater Los Angeles area. Write for more information.

# Awesome Advertising

## Worldwide Adcorp. Inc.

*P.O. Box 8120, Palm Springs, CA 92263*
*(619) 322-5092*

An advertising agency that specializes in classified and display advertising for the 800, 900 and mail order adult entertainment industry. For those of you running an adult business, check them out.

# Eternal Beauty

## Contours By Carlson

*P.O. Box 5057, Beverly Hills, CA 90209*
*(310) 276-3622*

Julie Carlson is a unique artist who creates body contours . . . basically body casting sculptures. You or your mate or both can have body casts made for gifts or to preserve that youthful body you won't have forever. The session usually takes about an hour and is relaxing, comfortable and fun.

# Slide into Bed

## Sportsheets International Inc.

*P.O. Box 7800, Huntington Beach, CA 92646*
*(714) 962-8946 (800) 484-9954*

An innovative product that can help increase your fun in the bedroom. The sportsheets product includes 4 sportcuffs, 4 anchor pads and 1 fitted bed cover. You use it for a little bondage fun or whatever your heart desires. The cuffs are made of nylon with a velcro closure, and they are completely adjustable. The sportsheet really ads some excitement to your love life . . . take it from the voice of experience.

# Strange Gifts for Strange People

## Falcon Enterprises

*P.O. Box 361118 Los Angeles, CA 90036-9517*

They have a variety of collector's items such as a custom-made patent leather S & M diary. T-shirts and more available. Write for information.

## Raffaelli 3-D Classics

*190 West Kern St., McFarland, CA 93250*

They offer erotic art sets that the master artist Raffaelli has created from explicit photographic sessions with his naked models. For a catalog, send $3.

# It's Your Move

## Passion Play

*P.O. Box 1027, Union City, CA 94587-1027*
*(800) 414-7529*

An adult board game that creates all sorts of interesting situations. Can create that special mood. For adults only!! I was part of three couples playing this game once . . . and after an hour or so of playing everyone was naked and playing other adult games!! They also have a special "gay" game.

# Let Them Do It

## Custom Party Planning

*716 N. Ventura Road #285, Oxnard, CA 93030*
*(805) 486-0971*

They will cater your next event from the intimate to the elegant.

# Feel the Spirit

In the "good-ol-days" sex used to be a very important part of the religious experience. The male phallus used to be worshipped by everyone . . . I know I still worship mine. If you want to put sex back into the spirit, check out —

## The Church of the Most High Goddess

*Post Office Box 1704, Canyon Country, CA 91351*

Is it a church? Is it a cult? I don't really know. They preach the religion of the goddess, which they claim to be a sex-positive religion. They preach the positive and beautiful about sex . . . and I think we can all agree on that! The leader (priestess?) of this religion is Sabrina Aset who gives lectures, does television shows and sends out literature to educate the public.

They are currently engaged in action to have prostitution laws repealed. And they will certainly appreciate your donations to further their cause. Write for more information about what they do and how you can be involved.

© 1995 DR Tupper

Fighting For Your Freedom          *Photo by Adult Video Association*

# CHAPTER NINETEEN

# Censorship

> . . . Almost no legitimate researcher now gives credence to the notion that nonviolent sexual material causes anything but sticky paper.
>
> — *Marcia Palley*

**I**'m quite certain there are many people out there who would love to censor this book. *Lust Angeles* certainly doesn't appeal to everyone's tastes. I suppose, there are many that it offends. And of those whom it offends, many would like to pull it off the shelves and throw it into a raging fire.

Of course, I don't mind if you throw it into a fire and reduce it to ashes, as long as you buy it first! Once you purchase it and put money in my pockets . . . you can do whatever you want with it: read it, utilize the material, use it as toilet paper, whatever!

If you don't want to read this book . . . don't buy it (too late, you already bought it). If you don't want to patronize stores that sell it . . . don't! That's not censorship, that's personal choice.

Censorship is when the government or any government-sponsored group removes material from open access; when government authority denies my right to write this book or a bookseller's right to sell this book; when government bows to pressure from special interest groups to censor books, movies or art.

In the dictionary meaning of the word, to censor is "to examine in order to suppress or delete anything considered objectionable." The word "censor" originated in ancient Rome. Censors were government-appointed officials who took the census and supervised public morals. We should all be opposed to any government intervention in ideas, whether it be by the written word, picture, sound or electronic form.

Though at times it seems as if the religious right and moral do-gooders have become the majority in this country it isn't necessarily so. A July 1990 *Newsweek* poll showed that 75% of felt that the rights of adults to determine what they may see and hear was more important than society having laws to prohibit material that may be offensive to some.

Another poll showed that 62% of Americans thought that people have the right to view whatever type of movie they desire. Other polls done in the last ten years also show this to be true. Many are concerned about the decay of ethics, the lack of responsibility and the increase in crime in our society . . . but they do not feel that censorship is the answer.

# Remember the First Amendment????

"Congress shall make no law respecting an establishment of religion, or prohibiting the free exercise thereof; or abridging the freedom of speech, or of the press; or the right of people peacefully to assemble, and to petition the Government for a redress of grievances."

This Amendment wasn't created to protect speech that is popular . . . it was created to protect speech and activities that are unpopular (and pornography and the commercial sex industry may possibly be considered unpopular activities . . . though sales figures may dispute this).

When a government limits free speech . . . no matter how unpopular or objectionable . . . all our other liberties tend to disintegrate like dust in the wind. Perhaps that's why it is the **"First"** Amendment.

Should the First Amendment protect our right to create and read or view pornography? There are many out there in the Land of Liberty who say no. In fact, the Supreme Court has said no on many occasions. Obscenity and sex receive separate and very unequal treatment under the First Amendment. In a landmark 1957 case, *Roth vs. United States*, a majority of the judges ruled that an obscenity exception does exist, and obscenity is defined as speech about sex that is "utterly without redeeming social importance."

The next landmark case was *Miller v. California (1973)*, which more or less defined obscenity as material that "lacked serious literary, artistic, political or scientific value." This made the meaning of obscenity much broader and created more room for prosecutions . . . and censorship!! According to our great legal system, pornography is not covered as free speech by the First Amendment!

# What Harm Pornography?

> Censorship, like charity, should begin at home; but unlike charity it should end there . . .
> — *Clare Booth Luce*

There are numerous social science studies that have concluded that pornography does not increase crime or intensify levels of rage toward women. The landmark *1968 President's Commission on Obscenity and Pornography* took over two years, a massive budget and thousands of surveys and laboratory studies to reach the conclusion that explicit sexual material does not play a significant role in the causation of criminal behavior in adults or youths.

Of course, the infamous Meese Commission, which operated during the Reagan administration, reached different conclusions. But there were many who worked for the Meese Commission who found no evidence to support the correlation between obscenity and criminal activity; their conclusions were conveniently ignored.

In 1985, the Institute of Criminal Science, University of Copenhagen, reported that in European countries where restrictions on sexually explicit material have been eased or erased, incidence of violent sex crimes has remained constant or decreased. British and Canadian commissions on pornography have also found no evidence that there is a link between watching *Debbie Does Dallas* and sex crimes. Many other studies by doctors and social science researchers have reached the same conclusions: there is no link between pornography and criminal behavior or violence toward women.

One interesting 1990 study by Dr. Larry Baron (Yale University) found a positive correlation between sales of sexually explicit material and high gender equality. Now that one may shake up a few feminists who believe all pornography degrades women and gives men the impression that all women are merely subservient sex slaves.

Men don't rape because they read or view pornography. Rage and hatred toward women existed long before pornography. If a society wants to reduce the incidence of rape it must deal with high levels of misogyny in this country and many others and solve the psychological and social conditions that cause men to feel rage toward women.

Violence toward women and rape should stop!! Rapists are serious criminals and should be put away for a long time. Women should be treated equally and fairly under the law and in the workplace. These are issues vital to our continuation as a democratic and free society . . . but they are not issues directly related to pornography as some feminists believe.

# What Harm Censorship?

We should all be concerned with censorship . . . whether we like pornography or not. Censorship has a way of creeping into the lives of everyone. How would you feel if the following books were banned: *1984, Of Mice And Men, Gone With The Wind, The Catcher in The Rye, The Diary of Anne Frank, One Flew Over The Cuckoo's Nest,* and *The Adventures of Huckleberry Finn?*

Well, these classics of literature have all been banned at one time or another. And not in the distant past . . . right here in the 1990's. How would Christians feel if the *Bible* were banned? Well, it's almost been the victim of censorship. It has been challenged as "obscene and pornographic" by several communities in the past few years. I bet those good Christians and religious right fanatics wouldn't like that at all! And I wouldn't either. Censorship is wrong, immoral and detrimental to a society.

> . . . she lusted after lovers, whose genitals were like those of donkeys and whose emissions were like that of horses . . .
> — *Ezekiel 23:20*

As Marcia Palley stated in her excellent book on censorship, *Sex & Sensibility*, censorship has always been more problem than solution. It purges society of books, movies, and music, leaving hate, racism, sexism, drug abuse, poverty, and violence flourishing as they did before the printing press and movie camera. It flatters the nation into thinking it has done something to better life while it ignores what might be done.

# Freedom Isn't Free

Sometimes it seems as if freedom just is. This is one of the greatest attributes about this country. But freedom isn't absolutely free; it didn't just happen and it needs to be protected and preserved. You should be able to read or watch whatever you desire in the privacy of your own home.

There are many groups in this country and the rest of the world fighting for your freedom; your freedom to read, to view, to write, to paint, to listen to, to create what you want. All these groups need your support. All of these groups welcome your support with open arms.

## American Civil Liberties Union (ACLU)

*(213) 977-9500*

Thank goodness (or whatever) for the ACLU. They have been supporting our rights for many years. With your help they will continue to fight for "justice, freedom and the American way" against those who would like to take it away from us.

## Californians Against Censorship Together

*2550 Shattuck Ave. #51 Berkeley, CA 94704*

Their annual membership is $15.00.

## Free Speech Coalition

*22968 Victory Blvd., Suite 248*
*Woodland Hills, CA 91367*
*(818) 348-9373 or (800) 845-8503*

A group for people in the industry dedicated to protecting your rights to speak, write, read and view what you like. This is a trade association and not for the general public. These are adult actors and actresses, directors, producers, distributors and more who fight a constant legal battle to keep intact your rights to watch what you want.

## F.O.X.E.

*8033 Sunset Blvd., Suite 851, Los Angeles, CA 90046*

Acronym stands for *"Friends of Adult Entertainment,"* and it's a group dedicated to the preservation of our right to watch X-rated movies and shows. They publish a newsletter and offer merchandise for sale to help raise money to fund the many ongoing legal battles to protect your rights to see, hear and read what you want.

It's run by Bill Margold, a veteran of the X-rated industry who's done it all. Even if you haven't heard of him, he's been working hard to protect your rights. Help him help you. For more information write to the address above.

## Naturist Action Committee

*Post Office Box 132, Oshkosh, WI 54902*

A group dedicated to preserving the free status of nude beaches around the country and to guarding against any legal intrusion into the right to visit those beaches. Their principal goal is to demonstrate to public and government officials that nude recreation on appropriate public land should be accepted, and that places for these activities should be provided.

## The Defender

*Post Office Box 67398*
*Los Angeles, CA 90067*
*(800) 752-6562*

A periodical published by the Center for the Study of Popular Culture. It is dedicated to the First Amendment and informing concerned citizens about threats to our rights, restrictions and other pertinent details about our chershed freedoms.

## The Erotic 11

*1442A Walnut Street, #242*
*Berkeley, CA 94709*

Eleven girls were charged with acts of prostitution and lewd conduct at the *Pure Pleasure* adult bookstore in Las Vegas in January, 1993. After several months of legal hassles and mounting bills, the girls pleaded guilty to "performing in an obscene or immoral or indecent performance."

The host of the show, Bill Margold, was also charged with many crimes including pandering. He finally pleaded guilty after staring the law in the eye until they blinked, with "conspiracy to promote an obscene, indecent or immoral show, acts or performance," which is a gross misdemeanor (How ironic that "gross" is a legal term used to describe the crime).

Margold was sentenced to three years summary probation, $1000 fine and ordered to donate $3,500 to a fund for abused children. Margold is also prohibited from participating in any performance similar in nature for three years.

However, he can be a host for similar shows. Which according to Bill means, "I'm allowed to speak there all I want, I just can't get my dick sucked on stage." Since the legal bills were so exorbitant, the girls are still seeking contributions. Send your donations to the above address.

# Other Groups . . .

### Americans for Constitutional Freedom
*900 Third Avenue, Suite 1600, New York, NY 10022*

### Against Censorship Together
*1800 Market Street, #1000, San Francisco, CA 94102*

### National Coalition Against Censorship
*2 West 64th Street, New York, NY 10023*

### The Freedom Writer
*Post Office Box 589, Great Barrington, MA 01230*

### No More Censorship Defense Fund
*Post Office Box 424756, San Francisco, CA 94142*

### People For The American Way
*2000 M Street N.W., Suite 400, Washington, D.C. 20036*

### Rock Out Censorship
*Post Office Box 147, Jewett OH 43986*

### Video Software Dealers Association
*303 Harper Drive, Moorestown, NJ 08057-3329*

© 1995 DR TUPPER

# Religion & Censorship

> . . . religion is what keeps the poor
> from murdering the rich.
> — *Napoleon*

It seems as if many of the groups seeking legislation to promote censorship are religious in nature. They believe in the (selective) literal word of the Bible and desire to impose its values and laws on our entire society. On one hand, these moral crusaders have a point when they emphasize the breakdowns in ethics and responsibility in our society.

However, I do not believe that by censoring our speech or the written word or the visual arts, we will create a better society. True freedom has some rough edges; true freedom means that other people can do what they want or watch what they want or read what they want or listen to what they want even if it clashes with your beliefs and values. True freedom is always a struggle.

Religious fundamentalism is certainly antithetical to the existence of adult entertainment and this book. But it is also in opposition to a free and tolerant society. Religion and spirituality can exist in a free nation, but it must be devoid of fanaticism and intolerance.

We should all respect the rights of others to believe in their own sense of morals and code of ethics. We should respect everyone's right to believe in their chosen god or to select the appropriate path of spirituality. Christians, Hindus, Moslems, Buddhists, Humanists, Atheists, Pagans, Flat-Earth Believers, whatever . . . a heterogeneous mix of beliefs and peoples and groups make up a truly free society. Whatever you believe or whichever group you belong to . . . live peacefully and happily and respect everyone's right to their own peace and happiness.

Don't force your beliefs down someone else's throat, don't claim moral superiority over others, don't damn the rest of the world because they think differently than you do. Tolerance and understanding are the building blocks to respect, individual privacy, freedom . . . and peace!!

# Freedom to . . .

It's all about freedom: freedom of expression, freedom to live as you like, freedom to do what you like, freedom to read what you want, freedom to view what you like, freedom to sleep with whom you wish, freedom to be you! But even staunch believers in the First Amendment such as myself realize that freedom is not absolute. It should be as absolute as possible – but when it infringes on someone else's freedom or privacy, then there are problems. Only if you step over that line and invade or violate someone else's freedom and rights, should your freedoms be limited or taken away.

Our First Amendment to the Constitution is the most wonderful and powerful paragraph in the history of writing. Let us all respect it and uphold it and cherish it. Are any politicians listening out there??

# Freedom from . . .

**EDITOR'S NOTE:** Eveyone should study the *Bible, Koran, Book of Mormon,* or whatever, with an open mind. Those who do will find that religious writings disprove themselves with their inaccuracy, and immorality. How can you base your life and morals on a book or prophet if even one thing it says is incorrect? LIve your life with fun, logic and compassion!!

# Freethought Books and Publications

## Prometheus Books

*59 John Glenn Drive, Amherst, NY 14228-2197*
*(800) 421-0351*

If you want to learn more about the truth of religion, send $1 for a catalog. They have a large selection of freethought and even some books on sexual subjects. The famous comedian, Steve Allen, is one of their best known writers, along with Gore Vidal, Carl Sagan and the Amazing James Randi.

## Warren Communications

*Post Office Box 620219, San Diego, CA 92162*

In addition to this book, Warren Communications has other books for sale on freethought, such as *The Book Your Church Doesn't Want You To Read* and *Sex In History*

See our ad at the back of this book or check out *Lecher McRich's Mansion* on the InterNet.

## The Skeptics Society

*2761 N. Marengo Ave., Altadena, CA 91001*

This is a very scholarly organization that publishes *Skeptic, a* quarterly devoted to the investigation and promotion of science and rational skepticism. A single copy costs $5. They also sell many book and reprints of their articles.

## The Truth Seeker Company

*Post Office Box 2872, San Diego, CA 92112*
*(619) 676-0433 — Email: TSEditor@aol.com*

They publish the *Truth Seeker* magazine, the oldest, continually published free thought publication in the world. Send for sample copy or you can read them on *America OnLine* in the *Freethought Forum* located in the *Capital Connection* area (keyword Capital).

If you have any questions about religion, you can email them to their religious scholar and associate editor, William Lindley, at TSLindley@aol.com.

# Local Freethought Organizations

There are too many organizations for me to list all of them. However, you can contact —

# Alliance Of Humanist, Atheists, and Ethical Cultural Organizations of Los Angeles County

*8491 Sunset Blvd., Suite 240, West Hollywood, CA 90069*

This group is an alliance of freethought organizations in LA County and helps to publicize their joint activities.

**Or send for a copy of:**

## The Freethinker's Directory

*Rt-1, B-45, Craftsbury, VT 05826*

They publish a directory of most freethought organizations in the country including Rational Recovery chapters for those suffering from substance addictions.

## Humanist Association of Los Angeles

*Post Office Box 800148, Santa Clarita, CA 91380-0148*
*(805) 297-3289*

A local chapter of the American Humanist Association.

## Gay and Lesbian Atheists and Humanists[*]

*Post Office Box 15803, Los Angeles, CA 90015*
*(213) 851-5244*

The title explains it all and they put out a great little newsletter.

---

[*] Although gays and lesbians have been persecuted for centuries by most religions, it hasn't always been that way. It has been discovered that in the early church, gay weddings were performed and that in one of the book that was not included in the Bible by the Catholics, The Secret Gospel of Mark, shows that Jesus could have been gay. There was even at least one openly gay Pope.

Cartoon character based on the real-life, Capt. Sticky, famed Southern California caped crusader

# National Groups

## American Humanist Association

*7 Harwood Drive, Post Office Box 146, Amherst, NY 14226-0146 — (800) 743-6646 Email: Ap818@Freenet.buffalo.edu*

A group dedicated to free thought and to the tenet of allowing human beings to determine the moral principles by which they live. There are humanist chapters all across the country. They publish books, videotapes, films and magazines. If you believe more in the here and now than the afterlife, this group is worth looking into.

## Council for Democratic and Secular Humanism (CODESH) Inc.

*Post Office Box 664, Amherst, NY 14226-0664 (716) 636-7571*

They publish the Free Inquiry magazine. The editor, Paul Kurtz, Ph.D., is also the president of Prometheus Books. CODESH also has chapters in most major cities including Los Angeles.

# CHAPTER TWENTY

# Sexual
# Celebrities

> . . . being a celebrity is like rape.
> — *John McEnroe*

## Heidi Fleiss

**F**or over two years this woman in her late twenties ran a business that provided some of L.A.'s richest and most famous men with expensive call girls. But, she was too above ground in a profession where she should have stayed low keyed. Her exclusive escort service was busted, another infamous madam became news and another Hollywood (behind the scenes) story was made.

Heidi is the daughter of a prominent pediatrician and a former school teacher. She's an L.A. girl all the way. Stories vary how she got into the escort business. She claims she was "sold" to Madam Alex, then the most powerful madam in Los Angeles, but this is denied by the other parties involved. It is known that she worked for Madam Alex for a time but eventually branched out on her own (Madam Alex claims that Heidi stole her clients).

Heidi's standard fee for a call was $1500, but many of the calls were for a great deal more money. She made enough money to buy a mansion from actor Michael Douglas for a $1.6 million. Heidi was a socialite, a go-getter, a party girl and she was always out and about, clubbing, meeting celebrities and increasing her business. As her business grew, so did her list of enemies, including the LAPD.

In 1993, her world came crashing down around her and her name became a tabloid fixture. The police set up a sting and busted some of her girls. Some drugs were seized and so was her black book. And that was the end (and the beginning) for Heidi Fleiss. Heidi seems to be capitalizing on her new fame with a line of clothing (pajamas) and some other ventures, but legal prosecution is a high price to pay for business success and notoriety.

Heidi admits that most of her high-money business came from the Middle East. She also says that she supplied girls for the Bush and Clinton Administrations (some surprise there — politicians using escorts!), a horde of celebrities and many other movers and shakers in Los Angeles. It is doubtful whether any of the names will be released to the public so we will leave it the tabloid shows to speculate on the rumors.

So far, Heidi has been sentenced to three years and some heavy fines by the state. She also must watch out for those beady-eyed creatures at the IRS who are always waiting in the wings when there is big money involved. Her Federal trial involves money laundering and lying on tax forms.

But, Heidi has provided us with some entertaining television over the past several months and is another example of how much time and energy is spent busting prostitutes and madams while violent crimes paralyze good citizens with fear. Their clients are rarely prosecuted. I don't know Heidi, but I do know some women who were busted for prostitution or pimping and pandering. They are not a threat to anyone, but I do know the hassle and suffering they went through at the hands of law enforcement and our justice system.

Bill Margold and friend

# Bill Margold

As a veteran of 25 years in the X-rated industry, Bill Margold has seen it all. He has done it all, too. He has acted in, directed, written for and even reviewed adult films in his long career. He is affectionately known as "Papa Bear" because of his size and the fact that he is a helping hand and guidance counselor to many in the industry. He is also a devoted and dedicated and usually depressed Detroit Lions fan; his one goal before he dies is to see them play in a Super Bowl. The team is even aware of his devotion and has sent him a few team balls!

Bill graduated from Cal State Northridge and worked as a film reviewer, a probation officer, a salesman and an editor before jumping into bed with X-rated starlets. Bill was acting in films when the X-rated industry was in its embryonic stage, before it became a billion dollar per annum industry. "I was an outlaw" he says. "And I love being an outlaw. The X-rated industry is such a big business now that the feeling of rebellion is lost."

Bill remains a rebel with a cause. As the adopted son of a judge and a civil rights activist, he knows what the struggle for freedom is all about. He is the founder and head of F.O.X.E. (Fans of X-Rated Entertainment), an organization dedicated to preserving the X rated industry and fighting censorship around the country. It's a fan-based group whose membership is growing every year. F.O.X.E. presents the Adult Film Awards Show every year in February. (Don't look for it on TV– they wouldn't dare show it!)

Bill is a straight-shooter who has had some great times in the industry and is giving something back to the world that has been so good to him. He is rebellious and blunt and takes great pleasure in exposing the hypocrisy of people. He's articulate and extremely quick-witted and has proven his debate capabilities on a variety of talk shows with those who preach against the "evils" of pornography.

Most of the moral do-gooders are now afraid to debate him – they know he's too damn good!! If Bill Margold is scheduled to be the opponent, those right wing-zealots and First Amendment bashers politely decline. But "Papa Bear" keeps plugging along, never hibernating, always pursuing something, always rebelling, always teaching us what freedom is all about. Never stopping until the world is rid of hypocrisy and the Lions win the Super Bowl!

# Norma Jean Almodovar

Norma Jean has been a religious cult member, a police officer, a call girl, a political candidate and an author. She's a busy woman!

After her cult experience and brief marriage, she joined the LAPD. On April 18, 1982, after ten years, three traffic accidents and years of disillusionment and anger at her co-workers' corrupt and illegal activities, she tore up her uniform and quit. After her disability benefits were cut off, she spun the career wheel of fortune and decided to become a high-priced Beverly Hills call girl. She also had a doll business and was working on a book about her experiences as an LAPD officer.

On September 17, 1983, she was arrested on a charge of pandering, and her unfinished manuscript was confiscated by the cops. It seems that she attempted to fulfill a sexual fantasy of a friend who was still a traffic officer, but that "friend" was wired and later admitted during the trial that she had done this to try and prevent Norma Jean from writing an expose of the LAPD. Norma Jean was convicted of one count of pandering and went to prison for a psychiatric evaluation. (Is 50 days in solitary and isolation a proper psychiatric evaluation??)

After she was released, the judge decided that her sentence constituted "cruel and unusual punishment" and gave her three years probation. However, the L.A. District Attorney appealed her probation sentence on the grounds that the law mandates a minimum three year prison sentence and that her crime was "worse than rape or robbery" and that she compounded her crime by writing a book which would "cause disrespect for law and order." We always somehow get back to the evils of books and writing, don't we??

In 1986, Norma Jean received the endorsement of the Libertarian Party of California for lieutenant governor; she didn't win, but her showing was quite impressive. After the election campaign, the appeal of her sentence was heard . . . and guess what? The court overturned her probation sentence and even though she had gone almost three years on probation with no violations, she was thrown back in prison for 17 months. (Well, don't we all feel much safer when real criminals are behind bars!!)

Norma Jean has been active in several prostitutes' rights groups, and has appeared in over 200 radio, television and print media interviews all over the world. She also lectures at colleges and universities all across our great land of liberty. She is the director of C.O.Y.O.T.E. LA, a sex workers' rights group. She is working on her second and third books; Prose and Cons (about her experiences in prison) and Police, Prostitutes and Politics – 20th Century Sex Scandals in America. She is doing a series of educational fantasy videos and interactive CD's based on the fantasies of her clients and also has a ceramics and jewelry design business.

She was nominated to appear in Who's Who in American Women and Who's Who in Business and Professional Women. We should all nominate her for our own personal "Hall of Fame" as she has suffered and persevered in defense of our rights and freedom

# Mistress Jayne Alexander

Mistress Jayne is the owner of a unique phone sex service in the Los Angeles area: The Velvet Voices. Her service specializes in phone domination, slave training, bondage and many more fetishes. She runs a first-class operation and has top-notch girls working for her.

She is a nationally known mistress who is in great demand and has a large following. She is has written columns for several publications offering advice on the fetish scene, including Corporal, The Dominant View, Leg Tease, and many others. She is a busy active model who has worked here and abroad for over fifteen years. Her beauty has graced the pages of numerous publications including Penthouse, Playboy, and an international bikini calendar (and she does look great in a bikini!!).

Mistress Jayne offers clients a safe form of fantasy and sex. She realizes that today, safe fantasy or phone sex is an important expression of sexuality. Of course, we all must be concerned with protecting our right to talk dirty on the phone in a consenting business or personal relationship. Mistress Jayne is doing her part for your freedom and fantasy by offering a first-class operation and phone line. Check her out in our chapter on Aural Sex.

# Robert L. McGinley, Ph.D.

Dr. McGinley is president of one of the most unusual companies in the country; The Lifestyles Organization (TLO), also known simply as Lifestyles. TLO sponsors the world-renowned annual Lifestyles Convention which, for more than 20 years, has attracted couples from all parts of the world. The convention has been held in Las Vegas, San Francisco,

Miistress Jayne Alexander

Los Angeles and San Diego, where it will be until 1997. TLO also holds dances for couples, in addition to Halloween, New Year's Eve, Valentine's Day and Mardi Gras balls.

Robert is also the co-director and co-founder of Club Worldwide, one of the nation's oldest and continuously operated private membership swing clubs. He is president of Lifestyles Tours & Travel, the nation's first full-service, fully accredited travel agency that specializes, indeed, invented, exotic and erotic lifestyle-oriented couples tours. He is founder and president of NASCA, Inc. (North American Swing Club Association International), an association of clubs, publications and individuals in the swing community.

Dr. McGinley holds an M.A. and a Ph.D. in counseling psychology and has written numerous articles on swinging, relationships, society and sexuality. He has appeared on numerous talk shows including Phil Donahue, Hour Magazine, Sally Jesse Raphael, Geraldo and many more. He has been interviewed by USA Today, the Los Angeles Times, Time, Penthouse and more. He has traveled extensively and is known worldwide as a personal freedom activist.

It is people like Dr. McGinley, putting his lifestyle out in full public view, who help protect the rights of the silent majority who just want to live their lives as they choose. You can find more on his organization TLO and Club Worldwide in the chapter on swinging. He's out there expressing his freedom to protect yours!

# Jim South

Jim has been a fixture in the adult entertainment industry for many years, working with many of the biggest stars in the business. He has provided talent through his modeling agency, World Modeling Talent Agency, for thousands of X-rated films and mens' magazines.

Jim grew up in Dallas, Texas and worked in a variety of sales jobs including insurance. And then moved to the Southern California area in 1968 where he worked for a modeling school/agency. Jim eventually managed all five of the company's offices before branching out on his own. He was getting $20 per person per day back then to provide models. Someone offered him $50 per person per day to procure women for pornographic films and magazines. Jim turned him down. The guy upped the price to $100, but Jim still declined. When the guy raised his price to $200, Jim saw a financial opportunity too good to ignore. Jim was in the adult entertainment industry . . . and there he has stayed.

Jim has been in business for 18 years in the same location. World Modeling is a licensed and bonded agency that charges no fee. Many modeling agencies come and go, many are scams, many exploit the women, but Jim continues to run a legitimate agency that is a major force in the adult industry. He procures models for adult films, R-rated films and the leading men's magazines including Penthouse, Chic and Hustler. He has worked with such major stars as Ginger Lynn, Amber Lynn, Christy Canyon, Ashlyn Gere, Marc Wallice, Tom Byron, Peter North and the infamous Traci Lords.

If you are a woman, 18 years or older who is interested in nude photo work, you can contact —

## World Modeling Talent Agency

*4523 Van Nuys Blvd. Sherman Oaks, CA 91423.*

# Candye Kane

Candye is currently the lead singer of the group *Candye Kane & The Swingin' Armadillos*. She has also been involved in the adult entertainment industry. She worked as a stripper and as a  phone sex girl for several years. She also performed in a few X-rated videos and has appeared on the cover of *Hustler* and other men's magazines..

Born and raised in Los Angeles, she first made her mark in the local music scene singing for several groups. Nominated twice for best country vocalist by the *L.A. Weekly Music Awards*, she has achieved cult status for her involvement in

Candy Kane — The Boogie Woogie Country Girl

both the music and sex industries. She worked for several years as a receptionist for the *L.A. Weekly.* She even appeared on the television show, *Love Connection.*

Candye rubbed elbows with quite a few of the groups to come out of the early L.A. alternative music scene, such as *The Go-Gos* and the *Blasters.* She hung out with the late comedian Sam Kenison and porn stars such as Ron Jeremy.

She was in her punk rock era then and had purple hair and that total punk-rock look. But, now all is well with Candye. She and her group have just released a new CD. They perform mostly in the San Diego area, but they do travel to Los Angeles in addition to other parts of the U.S. and overseas on tour. Candye has had a vary varied career. She is talented, outrageous and you better run out right now and pick up her CD. I also want to thank her for her help in completing this book. Thanks, Candye!

Danyel
Cheeks

# Adult actresses

Following are short bios on a few of the starlets who moan and groan on screen for your viewing pleasure. Buy or rent their movies - support their right to act in them and your right to watch them. The more we buy or rent, the more influence we have.

## Danyel Cheeks

She's one of the hottest stars in the adult market: a beautiful blonde with a great body and, well . . . great "cheeks." She was born in India and came from a rather tumultuous background. She was discovered simultaneously by John Stagliano (of the Buttman series fame) and Mark Carriere, and was in great demand early by the makers of adult films. She was helped

along by Bill Margold who refers to her as "the Will Rogers of X" because of her down-to-earth nature. She is also endowed with an interesting and unique combination of animal magnetismand tremendous class.

She was arrested as part of the notorious "Erotic 11" in Las Vegas a few years back, charged with "felony lesbianism" (is there really a charge called "felony lesbianism" and if so, how do I find out more about it!!!); though her "crime" was later reduced to a misdemeanor obscenity charge.

She has appeared in at least 100 major titles including *Theory of Relativity, Everything's Relative, Analholics, Bend Over Babes 3, Buttwoman 2*, and the soon-to-be-released *Desire Kills.* She has recently moved to Las Vegas where she lives with her Himalayan cat, and is a featured dancer in some of the clubs. If you ever meet her, don't say anything bad about "America's team." She's a diehard Dallas Cowboy fan (I'm a diehard Dallas Cowboy cheerleaders fan!!). She won the

F.O.X.E. *Vixen of the Year* award in 1993 and is considered one of the top stars in the industry. You can write to her fan club at —

*8033 Sunset Blvd., Suite 851, Los Angeles, CA 90046.*

# Alicia Rio

A very popular and exciting star on the adult silver screen. She is one hot Latina who is both gorgeous and personable. She has been in many pictures including *Reflections of* Rio, A Weekend With Alicia & Sheila Stone, In Living Color Pt. 2, Almost Home Alone, Nookie of the Year, and many, many more. She enjoys her job . . . and it shows on the screen. She has appeared in many magazines including *Hustler, Genesis* and *High Society,* and travels around the country as a featured dancer at a variety of strip clubs.

She was born in Mexico, but grew up in Los Angeles and graduated from Cal State Los Angeles with a degree in business. She's smart and sexy!! She worked as deputy city treasurer for a city in the San Gabriel Valley, but when she was passed over for a promotion even though she was more qualified than the person who received the job, she filed a racial discrimination suit against the city. During the long tedious legal process, she decided to answer an ad in the *L.A. Express* looking for models. Believe it or not, she did her very first tape the day she went in for the interview!

She loves working in the X-rated industry, and has no regrets about making the move from working class hero to porn starlet. However, she knows that the world of porn and showbizz can eat you up and spit you out if you lose your focus and foundation. She credits her long-time partner for keeping her grounded and free of an attitude. Many people say "Alicia, you're a big star," but she responds, "No, I'm just a horny girl who does movies."

I personally think that Alicia is one of the hottest and sexiest women in porn. She's got a great head on her shoulders . . . and everything below her shoulders is great, too! And for all you nerds out there; Alicia says that guys in nerdy glasses and

Steve
Houston

ties really turn her on. Just my luck . . . I had to be such a stud!

She has a fan club you can join for $20. Write to her at —
*Post Office Box 9656, Canoga Park, CA 91309.*

## Steve Houston

Sorry guys . . . Alicia's spoken for!! Her long time partner is Steve Houston who was Alicia's companion before she got into the X-rated industry. Now he's a star, too! What a lucky guy . . . he's performs in sex videos and makes love to Alicia every night (well, almost every night!). He graduated from the police academy and was a police officer for two years before following Alicia into the business.

They are two conservative city employees who made the switch to X-rated entertainment: The American Dream at work! Alicia and Steve enjoy working with each other on screen

Taylor
Wane

and she credits him with keeping her focused and from being wrapped up in the industry and all its pitfalls. They live in the Big Bear area now and are enjoying their life together away from the L.A. rat race.

# Taylor Wane

Taylor is Europe's most popular XXX rated superstar. She worked in Great Britain as a photographic model, and eventually began doing erotic fashion and dance shows. That lead her to the adult film industry for which she has done over 300 adult movies including her very own production called *Secret Diary*. She has been featured in many magazines and has been in the centerfold or on the cover of such magazines as *Penthouse, High Society, Swank, Fox* and many more. She has appeared on many television shows such as *48 Hours, Hard Copy, The Jerry Springer Show,* and even *People's Court.* She has also appeared as a sexy vixen in several rock videos. And she has also appeared in many T.V. movies. She's been a busy girl for the past few years!

Brooke
Waters

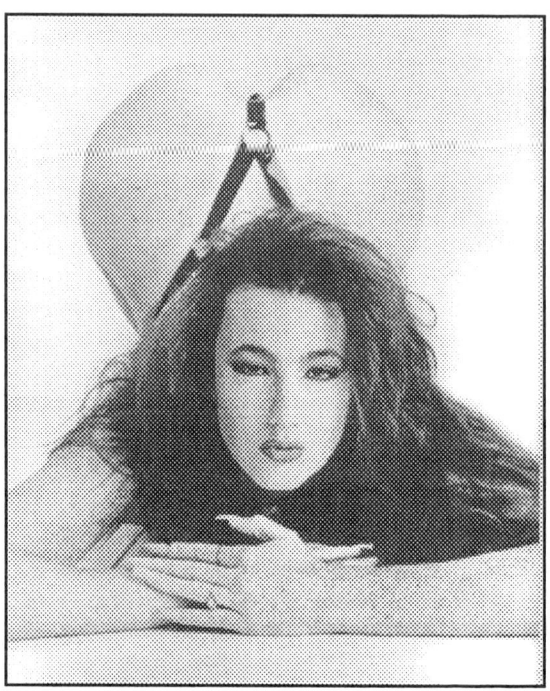

She is beautiful, well-spoken, classy; far from the stereo-typical blond bimbo that many people visualize when they think of porn starlets. She is one of the many women in the industry who pave their own way and debunk the theory that all women in the adult field are being exploited by men. Pick up one of her movies and check out this very sexy woman. You can write to her at —

*Post Office Box 57229, Tarzana, CA 91357-2229.*

## Brooke Waters

She's a relative newcomer to the silver screen. A native Californian who once worked as an insurance agent for a mortuary, she used to be too shy to be seen in public in a bathing suit. But she got out of her shell (and her clothes) and became a nude dancer. However, she got kicked out of many clubs; it seemed she had this problem – she couldn't stop touching herself in all the wrong places on stage! She's basically an ordinary girl with an ordinary life. She has a wonderful husband and two beautiful kids and three purring cats. Though sex in the porn business can be "like shaking hands," she truly loves sex and is a very erotic and sensual person. She's been in over 60 films and can be seen in *Babe Watch, Babes Illustrated Part II* and *A Dirty Western Part II.* Look for her in many more films in the future.

# Traci Lords

Traci has become a legend in the industry . . . not because of what she did, but because of when she did what she did. She was born Nora Kuzma in Ohio and came to Los Angeles when she was 12 to make a name for herself. She obtained a fake ID and entered the world of porn. Traci appeared in nearly one hundred films before it was revealed that she was still a minor. She had tricked the porn industry . . . though the media made it seem as if the adult industry had exploited a naive young girl. She even tricked the government when she showed a fake birth certificate and driver's license to obtain a passport!

A federal case was brought against the producers of one of her early films. Even though the case was dropped, the porn industry looked bad and took the blame for a fifteen year old girl appearing in sex films. Another case involving her video tapes went all the way to the U.S. Supreme Court.

That case involved a video company owner, Rubin Gottesman of X-Citement Video, Inc., who sold her tapes to undercover officers in 1986 and 1987 even though he knew she was underage. The U.S. Supreme Court upheld his convictions and Gottesman is facing fines and imprisonment.

Traci has come a long way from acting in porn films to being busted by the Feds to appearing on the evening news to a stay in the suicide ward. Traci has made the transition to mainstream films including *Not Of This Earth* and *Cry Baby.* She has also appeared on television and has released an exercise video.

Kylie Ireland

She is currently making a dance record and is up for parts in other films. Only one adult film in which Traci appears is still on the shelf. *Traci, I Love You* was made after she turned eighteen; all her other films were made prior to her eighteenth birthday and were pulled off the shelf and lost forever to the horny public.

Unless you have an old copy or know someone who does, or you're a government official (you can't tell me that some of them didn't keep confiscated copies), there's only one film left to memorialize Traci's exploits on film.

Traci can now be seen as a permanent character on the popular TV show, *Melrose Place.*

# Kylie Ireland

Kylie is one of the hottest girls in X-rated entertainment. She burst on the scene only a little over a year ago and has turned out numerous movies and won many awards, including this past year's *F.O.X.E. Vixen of the Year Award.* She worked as a dancer for a few years in Denver and decided to do some magazines and go on the road.

While in California, someone suggested she do movies. After some serious conversations with her husband, she tried it. She tried it . . . and liked it!

Kylie is from a small town and remains a small town girl. After living in San Diego and Los Angeles for a time, she has moved back to small town life. She loves the mountains, the bright blue skies, the seasons, the slower pace. However, she does keep busy traveling around the country as a featured dancer and going to L.A. to make more movies.

She is truly one of the nicest and sexiest people in the adult business . . . she is bright, honest, open and friendly. She looks and acts like the All-American girl.

She never expected to become a big star in the adult business. She thought she would do a few films, make a little extra money and then continue on with her dancing career. But, lucky for her fans, she liked it so much she decided to stay longer than expected.

Some day she wants to get out of the adult business and open a cozy sports bar in a small ski town in Colorado. We hope she stays in the business for a while longer. We would certainly miss seeing her!

Some of her films include *Lil Ms. Behaved, The Passion, The Star, Blonde Justice 3* and *Enter The Dragon Lady.* She has also crossed into mainstream acting having appeared in various specials on HBO and in a mainstream movie entitled *Strange Days.* You can write to her fan club at:

*Post Office Box 1795, Longmont, CO 80502.*

Mistress
Brandy

# Mistress Brandy

She is known as the dominatrix grandmother. She is a sixty-year old woman who was the subject of headlines in Orange County newspapers this past year. She was arrested and accused of prostitution, conspiracy to commit prostitution and operating without a business license(how come my grandmothers were never that much fun!!)

She had been working as a dominatrix for 19 years out of her upscale condo only a quarter-mile from the Sheriff station. None of her neighbors had a clue that there was an dominant's dungeon in their quiet suburban neighborhood. She always kept to herself and never bothered anyone. The perfect neighbor. Until the law and one disturbed woman changed all that.

A harbinger of bad things to come for Brandy was when a good friend and slave of hers died accidentally in her dungeon. Not only was it a tragic end for the man, it was also the beginning of the end for Brandy's dungeon days in southern Orange County.

She was actually set up by a woman who had been stalking and harassing her for some time. Brandy obtained a restraining order against this woman, who was in love with Brandy and had a "fatal attraction" for her. This woman, who also worked in the B & D scene, then began feeding information to the cops. Though she acted in more of a criminal manner than Brandy, the cops relied on her information and conducted an elaborate sting operation to entrap and bust Mistress Brandy.

Her equipment was confiscated and her name was splashed all over the newspapers and heard on television news across the country. She became notorious; for being a dominatrix in quiet conservative Orange County, and for being a grandmother dominatrix!

No charges were ever filed and most of her equipment was eventually returned (wonder what the cops did with it while they had it??). Currently, Brandy is attempting to put her legal hassles behind her while selling videos, waiting for her book to come out and doing television interviews. And for those of you interesting in serving one of the best, she is also seeking quality upscale slaves! You can write to her at:

*Post Office Box 3923, San Clemente, CA 92672*

© 1995 DR TUPPER

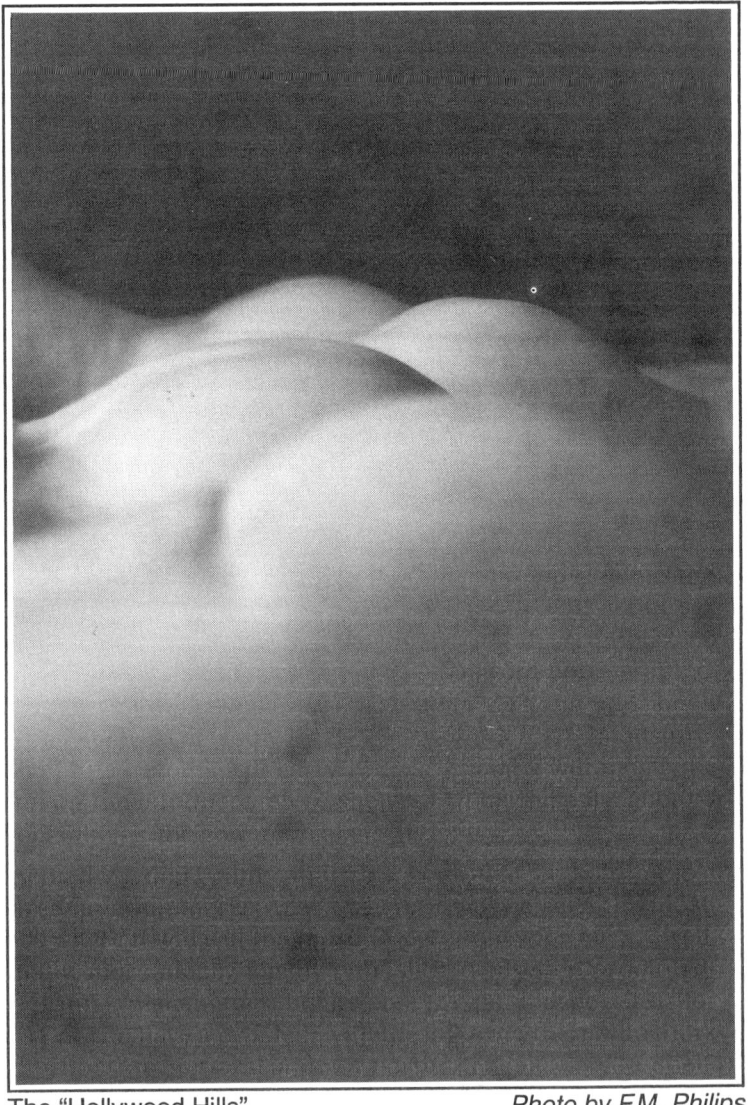

The "Hollywood Hills"                    *Photo by F.M. Philips*

# CHAPTER TWENTY-ONE

# The Rear End

> . . . a little government and a little luck are necessary in life,
> but only a fool trusts either of them.
> — *P.J. O'Rourke*

**T**his book is a compendium of trash and sleaze to some. It's a guide to sin and evil and immorality and those things not considered appropriate for "polite society". It's all about sex and sin, yet it has very few sexually explicit descriptions, no explicit photos, is not graphic, and is far from pornographic. However, you will have to search far and wide to find this book on the shelves of your local "general interest" bookstore, though a few stores will carry it. *Lust Angeles* will mostly be stuck on the adultbook store shelves. All because it's about a taboo subject: the commercial sex industry.

Actually, I don't mind that this book will be sold almost entirely in adult stores; that's where it will be seen the most, that's where it will sell the most. (More money for me . . . well, actually, more money for my publisher, typesetter, proofreaders, printer, distributors, bookstores . . . and maybe a little for me.) But I do have a problem with the folks out there who think of this book as immoral and not worthy of a place on the shelf. Sure, it's not for children . . . I didn't write it for children, yours or mine, I wrote it for adults.

My previous book, *Sin Diego*, a guide to the adult entertainment industry in San Diego, has sold well in adult stores and has even been picked up by a few brave general interest stores in the area. However, our general interest distributor had a little problem with two of its employees when they obtained the book for distribution. The employees presented their employer with an ultimatum: the book goes or we go! Luckily for us, and luckily for everyone's First Amendment rights, the brave employer said . . . "see ya" to the employees!

We do our best to legitimatize and categorize activities that millions of Americans partake of each and every day. The pornography industry is a $10 billion a year business. You can't tell me that there are ten perverts out there spending $1 billion each on all those dirty movies and pictures.

Our book is just about having fun and being safe and sane. It's about exercising your rights of freedom of expression without hurting yourself or others. Who cares if someone down the street is watching an X-rated movie? Who cares if your neighbor is entertaining (or being entertained by) a call girl? Who cares if someone you work with has a stack of dirty (erotic) magazines at home?

I don't care if you buy this book or not (except that I'm broke and I need a new car and my dog needs an operation and my kid's college fund is on empty and my . . . ), just don't deny my right to publish, write or read it!

Have fun, be careful and conscientious, exercise your freedom of expression and vote those bureaucrats who aim to take away your rights, out of office!

# Publisher's Note:

This is not the end . . . it is just the beginning. Wherever there is sin in Southern California, we will root it out and tell you about it. You can help us in this quest by sending us your address so we can mail you a notice when the next edition comes out. Also, even though F.M. is one of the most sinful and debauched guys I know, unlike the devil, he can't be everywhere. It is up to you to send us new ideas, suggestions and additions. And for you net surfers, check out *Lecher McRich's Mansion.* on the Net.

# The Author

## F.M. Philips

. . . is the author of the hugely-popular, highly-successful, critically-acclaimed, award-winning, blockbuster book of the year *Sin Diego*.. He also tends to exaggerate at times. He was hoping that *Sin Diego* would lead him to women and wealth and a lifestyle of the rich and famous, but since it didn't, he's still plugging away at his computer in pursuit of that great American novel (and more guide books to fun and fantasy). Philips also writes for the *Climax Times* in New York.

He strongly believes in freedom and wishes that our leaders would see the absurdity of consensual crimes in a free society. He wants to prove that one can indulge in adult fun and still be ethical and moral; goodness and decadence are not mutually exclusive terms.

If you want to drop Philips a line to tell him how good he is or to give him some hints on how to improve the next edition, E-mail it to him at SinDiego@aol.com or snail mail it to: Warren Communications, P.O. Box 620219, San Diego, CA 92162-0219 (warren@cyberheads.com).

F.M. Philips and his assistants doing research

# INDEX

As many people mentioned in *Lust Angeles* use only their first name or a *nom de plume,* names are listed by first name first.

$99 Outcall............................. 100
1 Hour Photo Plus.................... 269
1350 Club ............................... 167
1st King................................. 27
4 Play Video........................... 47
550 Resort ............................. 178
69 Fantasy Line ...................... 73
7969....................................... 155
900 numbers........................... 61
976-CREW.............................. 169
976-HUNK ............................. 170
976-MUSCLE.......................... 169

**A** A Different Light ..................... 165
A Dirty Western Part II ........... 317
A Mystic Arousal Entertainment ........... 101
A Weekend With Alicia & Sheila Stone . 313
A-1 Teasers............................ 104
A.A. Video & Novelty............... 21
A6 CD ROM............................. 75
Abalone Cove ......................... 203
Absolutely The Best ............... 103
abstinence ............................. 7
Abyss ..................................... 187
Academy Video....................... 17
Ace Dawson............................ 274
Acety...................................... 248
ACLU ..................................... 292
ACLU- Lesbian & Gay Rights Chapter . 175
Action (tabloid) ............... 133, 149
ad analysis and writing ......... 263
Adam & Company.................... 179
Adam Film World Guide............ 56
Adam Magazine ............... 136, 149
Adam Presents Amateur Porn ......... 57
Added Dimensions Publishing ........... 267
addictive................................. 230
ads, personal ......................... 141
adult amateur images software........... 75
Adult Books..................... 14, 15
adult CD ROM images............. 75

Adult Coupon Book................... 280
Adult Exchange ...................... 150
Adult Film Awards Show............ 304
adult GIFs & images............ 70, 75
adult jewelry........................... 258
Adult Services BBS ................. 73
adult stores ............................ 163
Adult Video News (AVN).......... 55
Adventure Line Newsletter ........ 137
Adventures of Heather............. 276
advertising agency................... 283
After Hours BBS ...................... 73
After Midnight Parties ............. 132
after-hours clubs.............. 155-157
AFVC & AFV Releasing............ 43
Against Censorship Together ...... 294
Age of Travel ......................... 210
Agua Caliente Palm Springs ...... 221
AIDS .......... 1, 7, 9, 86, 126, 167, 236, 268
AIDS Health Care Foundation ......... 176
AIDS Walk .............................. 175
Air-A-Tans............................... 210
Al Spencer ...................... 205, 212
Al-Anon................................... 242
Al's Bar.................................. 187
alcohol................................... 230
Alcoholic Anonymous .............. 241
Alcoholic Anonymous For Deaf Callers . 241
Alcoholic Anonymous For Spanish
    speakers ........................... 241
Alcoholism Center For Women ......... 241
Alejandro Photo Studio............. 273
Alibi East................................ 160
Alicia Rio............................... 313
All Nighter BBS ...................... 72
Alladin ................................... 24
Alliance Of Humanist, Atheists, and
    Ethical Cultural Organizations of
    Los Angeles County............. 298
Almost Home Alone ................. 313
Alternate Lifestyles BBS ......... 176
alternative lifestyle community ......... 72
Amanda .................................. 26

Amateur Connection (tabloid) ............... 149
Amateur Connexion (phoneline) ........... 137
amateur contests ................................... 35
Amateur Lesbians series ........................ 47
Amateur Orgies...................................... 43
amateur photographers ........................ 272
Amateurs in Action .............................. 136
ambergris............................................. 233
America OnLine ....................... 68, 76, 297
America's Raunchiest Home Videos...... 55
American Civil Liberties Union.............. 292
American Connection Video Magazine... 55
American Humanist Association ... 298, 299
American Sunbathing
   Annual Convention.......................... 255
Americans for Constitutional Freedom . 294
AmFAR ...................................................... 9
amphetamines ............................. 228, 230
Amsterdam ............................................. 85
amyl nitrite ........................................... 230
Anabolic Productions ............................. 43
anal features .......................................... 51
Anal Gangbangs ..................................... 55
anal intercourse ................................. 4, 11
Anal Knights........................................... 46
Analholics ............................................. 313
Analvision .............................................. 49
Andy's Adult World......................... 14, 163
Angel...................................................... 35
Angels Nite Club .................................... 24
Angie..................................................... 102
Annex...................................................... 72
answering service ................................ 263
Anthony Yazzolino ............................... 274
anti-aging substance........................... 247
Anti-club .............................................. 187
Apache.................................................. 157
aphrodisiacs ................. 227, 246, 247, 267
aphrodisiacs, herbal............................. 228
Arena ............................................ 154, 187
Arrow ..................................................... 43
Art Gallery – South BBS ........................ 73
Ashley:.................................................... 25
Asia...................................................... 118
Asylum ................................................. 154
Ataxi....................................................... 44
Atlantic City ......................................... 215
Atlantic World......................................... 15
audio cassettes for fetish ..................... 276
aural sex ................................................ 61
Avalon Video International ................... 179
Avanti .................................................. 178
Avica Entertainment............................... 44
AVN (Adult Video News) Awards .......... 256

AVN Presents Deep Inside
   The Adult Video Industry................... 256
Axis...................................................... 154

**B** B & D ................................ 52, 121, 136
B & D Enterprises................................. 259
B & D films............................................. 44
B & D parlors........................................ 117
B & D Pleasures ................................... 137
B & D Vending & Distributing............... 259
B/D & S/M Hotline ................................ 149
Babe Watch .......................................... 317
Babes Illustrated Part II ........................ 317
bachelor parties..................................... 97
Backdoor, The ...................................... 161
Bailey's 2020 ......................................... 39
Bailey's Twenty-Twenty
   Gentlemen's Club .............................. 24
Baja ........................................................ 85
Ball Bizarre .......................................... 255
banana eating contests ......................... 35
Bangkok ............................................... 268
Barbary Coast ....................................... 25
barbiturates ......................................... 230
Bare Elegance........................................ 25
Barona Indian Reservation................... 222
bars and clubs ..................................... 187
Baseline Books...................................... 19
Basic Plumbing..................................... 167
bathhouses........................................... 167
Baudtown .............................................. 72
bawdy books ........................................ 279
BBS ...................................................... 138
BBS, nudist.................................... 72, 210
BBS's...................................................... 67
Be Careful What You Wish For.............. 54
beach etiquette..................................... 201
Bearly Decent Enterprises.................... 279
Bearwithme Productions, Inc................ 272
Bedtime Stories ..................................... 64
Bend Over Babes 3 .............................. 313
bend-overs ............................................ 38
Benny Hill .............................................. 23
Best Buddies ....................................... 177
Best Care Medical Clinic ...................... 265
Betel .................................................... 229
Betty Ford Center ................................ 242
Bev Carlson ........................................... 65
Beverly Hills Matchmaker..................... 151
BFI Publications ................................... 177
BG Enterprises ..................................... 179
Bi Bi Love .............................................. 52
Bi-Sexual Support Services.................. 176
Bicycle Club.......................................... 217

Big & Little Caliente Hot Springs........... 205
Big Bust Screentest ................................. 50
Bikini Girls.............................................. 50
Bill & Debbie Majors Enterprises .. 270, 276
Bill Clinton............................................. 174
Bill Margold .......... 279, 292, 293, 303, 311
Bill Wilson ............................................. 279
bingo ..................................................... 221
birthday suits......................................... 202
bisexual series ........................................ 52
bisexual women ........................... 126, 138
bisexuality ............................... 11, 145, 153
Bits and Bytes ........................................ 71
Bizarre Erotic Fantasies........................ 137
Black Debutantes.................................... 47
Black Orgies ........................................... 43
Black Peppers......................................... 44
Black's Beach ....................................... 205
Blacks & Blondes ................................... 54
Blacks' Beach Bares .................... 205, 212
Blix Mail & Answering Service ............. 263
Blonde Justice 3 ................................... 319
blow up dolls ........................................ 261
blues ..................................................... 189
board game............................................ 284
Bob's Classy Lady .................................. 30
Bodacious Boat Orgies ........................... 47
body casting sculptures ....................... 283
body jewelry.......................................... 258
body massage ........................................... 3
body piercing ........................................ 275
Body Shock............................................ 251
Body Shop .............................................. 25
Body Shop Tattoo.................................. 278
body worship.................................. 63, 122
bodybuilder ........................................... 102
Bon-Vue Enterprises ............................... 44
bondage .................. 11, 63, 122, 283, 306
   (see also: B&D)
Book & Video Stores............................. 163
Book Soup ............................................. 165
Book Store, The....................................... 16
Book Your Church Doesn't Want You To
Read, The ............................................ 297
books for women .................................. 166
bookstores .............................................. 11
Boom-Boom Room ............................... 162
Bourbon Square..................................... 188
box rentals ............................................ 263
boy-boy videos........................................ 54
Brandy .................................................. 320
Breaking Into XXX ................................ 279
Brendan Francis ................................... 199
Brent Bolthouse Productions ............... 188

Brittany ................................................. 105
Broadway............................................... 158
Brooke Waters....................................... 316
Bruce Seven Productions ....................... 46
Bulldogs................................................. 158
Bun Busters ............................................ 49
burlesque house ..................................... 25
Bust Line................................................. 53
Butch's BBS........................................... 176
butt fun.................................................. 177
Buttwoman 2 ......................................... 313

**C** C West Books........................................ 13
C.O.Y.O.T.E. .......................................... 305
Caballero ................................................ 44
Caballero Direct.................................... 180
Cabaret bar............................................ 163
Cabazon Casino .................................... 221
Cahuilla Indians .................................... 221
Cake and Art.......................................... 263
calendars, nude .................................... 270
California Council on
   Compulsive Gambling....................... 225
California Girls ......................... 32, 72, 99
California NORMAL ............................... 238
California Self-Help Center.................... 241
California's Nude Beaches ........... 205, 213
Californians Against
   Cencership Together.......................... 292
Caligula's Dungeon ................................ 71
call girls............................................ 83, 305
call guys............................................... 170
Camp Palm Springs ............................. 179
Camping Bares...................................... 211
Candy Cat I & Too ........................... 30, 31
Candye Kane & The
   Swingin' Armadillos .......................... 309
cannabis sativa ..................................... 235
cantharis vesicatoria beetle.................. 232
Canyon Boys Club................................. 178
Canyon Sun Club .................................. 211
Cap d'Agde........................................... 200
Capones ................................................ 154
Captain Cream's...................................... 33
card rooms ............................................ 217
cards ..................................................... 221
Carlos O'Brien's..................................... 194
Carnal Cakes......................................... 263
Carnal Clothing..................................... 251
Carol ..................................................... 101
Carpinteria Beach................................. 204
Casanova's Adult World ......................... 13
Casino Morongo .................................... 221
casinos .......................................... 216, 220

Castle........................................ 70
Catalina Video................. 44, 180
Catch One............................ 156
cater...................................... 284
catfighting films..................... 45
Cathouse Guide Hoyål.......... 200
Catovit.................................. 248
Cave........................................ 12
Cave Theater.......................... 25
CC Construction ................... 163
CD ROM images..................... 75
CD-ROM adult-oriented software .......... 49
CDI Home Video catalog ......... 44
celery seeds......................... 233
Cemetery Beach ................... 204
censorship .............. xiv, 287, 304
Center for Men...................... 265
Center for the Study of Popular Culture 293
Centers for Disease Control
    and Prevention ..................... 5
centrophenoxine .................. 248
Centurian-Spartacus Distributors.......... 261
Century Acupressure ........ 109, 115
Century Theater 7 Lounge ...... 26
cerebroactive ...................... 247
chain g-strings ..................... 251
Champions Video of America ........... 180
Charles Pierce ..................... 153
Chase & Associates.............. 262
Chateau Computer BBS .......... 70
Chateau Phone Fantasies ...... 64
Chateau, The .................. 73, 118
Chaynelle............................. 102
Che Che Club ........................ 33
Checca.................................. 188
Cheetah's.............................. 25
Cherry Peppers...................... 44
chicks with dicks ................... 49
Chillers............................... 194
Chippendale's ....................... 39
chlamydia................................ 6
Choice (tabloid)............... 133, 149
Choices............................... 163
choline................................ 247
Christopher Street West ........ 175
Christy Canyon ...................... 64
Chuck Thompson................... 174
CHUMS................................ 171
Church of the Most High Goddess........ 285
Cinderella.............................. 44
Cinderella/CDI Video ............. 180
Cinema Motel........................ 281
circle jerks........................... 177
Circle P Ranch ...................... 179

Circumcised Celibrities.......... 174
Circus .......................... 154, 187
Circus of Books ............... 14, 165
Clare Booth Luce.................. 289
Class Act Dancers ................. 98
Classy Lady, The ................... 31
Climax Times........................ 322
Clinic For Male Cosmetic and
    Sexual-Medical Needs.......... 265
clitoris jewelry...................... 258
clothing-optional ............ 201, 206
clothing-optional vacations .... 210
Club 22............................... 157
Club 369.............................. 196
Club 3772............................ 159
Club Exposure ..................... 188
Club Fantasy ....................... 258
Club Fetish ......................... 192
Club Lingerie ....................... 188
Club Paradise....................... 194
Club Sun (tabloid)........... 133, 149
Club Worldwide ............. 129, 308
Coach House........................ 196
cocaine ................. 228, 230, 234
Coconut Teaszer................... 188
CODESH .............................. 299
cognition enhancement ......... 249
Colossal Collection BBS.......... 71
Colt Studios ........................ 180
Columns Resort.................... 178
Commerce Casino................. 219
Communaphone...................... 65
companionship service........... 103
Compu-Net............................ 73
Compu T's............................. 75
CompuServe .................... 68, 76
computer bulletin boards (BBS) ....... 67,138
Concept St. James ............... 169
Condom Revolution ................ 18
condoms................................. 5
Condor Club .......................... 42
Confidential Connection, The ....... 145, 168
Connection .......................... 156
Constitution, The ..................... xv
Consumer's Research (magazine)........ 224
Contours By Carlson ............. 283
Copper Canyon ..................... 171
cops.............................. 87, 242
costumes............................ 252
Council for Democratic and Secular
    Humanism (CODESH) Inc......... 299
country & western bar ........... 163
country music ...................... 189
Couple Costume Ball............. 255

couples ............................ 125, 127, 145
Couples Lifestyles Organization .......... 255
covergirls ............................................. 101
crack .................................................... 230
craps .................................................... 224
Crazy Girls ............................................. 26
Crenshaw Adult Books............................ 15
crime ...................................................... 87
cross-dressing ............. 117, 121, 122, 136
Crossdresser's International
    Shopping Guide ............................... 182
Crossdresser's Quarterly ..................... 182
Cry Baby .............................................. 317
Cuffs..................................................... 157
cults ..................................................... 285
Curtis Dupont......................................... 45
Custom Party Planning ......................... 284
cybersex ................................................ 71
cyberspace ............................................ 67

**D** D.G. Distributors ..................................... 45
D.J.'s ................................................... 131
D.O.M. Corporation................. 45, 275, 279
D.T ....................................................... 271
damiana ............................................... 229
dance club/party .................. 154, 187, 188
dancers .................................................. 93
Danyel Cheeks ..................................... 311
Dating Services ................................... 150
Dawn Media .......................................... 135
Deep Creek Hot Springs.............. 204, 211
Deep Inside Dirty Debutantes................ 47
Defender .............................................. 293
Deja Vu .................................................. 35
delta-9-tetrahydrocannabinol ............... 235
depressant............................................ 230
desert area............................................ 104
desert cities............................................ 35
Desert Shadows Inn ............................. 207
Desire Kills .......................................... 313
Diamond Adult World ..................... 16, 165
dildos ................................................... 259
Directory of Adult Films, The................ 57
Directory of Tattoo Artists ................... 278
dirty dime-store novels........................... 11
dirty movies............................................ 54
Discount Dolls...................................... 261
disease ................................................... 86
Diva's Dungeon..................................... 118
DMAE .................................................. 248
Doc Johnson Products........................ 260
Dolly..................................................... 104
Dolly Parton ......................................... 251
dominance .............................................. 99

Dominant View ..................................... 306
domination............................................ 306
Dottie ................................................... 130
Down & Dirty.......................................... 43
downers................................................ 230
Downtown BBS, The .............................. 72
Dr. John's Tattoo American.................. 277
Dr. Larry............................................... 290
drag shows ................................... 154, 187
Dragonfly .............................................. 189
Drake's .................................................. 14
Dream Makers ...................................... 132
Dressed to Thrill Versatile Fashions ...... 255
Drug Policy Foundation ........................ 238
drug policy ........................................... 238
Drugbusters International ..................... 241
drugs................... 87, 129, 228, 230
drugs and nutrients.............................. 245
drunk drivers........................................ 239
dry sauna.............................................. 111
dry social kissing .................................... 2
DUI ...................................................... 240
dungeons.............................................. 117

**E** Earring Collection ................................ 275
Easyriders............................................ 277
Eat My Shorts BBS................................ 73
ecstasy ........................................ 229, 231
Ecstasy Audio ...................................... 276
Ed Lange ............................................. 208
Eden BBS .............................................. 71
Edge (magazine) ......................... 150, 172
Edge Male Call ..................................... 169
El Dorado Club ..................................... 219
El Mirasol Villas .................................... 179
Elbert Hubbard .................................... 215
Elegant Angel ........................................ 46
Elegant Connections ............................ 147
Elise....................................................... 33
Elysium Fields ...................................... 207
Encounters ........................................... 159
enemas................................................. 121
Ensenada ............................................... 85
Enter the Dragon Lady ......................... 319
Entre Nous............................................ 155
erection enhancement.......................... 267
Erotic 11...................................... 293, 313
erotic art sets ....................................... 284
erotic ball ............................................. 138
Erotic Connections:
    Love and Lust on the
    Information Highway........................... 69
erotic dancers ....................................... 83

erotic dancing men ................................ 39
erotic edibles........................................ 263
erotic entertainment ............................. 188
Erotic Events......................................... 255
Erotic Masquerade Ball......................... 256
erotic messages.................................... 65
erotic snapshots.................................... 269
erotica .................................................. 105
Eroticard DataDriven Inc....................... 65
Eruption ................................................ 43
escort services ...................................... 92
Escorts............................................. 92, 93
Especially For Me ................................. 254
Europe .................................................. 85
European Amateurs ............................... 49
Eve's Room .......................................... 71
Everything You Always Wanted To
    Know About The X-Rated Industry .... 279
Everything's Relative ............................ 313
Evil Angel Video .................................... 46
Excalibur Films ..................................... 46
Exceptions Enterprises ......................... 51
Executive Suite ..................................... 158
exhibitionism ............................... 126, 125
Exotic Cakes ........................................ 263
Exotic World Burlesque Museum.......... 257
experimental drugs .............................. 246
Expressions West BBS ......................... 72
extasy .................................................. 27
Eye Shadow........................................... 46
Eyefull, Inc ........................................... 35


**F** F.I.G.H.T ............................................. 174
F.I.N. Entertainment ............................. 46
F.M. Philips ..................................... 81, 321
F.O.X.E. ............ 57, 256, 292, 304, 313
F.O.X.E. Vixen of the Year Award ........ 319
face lifts................................................ 265
Faces.................................................... 169
Factory Home Video ............................. 46
Falcon Enterprises ............................... 284
fanaticism............................................. 295
Fans of X-Rated Entertainment .... 256, 304
Fantasia BBS ....................................... 73
Fantastic Pictures ................................ 46
Fantasy 66 ........................................... 19
Fantasy Fashion Digest ........................ 123
Fantasy Island ...................................... 31
Fantasy Lingerie ............................ 252, 261
fantasy outcall service ......................... 99
fantasy shows ....................................... 99
Fantasy Springs Casino........................ 221
Fantasy Topless Theatre....................... 35

Fashions Niteclub................................. 194
Faultline ............................................... 157
FDA ...................................................... 245
Female FYI............................................ 172
female impersonators........................... 158
female over male dominance             117
female wrestling ................................... 45
feminization .................................... 63, 122
fetish/fetishes .............. 117, 155, 251, 306
fetish and bondage board...................... 70
fetish fashions ...................................... 123
fetish magazines and books................. 252
fetish videos ................................... 50, 55
FilmeXpert ........................................... 269
filming.................................................. 275
First Amendment ........................... xv, 288
First Date .............................................. 170
Fit To Be Tied ....................................... 252
Five Star Entertainment........................ 257
FJS International ................................... 47
Flame ................................................... 43
Flamingo Massage & Sauna ................ 113
Flash Modeling Studio .......................... 38
Flex Complex ....................................... 167
foot fetish.................................... 117, 121
Foothill Club ......................................... 189
For The Ladies ...................................... 39
Foto Forge............................................ 273
Frat House Boys.................................... 180
Frederick's of Hollywood ...................... 252
Free Inquiry (magazine) ....................... 299
Free Speech Coalition .......................... 292
Freedom Acres ..................................... 129
Freedom From....................................... 296
freedom of expression.......................... 296
Freedom Writer ..................................... 294
Freethinker's Directory ......................... 298
freethought books and publications....... 297
French Connection, The......................... 64
French (wet) kissing ............................. 3
Frenchie's Fantasy Tales....................... 64
Friday Night Socials .............................. 131
Friends & Lovers (tabloid) ............ 135, 149
Friends of Adult Entertainment.............. 292
Friends of Deep Creek .......................... 211
friendship.............................................. 127
Fritz That's It ........................................ 27
From Cop To Call Girl............................ xvi
Frontera Gay (tabloid) ........................... 174
Frontiers (magazine) ............. 150, 170, 173
Frontview Cabaret ................................. 27
Fuck!.................................................... 192
Fuji Oriental Spa & Massage................. 109
Fuji Shiatsu & Massage......................... 112

Fun Company, The ............................. 100
Funhouse ........................................... 33
Funtime BBS ..................................... 72

**G** g-strings ............................................ 251
Gail McGee ....................................... 279
Gamblers Anonymous ......................... 225
gambling ........................................... 215
Gaming Registration Program ............. 217
gangbang flicks ................................. 47
Garbo Inn ......................................... 210
Gauntlet ........................................... 275
Gaviota Beach ................................... 204
gawkers ............................................ 202
gay/lesbian ................ 11, 145, 150, 153
gay & lesbian community centers ........ 175
Gay & Lesbian Times (tabloid)............. 173
Gay and Lesbian Atheists and
    Humanists ................................... 298
gay and lesbian literature ................... 165
gay bathhouses ................................. 167
gay computer bulletin boards .............. 176
Gay Connection .................................. 169
gay desert resorts .............................. 178
gay fiction ......................................... 165
gay mail order videos ................. 165, 179
gay male nude club news .................... 174
gay periodicals .................................. 150
gay phone lines .................................. 168
gay tourism ....................................... 171
gay/lesbian travel agencies ................ 171
gay/lesbian/bi/gender bender
    social clubs .................................. 183
gay game .......................................... 284
geisha girls ....................................... 107
Gemini Club ...................................... 130
gender-bending .................................. 136
Gentle Enemas .................................. 121
Gentlemen's Club ............................... 31
George Burns ...................................... iv
Gerovital ........................................... 248
GIF pictures ........................... 69, 70, 138
GIFshoppe ......................................... 71
gifts .................................................. 11
Gina ................................................. 102
Ginger Lynn ....................................... 64
Ginja Oriental Massage ...................... 112
Ginkgo ............................................. 248
ginseng ............................................. 248
Ginza Spa ......................................... 109
Girl Bar ............................................. 154
girl parties ........................................ 138
girl-girl wrestling flicks ........................ 44
Glam Slam ........................................ 189

Glamour Photographer Magazine ........ 272
Glen Eden Sun Club .................... 208, 255
Glitz Tits ........................................... 47
Glitz Video ........................................ 47
Global International, Inc ...................... 266
Global World Media ............................ 229
Gloria ............................................... 47
go-go boys ................................. 154, 155
go-go dancers ................................... 23
Golden Bares ..................................... 211
Golden California Girls ................. 270, 273
Golden Touch ..................................... 114
gonorrhea .................................... 6, 86
Good Art Comapny .............................. 258
Gourmet Video ................................... 47
Grand Central .................................... 160
grandmother dominatrix ...................... 321
Great Expectations ............................. 151
Greek freaks ...................................... 102
Green Garden .................................... 112
greeting cards ................................... 275
GRIDS .............................................. 2
group sex .......................................... 126
guides to nude recreation ................... 213

**H** Hamburg, Germany .............................. 86
Hana Acupressure .............................. 115
Happy Hour (gay bar) .......................... 161
Happy People Tours ............................ 171
Happy Tanner Inn ............................... 207
Harlow Club Hotel .............................. 178
Harry and Davids Goat Hill Tavern ....... 195
Harry Horndog ................................... 46
Harvey's Bar & Grill ............................ 33
hashish ...................................... 235, 228
head shop .......................................... 237
Head's Up Adult BBS ........................... 72
Health Center Oriental Massage .......... 114
Heartwood Whips of Passion ............... 254
Heather ............................................. 276
Heather & Jane .................................. 104
Heavenly Bodies ................................ 101
Hedonism BBS, The ............................ 70
hedonistic pleasure centers ................. 125
Hell's Gate ........................................ 189
hemp ................................................ 235
Hennessey's Tavern ............................ 194
herbal ecstasy ................................... 229
herbs ......................................... 228, 246
heroin .............................................. 231
herpes ............................................. 86
High Strung by Jolie ............................ 253
High Times (magazine) ....................... 238
HIS Video .......................................... 180

Hispanic ............................................ 111
Hispanic Orgies series ...................... 47
HIV positive ..................................... 176
HIV sex phone line ........................... 170
Holiday ............................................... 27
Hollywood Exposed ........................... 54
Hollywood Massage .......................... 109
Hollywood New Reality ............... 135, 149
Hollywood Park ................................ 223
Hollywood Park Casino ..................... 219
Hollywood Playmates ................. 97, 135
Hollywood Tattoo .............................. 277
Hollywood Times ............................... 147
Hollywood Tropicana .......................... 29
Hollywood Video ......................... 13, 47
Hollywood-A-Go-Go ........................... 31
Home Lodging ................................. 139
Homegrown BBS ............................... 72
Honey Bunnies, The ......................... 102
Hooker's Girls .................................... 83
hookers .............................................. 83
horny computer nerds ........................ 49
horses ............................................. 223
Hot Bodies ........................................ 99
Hot Body Video Magazine .................. 45
hot chat ............................................. 69
hot cream wrestling ........................... 33
hot hunks .......................................... 39
hot spring activities ......................... 211
Hot Springs SIG .............................. 211
Hot Springs World ........................... 212
hot table dances ................................ 27
hot tubs ..................................... 20, 130
Hotel California .................................. 73
House of Blues ................................ 189
House of Sex ..................................... 51
How to Make Your Own XXX
    Video for $$$ ................................ 48
Howard Stern Show .......................... 262
hug drug .......................................... 231
Hugging .............................................. 2
Humanist Association of Los Angeles ... 298
Humdinger ......................................... 32
Hung Jury ......................................... 267
Huntington Park Casino .................... 219
Huntress .......................................... 162
Hy-O-Silver ...................................... 101
hydergine ....................................... 2 47
Hyperion .......................................... 157

I   Ice House ...................................... 194
    Image Core ..................................... 72
    Image Experts ............................... 269
    Image King .................................... 274

Imagers ........................................... 274
impotence ........................................ 234
In Living Color Pt. 2 ......................... 313
Indian reservations .................... 216, 220
Indigo Jazz Club .............................. 194
Industrial Drone ............................... 192
infantilism ................................ 117, 121
Infinity Video .................................... 49
Infonet Publications ......................... 280
Inkslippers Ball ............................... 257
Inland Empire .................................... 35
Inntrique .......................................... 178
Insider Video Club ........................... 181
Inspiration Point .............................. 203
Institute of Criminal Science,
    University of Copenhagen ............. 290
Integrity ........................................... 170
Interludes .......................................... 73
International Directory of Swing Clubs &
    publications ......................... 139, 280
International Gay and Lesbian
    Travel Association ....................... 171
International Love Boutique ................ 12
International Wavelength ................... 181
InterNet .................................... 76, 176
interracial ......................................... 11
Interstate 1 ....................................... 73
intolerance ...................................... 295
introduction network ........................ 171
Iron Man Personal Workout ............... 266
IV drug needles ................................... 4

J   J. Heartwood Corsets of Desire ...... 254
    J. Wink Pleck ............................... 270
    J.B. Video ...................................... 48
    J.H. Phonics .................................. 64
    J.J.'s Pub ..................................... 157
    Jack Messick ................................. 274
    Jack Nicholson .............................. 234
    Jack Trimpey ................................. 242
    Jack's Sugar Shack ....................... 189
    jacuzzi suites ............................... 281
    jacuzzi ........................... 111, 127, 167
    Jade Massage ............................... 114
    Jai Alai ........................................ 224
    Jalapeno Peppers ........................... 44
    Jamie Summers .............................. 64
    Japan Shiatsu ............................... 115
    Japanese Bath Massage ................. 111
    Japanese Massage ......................... 113
    Japanese Shiatsu Massage ............. 114
    Jason's II ....................................... 16
    Jean Daniel Cadinot Videos ............ 179
    Jennifer Flowers ........................... 174

Jennifer West ... 103
jerk off ... 21
Jh Acupressure ... 115
Jim South ... 308
Jim Tobak ... 274
JMPG ... 182
Joan Rivers ... 259
Joel Kaplan, Dr ... 266
Joe's Adult Books ... 15
John Donne ... 107
John Leland ... 264
John McEnroe ... 301
John Stagliano ... 311
John T. Bone's Starbangers series ... 46
Johnny Depp ... 193
Joker's Wild Tattoo Studio ... 278
Joystick BBS ... 176
JR Brians ... 160
Judy Kirk Design ... 258
Julie Carlson ... 283
Jumbo's Clown Room ... 28

**K** KBBS ... 48, 70
keno ... 221
Kern Charter Service ... 282
KIKS ... 259
Kim Christy's She-Males ... 49
King of Hearts ... 167
Kinky (tabloid) ... 133, 149
Kiser Models ... 273
Kiss ... 279
Kissin' Sisters ... 103
Knave magazine ... 83
Knick Knacks 'N More ... 259
Knight Publishing Corp ... 56
Knight Publishing Corp. ... 136
Korean ... 107
KY Jelly ... 5
Kylie Ireland ... 319

**L** L.A. Connex BBS ... 72
L.A. Free Press ... 125
L.A. Girl Guide ... 150, 172
L.A. Reader ... 97, 186, 197
L.A. Reader Call Dating ... 145
L.A. Tattoo ... 277
L.A. Tower ... 191
L.A. Weekly ... 97, 145, 186, 197
L.A. Women ... 138
L.A. X-Press ... 97, 135, 149
LACE ... 75
ladies of the night ... 83
Lady Laura's Dominion ... 118, 121
Lake Elsinore Casino ... 219

Large & Lovely ... 101, 148
large breasts ... 53
Larry, Dr ... 290
Las Vegas ... 215
Las Vegas Video ... 48
Laser Disc Entertainment ... 49
laser disc releases ... 49
Late Show, The ... 73
latex condoms ... 5
latex ... 52, 117
Latinas ... 47, 157, 313
Laura Lynn ... 65
Laurie Lewis ... 103
lawyers ... 261
LBO Entertainment ... 49
Le Petit Chateau ... 208
Le Sex Shoppe ... 12, 15, 18
Leather Lovers ... 49
leather ... 12, 117
Lecher McRich's Mansion ... 80, 327
Lee Baxandall ... 213
Leg Tease ... 306
legalization of marijuana ... 237
legalized gambling ... 215
Legend Graphics On-Line ... 70
Leisure Time Entertainment ... 49, 181
Leo's ... 110
Leoram ... 49
lesbian ... 153, 158, 172
lesbian lingerie fantasy films ... 46
Lesbian News ... 150, 172
Letro Limited ... 49
levi and leather crowd ... 156
Libertarian Party ... 305
Liberty Books ... 20
Lifestyles ... 211
Lifestyles Convention ... 129, 138, 255, 256, ... 274, 308
Lifestyles Organization ... 131, 306
Lifestyles Tours & Travel ... 138, 308
Lighthouse Cafe ... 194
Lil Ms. Behaved ... 319
Lilly-of-the-Valley Oil ... 234
limos ... 20
lingerie ... 39, 92, 252, 259
Lingerie Dreams ... 39
lingerie museum ... 252
Lingerie Oasis ... 39
lingerie ... 12, 251
liposuction ... 265
Lipstix ... 161
Little Hong Kong Acupressure ... 111
Little Shrimp ... 162
live original music ... 187

Long Beach Lesbian & Gay Pride......... 175
Looking Glass ............................... 137, 149
loops ............................................... 41
Los Alamitos Race Track ..................... 223
Los Angeles AIDS Hotline............... 6, 175
Los Angeles Center for Alcohol &
    Drug Abuse ................................... 241
Los Angeles Love Connection ............. 148
lotions ............................................... 12
lotteries ............................................. 215
lottery................................................. 22 4
Love Bunnies ...................................... 46
love doll.............................................. 261
love drug ............................................ 231
Love Lounge ....................................... 155
Love Network...................................... 131
Loving Alternatives............................. 137
LSD.................................................... 231
lubricants ........................................... 165

**M** Mack Releasing ................................. 181
Madison's Avenue................................ 99
Mae West........................................... 11, 41
magazines .......................................... 11
Mahogany's Unlimited Productions ...... 155
Maid in LA.......................................... 263
mail box ............................................. 262
Mail Box Place ................................... 263
mail order companies ........................... 42
Main Street ........................................ 162
Main Theater....................................... 14
Majick & Fetish Shop .......................... 123
Making Contact Magazine ........... 136, 149
Male Clinic ......................................... 266
male dancers ................................. 39, 98
male genital stimulation device............. 259
male over female dominance................. 117
male videos.......................................... 44
Malibu ............................................... 102
Malibu Inn .......................................... 191
Mancini's Club ................................... 191
Mandrake........................................... 233
Marbles............................................... 33
Marcia Palley .............................. 287, 291
marijuana ................................... 231, 234
Marijuana Anonymous ......................... 241
Mariposa Foundation ............................ 6
marital aids ........................................ 11
Mark Carriere ..................................... 311
Mark Twain ........................................ 199
Mary Jane .......................................... 235
masquerade party............................... 138
massage parlor ................................... 107
masseuses................................... 83, 93

masters................................................. 148
masturbation club ................................ 177
Max Kauffmann ................................... 141
May West ............................................ xiv
Mayan................................................. 191
McConville.......................................... 208
MDMA ................................................ 231
Meese Commission.............................. 289
Melrose Baths ..................................... 167
Melrose Tattoo .................................... 278
Membership contact group................... 130
men with tits ....................................... 49
Men's Activities Hotline........................ 175
Menagerie .......................................... 161
mescaline ........................................... 231
methylene dioxy meth amphetamine .... 231
Mexicali ............................................. 85
Mexico ............................................... 84
Mia..................................................... 25
Michelle's Forbidden Pleasures ............. 64
MIDN .................................................. 266
Midnight Adult Book & Video ................. 17
Midnight BBS....................................... 73
Midnight Modeling ............................... 99
Midnight Rental & Preview Center ......... 17
Midtowne Spa...................................... 167
Mild to Wild......................................... 258
Mile High Club .................................... 282
Miller vs. California .............................. 289
Mimiko's ............................................. 111
Mineshaft............................................ 159
Miss Exotic World ................................ 257
Miss Nude America .............................. 47
Mistress Antoinette ...................... 55, 253
Mistress Aries ..................................... 122
Mistress Bijon ..................................... 119
Mistress Brandy................................... 320
Mistress Dee ....................................... 121
Mistress Elizabeth ............................... 121
Mistress Elvira .................................... 119
Mistress Jacqueline.............................. 64
Mistress Jayne Alexander ....... 63, 122, 306
Mistress Leah LeFleur.......................... 53
Mistress Nancy ................................... 69
Mistress Paloma .................................. 119
Mistress Roxanne................................. 103
Mistress Shannon................................. 121
Mistress Storm .................................... 119
Mistress Vanessa ................................. 121
mistresses .................................. 117, 148
Mitchell Brothers................................. 42
Modeling Studios................................. 38
models................................... 93, 272, 273
Modern Boy ................................. 71, 176

modem ...................................................... 67
Mon Cherie Lingerie Strippers .............. 104
Monte Carlo II ............................................ 28
Monte Carlo" nights .............................. 216
Moonlight Entertainment ........................ 49
Moose McGillycuddy's .......................... 191
MOR Enterprises, Inc ............................ 259
More Dirty Debutantes ........................... 47
More Mesa ................................................ 204
Morningside Inn ...................................... 208
Morongo 21 .............................................. 221
Motel Meetings ...................................... 281
motel with private jacuzzis ................... 281
motels with XXX videos ........................ 281
Mount Vernon News .............................. 19
Movieland Motel ...................................... 281
movies transferred to video ................. 269
Mr. Jay's .................................................... 34
Mr. Peepers Amateur Video ................... 49
Ms. Nude America ................................. 257
Ms. Nude Hollywood ............................. 257
musk oil & ambergris ........................... 233
Mustang Adult Books & Video .............. 19
mutual masturbation ................................. 2
Myako Massage ...................................... 114

**N** Nagoya Acupressure ........................... 115
Naked City .............................................. 209
Naked City L.A. ...................................... 257
Naked Magazine ...................................... 174
Nancy Novak ............................................ 54
Napoleon ....................................... 227, 295
Narcotics Anonymous ........................... 241
Narita Spa ................................................ 115
NASCA ............................... 139, 280, 308
Nasty Adults ............................................ 147
nasty or nude photos ........................... 270
National AIDS Hotline ..................... 9, 175
National Coalition Against Censorship .. 294
National Council on Alcoholism and Drug
  Dependency ......................................... 241
National Institute on Drug Abuse
  Help Line .......................................... 241
National Organization for the
  Reform of Marijuana Laws ............... 238
National Research Group .................... 282
Native American gaming places .......... 220
naturism ................................................... 199
Naturist Action Committee ................... 292
Naturist Penpal Club ............................. 212
Naturists Inc. ......................................... 213
Netherlands ............................................ 85
Nevada brothels ...................................... 280

New Age and alternative lifestyles ........ 207
New Fuji Spa ......................................... 115
New Jet Strip ............................................ 28
New Reality ............................................... 97
New Seoul .............................................. 114
New York style" dancing ......................... 32
Newport Station ...................................... 162
newsletter, swingers ............................. 137
Nichole's Therapy Massage ................. 114
Nick Lowe ............................................... 117
Night Rhythm ............................................ 98
Night, The ................................................. 73
Night Vision .............................................. 72
nightlife .................................................. 185
Nightline Service, The .......................... 147
Niki ........................................................... 38
Nikki's Bare Assets ................................. 98
Nina ........................................................ 118
nipple enlargement pumps ................... 266
nipple jewelry .......................................... 258
nitrous oxide ........................................... 231
No! No! Greetings ................................... 275
No More Censorship Defense Fund ...... 294
non-explicit videos ................................. 50
nonoxynol-9 ............................................... 5
Nookie of the Year ................................. 313
Nootropics, The ...................................... 247
Nora Kuzma ............................................ 317
Norma Jean Almodovar ................. xiv, 304
NORMAL .................................................. 238
Normandie Club ...................................... 219
North American Swing Club
  Association .................................. 139, 308
Northridge Video ...................................... 15
Not of this Earth ...................................... 317
nude BBS ...................................... 72, 210
nude beaches ........................................ 292
nude beaches & resorts ........ 199, 200, 201
  ..................... 202, 203, 204, 205, 206, 207
  ..................... 208, 209, 210, 211, 212, 213
nude beauty pageants ......................... 209
nude calendars ...................................... 270
nude city ................................................ 200
nude clubs ............................................... 23
nude dance shows ................................. 38
nude hiking ............................................ 211
nude hotels ............................................ 206
Nude Maids ............................................ 177
nude modeling .......................................... 92
Nude Models Directory ........................ 280
nude oil wrestling ................................... 29
nude photo ............................................ 263
nude resorts and hotels ....................... 206
nude swingers ....................................... 209

nude travel club ................................. 210
nude weddings .................................. 212
nudism ............................................. 199
nudist club ....................................... 211
nudist magazines .............................. 212

**O** O'Farrell Theater ................................ 42
Oasis Latex ...................................... 260
Odd Ball Cabaret .............................. 31
Odyssey ...................................... 69, 137
Odyssey Video ............................. 14, 16
Odyssey Video Group ......................... 50
Odyssey ............................................ 149
off-track betting ............... 216, 221, 223
Oil Can Harry's ................................. 158
oil of musk ....................................... 233
oil wrestling ...................................... 35
oils .................................................. 12
Okinawa Massage ............................ 115
Olive Dell Ranch .............................. 209
Olympian Club .................................. 212
Omnific ........................... 137, 138, 280
Ona Zee Productions ......................... 50
on-line games .................................... 69
On-Line Publications .......................... 136
open relationships ............................ 125
open-breast design outfits ................ 251
Oral Gangbangs ................................ 55
oral-anal contact ................................ 4
oral-genital .................................. 3, 11
Orange County ................................... 32
Orange County Close Encounters ........ 145
Orange County Cultural Pride ............. 175
Orange County Social Club ................. 151
organized crime ................................ 221
orgies ...................................... 11, 125
Orgy Club ........................................ 130
Oriental Acupressure ........... 113, 112, 115
Oriental Acupressure Massage ............. 114
Oriental Garden Spa .......................... 115
Oriental girls .................................... 111
Oriental massage & acupressure .. 112, 115
Oriental Shiatsu Clinic ....................... 113
Oriental Shiatsu Massage ................... 112
Oriental Spa Massage ............... 112, 114
Oscar Levant .................................... 255
Our Bang .......................................... 47
Our World (magazine) ....................... 171
Ovid ................................................ 258
OWE BBS ......................................... 71
Oxiracetam ...................................... 247

Oysters ............................................ 233
Ozz Supper Club ............................... 162

**P** P.I.C ............................................... 150
P.J. O'Rourke ............... 227, 245, 251, 325
Pacific Island Connections .................. 150
Pacific Media Entertainment ................ 50
Pacific World ..................................... 15
Pacificans ........................................ 212
Paddy Murphy's .................................. 34
Page One Books ................................ 166
pai gow ........................................... 217
Palace ............................................. 191
Palms .............................................. 155
Palomino, The .................................. 194
Panax .............................................. 228
Panther Palace .................................. 130
pantyhose worship videos .................... 48
Papa Bear ........................................ 303
Paradise Cove ................................... 203
paraphernalia: .................................... 12
Paris House ....................................... 38
Partnership For a Drug-Free America ... 241
Party House ....................................... 17
party houses ..................................... 125
Passion Play ..................................... 284
Passion, The ..................................... 319
patent leather ................................... 284
Pathway Communications & BBS ... 69, 138
Pattaya ............................................ 268
Paul Kurtz ........................................ 299
PC Group .......................................... 130
peep show booths ............................... 11
Pelican's Retreat ............................... 192
penis enlargement ............................. 264
Penis Power!! ................................... 264
Penis Power Quarterly ........................ 267
penises, large ................................... 267
penpal club, nudist ............................ 212
People for the American Way ............... 294
People ............................................. 149
Pepper Productions ............................. 44
Perfect Match Dating Service .............. 151
Personal Photography ........................ 177
personals ads .................................... 141
perverted talk ................................... 142
peyote ............................................. 231
phallic pastries .................................. 263
phantasy photographic models ............. 273
phenylalanine ................................... 248
phone dominance ............................... 122
phone lines and personals ........... 142, 168
phone sex .......................................... 59
phone sex card ................................... 65

phosphatidylserine ................................ 248
Photo Image Club .................................. 274
photo sets ............................................. 270
photographers, photography .......... 38, 271
............................................... 272, 274
photographic club ................................. 274
photographic modeling studios ............ 273
photographic prossessing .................... 269
Picasso's ............................................... 194
Pier 52 .................................................. 194
piercing ................................................. 275
Pink & Plentiful ....................................... 54
Pink Lady ................................................ 36
piracetam .............................................. 247
Pirate's Cove ......................................... 203
Pixis Interactive ...................................... 75
Planet Homo .......................................... 173
Planet Video Group .............................. 180
Platinum .................................................. 50
platonic ................................................. 103
Playboy and Penthouse videos ............. 45
Player's Club ......................................... 267
Playgirl Magazine ................................... 39
playmates ..................................... 145, 252
Playtime .................................................. 32
Playtime Kopies .................................... 270
Pleasure Chest ............................... 12, 253
Pleasure Products ................................ 260
Point Dume Beach/Paradise Cove ....... 203
poker ............................................. 217, 221
police ...................................................... 95
"Police, Prostitutes and Politics —
   20th Century Sex Scandals
   in America" ........................................ 305
pool tables ........................... 24, 27, 32, 33
Pope ...................................................... 298
Pope's Back Street ................................. 36
poppers ......................................... 13, 230
Porn Star Handbook .............................. 279
porno star, how to become one ........... 279
pornographic film industry .................... 41
pornography .......................................... 289
portfolios ............................................... 274
Portuguese Point ................................... 203
Positively Pagans ................................... 51
pot ........................................................ 235
Power House BBS ................................. 176
prescription drugs ................................ 246
President's Commission on
   Obscenity and Pornography ............. 289
priestess ............................................... 285
Prime Time .............................................. 72
Prime Time Slime .................................... 47
Prince .................................................... 189

Prissy's High Society ............................ 237
Pro Video ................................................ 50
Probe .................................................... 155
Prodigy ................................................... 68
Profiles Systems ................................... 145
Prolong SX ............................................ 267
Prometheus Books ....................... 297, 299
Prose and Cons ..................................... 305
prostitutes/prostitution ............... 83, 85, 92
provocative clothes ............................... 252
Pubic Hair Salon ................................... 264
public domain files ................................. 69
publications .................................. 133, 172
publications, gay, lesbian, bi ................ 172
Pure Pleasure ....................................... 293
Purple Panther Designs ....................... 277
purslane ................................................ 233
pyroglutamate ....................................... 248

Q Quaaludes .......................................... 231
   Quackenbush Video .............................. 51
   Que Sera Sera .................................... 159
   Queen Mary ........................................ 158
   Quicksilver Photo ................................ 269

R race tracks ......................... 219, 223, 224
   Raffaelli 3-D Classics ......................... 284
   Raffles ............................................... 209
   Rage .................................................. 155
   Raincoat Productions ........................... 51
   Rational Recovery ...................... 242, 298
   Raunch-O-Rama ................................. 49
   Raunchy Radio .................................. 262
   rave scene ......................................... 231
   Rawhide ............................................. 158
   Raymond Chandler ............................ 239
   recreational drugs ............................. 227
   Recycler ............................................ 147
   Red Lights of Baja .............................. 85
   red-light district ........................... 84, 85
   Redhead Bar ..................................... 157
   reefer ................................................ 235
   REG Publishing ................................... 75
   Regina ............................................... 118
   religion .............................................. 295
   religious right .................................... 288
   Renaissance ..................................... 192
   reservation ....................................... 220
   Reunion of the Diamonds of Burlesque. 257
   revitalizer ......................................... 228
   rhinoceros horn ................................ 232
   Richard Stevens ................................. 75
   Rincon Beach .................................... 204
   Rincon Indian Reservation ................. 222

Ripples .................................. 159
Risque Business ..................... 47
River Phoenix ........................ 193
Robbie's ................................ 161
Robert L. McGinley, Ph.D ..................... 306
Robert Rimmer's X-Rated
Video Tape Guide ................ 280
Rock Out Censorship ............. 294
Rodney Brown, Dr .................. 265
Rodney Dangerfield ................ 92
Roger Warren ........................ 81
role playing ..................... 63, 122
Roman Holiday Health Spas ............... 167
Romantics Line ..................... 145
Ronald Reagen ..................... 174
Rosarito Beach (Mexico) ........ 85
Rosebud Girls ....................... 51
Rosebud Productions ............. 51
Roth vs. United States ........... 289
roulette ................................ 224
Roxbury ................................ 192
Roxy ..................................... 192
Royal Roman Motel ............... 281
RTP ...................................... 51
Rubber & Rivets .................... 253
rubbers ......................... 52, 126
rubdown ............................... 92
Rubenesque women ............. 101
Rubin Gottesman .................. 317
Rude Dog .............................. 194
Rumors ................................. 158
Rump Humpers ..................... 47
Russian Romance .................. 151

**S** S & M ............ 63, 121, 122, 155, 169
S.B. Sales ............................. 52
Sabrina Aset ......................... 285
Sacred Beach ....................... 203
safe sex ............................... 167
Saks, Dr ............................... 265
Sally J .................................. 254
San Diego ............................ 105
San Francisco ....................... 42
San Francisco Lesbians series ............. 49
San Onofre Beach ................. 206
Sandi's Wounded Knee Cabaret ............ 34
Sandy's ................................. 52
Sandy's Modeling .................. 271
Santa Anita Race Track .......... 223
Sanwa Health Spa ................. 112
Sara ..................................... 102
sauna ................................... 167
SB Sales ............................... 51
Scannin .......................... 72, 210

Schizandra ........................... 229
scrotal enlargement .............. 267
Secret Diary .......................... 315
Secret Gospel of Mark ........... 298
Secret Pleasures .................. 261
Secrets of Attracting Beautiful Women .. 280
secular saviors ..................... 242
Sensations ........................... 104
Seventh Veil ......................... 28
Sex & Sensibility ................... 291
sex enhancers ............... 228, 232
sex flicks .............................. 11
Sex In History ....................... 297
sex shows ............................. 268
sex tours .............................. 267
sex toys ............................... 11
sex-positive religion .............. 285
sexual stamina increased ...... 267
sexually transmitted diseases ............ 6
Sexxy Sadies ........................ 105
Seymore Butts in Paradise ..... 46
Seymore Butts' Buttwatch ...... 46
Shadow Lane ........................ 52
Sharon Mitchell ..................... 54
she-male videos .................... 49
she-males ............................. 11
Sherman Boostore ................. 16
Shiatsu Japan ....................... 110
Shiatsu Massage and/or Acupressure
.............................. 111, 112, 113
Shiatsu Spa Center ............... 110
Sierra Pacific Productions ...... 181
Sigmund Freud ...................... 125
Silver Valley Sun Club ........... 210
Sin-a-matic At 7969 ............... 192
Sinclair Blue Productions ....... 52
single girl masturbation ......... 46
single men ............................ 127
single women ........................ 126
singles ........................... 142, 145
Sinners Repent ..................... 192
Sisterhood Bookstore ............ 166
Skeptics Society .................... 297
slave training .......... 63, 64, 122, 306
Slaveline .............................. 148
Sleepless Knights .................. 72
slides ................................... 271
slot machines ................. 221, 224
slutty attire ........................... 253
Sly Fox ................................. 28
smart & life extension drugs ........ 245-249
smart drink ........................... 246
Smart Drugs & Nutrients ........ 227, 249
Smuggler's Cove ................... 203

snow ....................................... 230
So I Married A Lesbian........................... 54
software .................................... 138
soliciting .................................... 87
Sorel Productions ............................. 53
Southeast Asian girls .......................... 107
Southern California Area
   Nudist Information Network........ 72, 210
Southland Social Club ......................... 131
Spanish fly ................................. 228, 232
Spanish language gay newspaper....... 174
spankings.................... 52, 117, 276
Spearmint Rhino Club........................... 36
sperm donors................................ 282
spermicide ...................................... 5
Spice For Life................................. 20
Spike........................................ 156
SPLASH................................. 281, 282
Sportsheets International Inc .............. 283
Spotlight 29 Casino.......................... 221
spreads ...................................... 38
Spurs ........................................ 163
stag" films .................................. 41
Stan's .................................. 13, 18
Star, The ............................... 53, 319
Star Garden ................................ 32
Star Strip................................ 29, 30
Starfire .................................... 271
state lottery ................................ 224
stationery .................................. 275
STDs.......................................... 6
steam sauna .............................. 111
Steve Houston ............................. 315
stimulants................................. 228
stoners .................................... 235
Stop AIDS L.A. ............................. 175
straight .................................... 145
Strand, The ................................ 194
Strange Days .............................. 319
Streakers on the Run ...................... 103
streetwalkers.............................. 83
strip clubs/shows .................... 24, 158
strippers .................................. 104
stripping telegrams ..................... 97, 105
Stryker Productions ....................... 181
studio figure shoots........................ 273
Studio One................................. 154
studio rentals ............................. 273
Studline .................................... 170
submission........................... 99, 117
Suburbs BBS ............................... 73
Success Motivation & Healing Institute. 266
Sue Acupressure ........................... 112
Summerland Beach .......................... 204

Sun Acupressure .......................... 113
Sun Massage ............................... 114
Sun Oriental Acupressure .................... 110
Sun Oriental Massage......................... 112
Sun, The (tabloid) ...................... 133, 149
Sun-Air...................................... 212
sunbathing .................................. 199
Sunset Strip ................................ 29
Sunset Strip Tattoo ........................ 277
Sunshine Gifts .............................. 18
super pan nine.............................. 217
Suzette's Studio............................. 38
Suzie........................................ 83
Swallows..................................... 209
swapping partners .......................... 125
Swedish Erotica (films) ...................... 44
Sweet Dreams ............................... 101
Sweet Pink................................... 44
Swing............................... 97, 135, 149, 237
swing houses/parties ........................ 125
Swingers Anonymous........................... 130
Swingers Hotline.................... 135, 149
swingers, nude ............................. 209
Swingers' Club.............................. 150
Swingers' News (tabloid) .............. 136, 149
Swingers' newspapers and magazines ... 11
swingers' nudist resort...................... 257
Swinging ................... 125, 133, 135, 149
switchhitters.................... 118, 125
Sybrians..................................... 131
Sycuan Indian reservation .................... 222
syphilis .................................. 6, 86
Syren ....................................... 254

T  T J's Theater................................ 35
T.C.E....................................... 269
Table Dance Delivery........................ 101
Taboo Topics............................... 176
Talk Dirty To Me ........................... 65
Talk of the Town ........................... 101
talking dirty ............................... 60
Tara ........................................ 26
tattoo artists directory ...................... 278
Tattoo Mania's Annual Inkslippers Ball .. 257
tattoo removal............................. 265
tattoos...................................... 277
Tawa's Shiatsu Massage .................... 112
Tawny's Twilight Liaisons...................... 99
Taylor Wane................................ 315
TC World ................................... 15
tea.......................................... 229
Teasers ..................................... 97
Telecompanions............................. 148
Telepersonals ............................... 148

Ten Plus Entertainment............................ 99
testicles................................................ 232
Thailand............................................... 267
THC ..................................................... 23 5
Theory of Relativity ............................... 313
thigh-high boots ..................................... 251
Think Pink Publications......................... 173
Three Star Adult News........................... 21
threesomes.................................... 11, 125
Threshold.............................................. 122
Tijuana .......................................... 85, 174
Tiki Theater ............................................. 29
Timothy Leary ...................................... 246
Tina ........................................................ 65
Titti-Twinkler........................................ 258
Toe's Tavern ........................................ 193
Tokyo Acupressure................................ 111
Tokyo Massage .................................... 111
Tokyo Spa ............................................ 114
Tom Cat Pictures ................................... 73
Tom of Finland Co................................ 177
topless clubs .......................................... 24
Topless Dancer World Championships. 257
topless .................................................... 23
Topper Video.......................................... 53
Tori Welles ............................................. 64
Totally Nasty........................................... 43
Totally Tasteless Video........................... 53
Townhouse Massage ............................ 112
Toy Box .................................................. 19
Traci Lords ........................................... 317
Traci, I Love You ................................... 318
transsexuals.................................... 91, 136
transvestites................... 11, 91, 136, 155
Trashies Lingerie .................................. 253
travel nudist club .................................. 212
Treehouse Fun Ranch .......................... 210
Treehouse Too Hotel & Resort.............. 209
Triangle Inn .......................................... 178
Tropical Lei ............................................ 37
Tropicana ............................................. 29
Troubadour ........................................... 193
Trunks ................................................. 156
Truth Seeker (magazine) ...................... 297
TV Epic ................................................ 136
Twist Productions................................... 53
Twisted Video.......................................... 16
two-girl shows ........................................ 38

U   U.S. Male ....................................... 181
Uncle Roy's Amateur Home Videos........ 54
uniforms............................................... 157
Unmentionables..................................... 19

UnReal .................................................. 149
UnReal People ..................................... 137
Unzip It.................................................. 72
Update............................................ 150, 173
urologists ............................................. 265

V   V & B Adult Book Store ................... 20
vacuum pumps ............................ 266, 297
vaginal intercourse ................................... 3
vaginal reconstruction .......................... 267
Valley Bookstore.................................... 16
valley girls............................................... 30
Valley West............................................. 72
Varsity Productions............................... 182
vasopressin .......................................... 248
VCA Pictures ........................................ 180
Velvet Voices ......................... 63, 122, 306
Venice Beach ....................................... 203
Venus Faire ............................................ 32
Versatile Fashions ......................... 253, 255
Versatile Productions............................... 55
vibrators........................................... 22, 259
vice cops ................................................ 92
Vicky.................................................... 272
Victoria ................................................. 101
Victoria's Videos ..................................... 54
video arcades ......................................... 11
video duplication and transfer .............. 269
Video Exclusives ............................. 49, 181
Video Fantasies....................................... 18
video games ......................................... 221
Video Software Dealers Association ..... 294
Video Vamps .......................................... 47
Video Vortex ........................................... 54
Video Vortex BBS.................................... 69
Video Xcitement ..................................... 56
Videoactive Annex................................ 165
videos, customized................................ 279
Viejas Indian Reservation..................... 222
Vietnamese ........................................... 107
Villa..................................................... 178
Villa-A-Go-G o ........................................ 37
vinopocetine ........................................ 247
Vip Massage.......................................... 111
Viper Room ......................................... 193
Virtual Connection ................................. 75
Visual Direct .......................................... 54
vitamin E............................................... 233
Vivid Interactive ..................................... 73
Vivid Video ..................................... 54, 182
Vixen of the Year award ....................... 313
voice mail ....................................... 142, 263

Voice Mail Bulletin Board ..................... 148
voluptuous ........................................... 102
voyeurism/voyers ......................... 125, 126

**W** wackos/weirdos ................................... 142
Warren Communications ..................... 297
Water sports......................................... 3
Waxing by Mistress Gloria ........... 182, 282
Wayfarer's Chapel ............................... 203
Web ...................................................... 119
weddings, nude.................................... 212
West Coast Swingers ................. 135, 149
West Hollywood ................................... 153
Western Photographer Magazine ........ 272
Western Visuals ..................................... 54
Westside, The ........................................ 70
Wet T-Shirt ............................................ 50
whippings ..................................... 117, 276
Whips & Chains (magazine) ........ 123, 136
Whisky a Go Go.................................... 193
White House ........................................ 196
Who's Who in American Women ......... 306
Whole Life Times ................................ 147
Wicked Pictures ..................................... 54
wife swapping ..................................... 125
Wild & Kinky......................................... 147
Wild Bill ............................................... 130
Wild Goose ............................................ 29
Will Durst ............................................. 281
William Lindley..................................... 297
William Randolph Hurst ...................... 235
Willis ................................................... 228
Winston Churchill................................. 185
Wolf's ........................................... 159, 163
Wolfline ................................................ 169

women fighting ...................................... 52
Women of Size ..................................... 254
Woody Allen.......................................... 153
World Guide To Nude Beaches
   and Recreation ................................. 213
World Modeling Talent Agency ............. 308
Worldwide Adcorp. Inc.......................... 283
wrestle ................................................. 122
Wynning Publications .......................... 280

**X** X-Citement Video, Inc...................... 55, 317
X-rated industry .............................. 42, 303
X-rated novelties................................... 11
Xaviera Hollander ................................. 92
XIS ........................................................ 75
XXX Connection .................................. 103
XXXtreme Fashions ............................. 254

**Y** Yellow Peppers................................... 44
yohimbine ............................................ 228
Your Search Has Ended ........................ 98

**Z** Zane Entertainment................................ 55
Zapper ................................................. 259
Zeb O'Brean ........................................ 195
Zeus Collection .................................... 182
zonas de tolerencia ............................... 85
Zone Club ............................................ 167
Zone Films/Zone Video Club ................ 182
zones of tolerance ................................. 85
Zuma Beach ......................................... 203

# D. R. Tupper

## Art Studio

**From the fertle mind from whence sprang forth *Lecher McRich* comes the:**

- **Best Dang Artist in the West!**
- **Custom Scrimshaw**
- **Pen & Ink Sketches**
- **Fine Art Paintings**
- **Advertising Art**
- **Water Colors**
- **Cartoons**
- **Logos**
- **Etc.**

© 1995 DR TUPPER

**Post Office Box 3171, Tustin, CA 92681**

## (714) 544-7111

# Lecher McRich's Library

For a visit to the old curmudgeon's mansion, access him on the InterNet at:

*http://www.cyberheads.com/~warren/index.htm*

## Books Available

Lecher would like to share some of his books with his fans (and make some money in the process). You can order from from the Net Site or you can order them the old-fashion way (see order blank next page).

- *Red Lights of Baja* ($12.95)
  By Roger Warren. A guide to Baja Mexico's Zones of Tolerances (red light districts).

- *Sin Diego* ($16.95)
  By F.M. Philips & Roger Warren. A guide to San Diego undeground – Sex, Drugs and Rock & Roll

- Lust Angeles ($19.95)
  By F.M. Philips, edited by Roger Warren. An underground guide to the Greater Los Angeles area.

- *Man's Guide to Mexico* ($16.95)
  By Hector Cardova. A gay/lesbian guide to Mexico.

- *The Book Your Church Doesn't Want You to Read* ($19.95) Edited by Tim Leedom. An enlightening anthology by world renowned historians and authors as Thomas Jefferson, Steve Allen, etc.

# Books In The Works:

- *Sex In History*
- *Baja's Best Bargains*
- *Sin Francisco*

# Other Services

- InterNet Web Sites & Design
- Desktop Publishing
- Book Publishing
- Happy People Tours
  (Gay Rail Cruise of the Copper Canyon
  Private tours of San Diego & Baja
- Publisher of: *FOCUS: San Diego Gay/Lesbian Community Pages* (InterNet E-Zine)

NAME: _____

ADDRESS: _____

CITY/STATE/ZIP: _____

PHONE: _____

EMAIL: _____

Add shipping cost of $1.25. Shipping free on two or more books. California residents add 7% sales tax.

**Mail with check to:**

# WARREN COMMUNICATIONS

Post Office Box 620219  •  San Diego, CA 92162

Lecher is now accepting
the following credit cards
for purchases
from his mansion
Gift Shoppe & Library

**VISA**
**MASTERCARD**
**DISCOVERY**
**AMERICAN EXPRESS**

CALL:
# 1-800-227-9858

and have the following
information ready:

**Name of Person on Card**
**Card Type and Number**
**Expiration Date**
**Address on Card**
**Shipping Address**
**Your Phone Number**
**Name of Books Ordered**

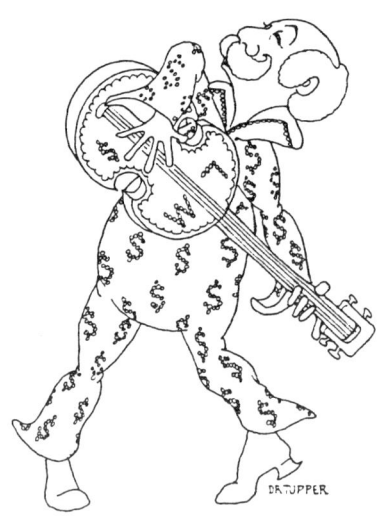

**Lecher wishes you a G-O-O-O-O-O-D!!! Night**